IRELAND:

A SOCIAL HISTORY

FROM THE CELTS TO THE
FOUNDATIONS OF
UNIONISM AND REPUBLICANISM

Jerry Shanahan

ISBN-13: 978-1-5272-8383-1

Comrades
'We meet beyond earth's barred gate
Where all the world's wild Rebels are.'
(Eva Gore-Booth)

CONTENTS

ACKNOWLEDGMENTS

Irish history is a subject which continues to engage and fascinate and this is evident from the regular emergence of new work. I am grateful to have had access to many of these through internet sites such as *JStor.org, Academia.edu* and *Project Gutenberg* without which the completion of this work would not have been possible. I am also grateful for the works from academics, researchers, and third-level institutions which have been published and made accessible. I would like to thank Vanessa Fox O'Loughlin at *writing.ie* and Tim Carey who looked at an earlier draft and provided valuable advice. I would also like to thank the National Library of Ireland for permission to use the image of The Siege of Limerick 1690 (dedicated to the Women of Limerick) for the cover of this book. Finally, my thanks to family, friends, and colleagues for all their support and encouragement.

INTRODUCTION

This work is an opportunity for readers to review Irish history from the first to the early nineteenth century from a social perspective and, in particular, to examine accepted narratives often considered to represent the dominant class understanding of Irish history or, as Gramsci observed; social constructs that benefit only the ruling classes – their view becoming the accepted view. I trust when readers have read this work they may commence a process of revisiting and examining these narratives, and better still, for those interested in the subject it will give rise to further examination and commentary. I have focused on social history as it is, in my view, a neglected area of examination, even if, in more recent decades, it has achieved a new and more nuanced level of interest. I will comment later on possible reasons for this. There are some works which can be considered to have approached long-term Irish history from a radical or Marxist perspective and these are referenced but they are not as plentiful as I would wish. There are exceptions such as Connolly's *Labour in Irish History*, Jacksons' *Ireland Her Own* and works by P Beresford Ellis and C Desmond Greaves on Liam Mellows and James Connolly. There are also some limited writings from Marx and Engels, who had commenced preparatory work on a History of Ireland which was never completed. There are works from Perry Anderson which are outstanding and I recommend these for those interested in gaining an understanding of the development of early and modern society.

More generally what readers are exposed to is a revisionist version of Irish history. This can be traced to some extent to the neo-liberal approach taken to the study of history over recent decades. More directly, revisionism was influenced post Irish independence (Free State-1922) and from the 1930s onwards, by the taught and written history which emerged from historians from the Institute of Historical Research in London and Cambridge, who produced a school of Irish historians who then went on to inhabit the History Departments of a number of Irish higher level institutions. These professional historians set about revising the narrative of Irish history and in particular revising in a more benign way the often malevolent role played by British colonialism and imperialism in Irish affairs. These were purportedly based on value-free judgements.[1] British policy towards Ireland was notably described elsewhere as *'a series of well-meaning blunders'*[2] and this bizarre distortion goes some way to sum up this approach.

It has also been argued that there is an English sense of historical continuity which sought to prevent *'the uprooting of things which have been organic to the development of the country'.*[3] This perspective has been influential and in this framework the struggle for national independence and self-determination are not considered part of a democratic process. The words of Marx and Engels should not be forgotten: *'the English working class will never accomplish anything before it has got rid of Ireland. The lever must be applied in Ireland'.*[4] Other misleading strands of revisionism fed into a pro-imperialist view of Irish history and support for a *'two-nation theory'* a theory which presented the view that Ulster Protestants constituted a separate nation on the island of

---

[1] Bradshaw, B., (1989), Nationalism and Historical Scholarship in Modern Ireland, Irish Historical Studies, Volume 26, Issue 104, November.

[2] Raftery, A., (1973), Introduction, Labour in Irish History, New Books, Dublin.

[3] Bradshaw, B, Nationalism and Historical Scholarship.

[4] Marx K and Engels F, *Ireland and the Irish Question*, R. Dixon (ed), Progress Publishers, Moscow, 1971.

Ireland. This theory re-emerged at the end of the 1960s but had its origins at the turn of the twentieth century when Ireland was still within the British Empire. It was condemned as a capitulation to British imperialism in 1971 by the then leader of Official Sinn Fein.[5] Over the past thirty years, as armed conflict has been replaced by the peace agreement, a less circumscribed debate has opened up. There is a growing amount of post-revisionist research and output which has overtaken the revisionists but they remain a distorting influence. It has also been argued not least that the most disturbing aspect of these professional historians is the credibility gap which exists between their versions of history and the general public. An associate plea to this narrative was for an account of Irish history capable of comprehending sympathetically the historical experience of both communities (on the island) and, by comprehending them, of mediating between the islands' past and present.[6]

It is a general observation, but it is not unusual now to see Marxism on third-level courses; however, actual written research, analysis, and end product are less plentiful.

In the case of this work it was not undertaken to address this lacunae but rather an opportunity for me to bring together the experiences of over forty years involvement with people in politics and the trade union and labour movement in Ireland, both jurisdictions, Great Britain, Europe, the USA, and to rely on these experiences to inform the social and economic approach taken. Due regard is also given to an international perspective which is often missing from the many inwardly directed histories of Ireland. There are references from authors who have provided revealing views of Irish history and may not be considered to be from a radical

---

[5] Tomas Mac Giolla, Irish Times, 25 October, 1971.

[6] Bradshaw, B., *Nationalism and Historical Scholarship in Modern Ireland.*

background. It is my view, to limit the field of examination would mean that this work would be a far shorter volume than it is. Additionally, to conduct research and produce evidence which supports a work of this kind it is necessary to cast the net as wide as possible. The underlying and most important point is as to how this examination is presented from a socially relevant historical perspective and to question not only the roles played by the *great men and women*' of history but more so question how the ordinary people who make up the great mass of society and create the wealth thereof, fared, as the social constructs of society changed from a clan system and onward through the centuries to capitalism. Specifically, how did the major events from Christianity to Feudalism, Absolutism, the English Revolution, Mercantilism, Colonialism, the rise of the Bourgeoisie, Unionism, and Republicanism develop, shape, and influence society on the island of Ireland.

Among the many issues examined are Christianity and the lingering cultural and superstitious influence of the Druids: did St Patrick really arrive in Ireland in 432 CE or was he a creation of sixth and seventh century clerical writers, supported by secular allies for the primacy of Armagh? Was it the Vikings alone or were there Irish chiefs and ecclesiastics who participated in church depredations, as these sites were known centres of wealth? Was the Battle of Clontarf the ultimate defeat of the Danes or rather an internecine war for the Irish kingship with Norse and Danes on either side? Was it the mercenary forces of Strongbow with Diarmuid Mac Murrough or Henry II who secured the Norman Conquest or was this conquest planned a long-time prior to the Mac Murrough invitation as part of European feudal transition and a religious reform process supported by the Pope? Why did the Irish chiefs pay homage and become vassals to Henry? What was the aftermath of the Tudors involvement

4

in ending the power of the old English feudal magnates and Gaelic clan strongholds and how did the new English Protestant Ascendancy class, introduced by Henry VIII and Elizabeth I, dominate Irish society for the next three centuries? Were the Flight of the Earls and Wild Geese events to be celebrated, or events which left the great mass of the population defenceless? Some of the other great narratives don't explain Papal support for the Crown and as to why a *Te Deum* was celebrated in the Vatican and other capitals in Europe following Protestant William's victory over Catholic James in 1690 at the Battle of the Boyne.

A further question posed is how did the Catholic Church survive in Ireland in a post-Reformation and penal climate yet went on to support the Crown, oppose rebellion, and still convince the great mass of the ordinary people that they were on their side? I was also interested to examine how land and land ownership had been so decisive a factor throughout Irish history. How the replacing of the collective ownership of the clan system was still socially relevant up to the nineteenth century. The changing character, ownership, and use of land and landlord and tenant relations has been a guiding thread throughout these centuries and in related class division. How did this give rise to a number of peasant rebellions and give birth to the Whiteboys and Steelboys? Why was there no alternative to work, even of a subsistence kind for the vast majority of the Irish population, other than on the land, and was this as a result of the prohibitions on economic and industrial development arising from English commercial and financial policy in the seventeenth and eighteenth centuries? Mercantilist policies that did not treat the Irish as they did other subjects in England, Scotland, and Wales but rather portrayed the Irish as an inferior race to be subjugated but yet were threatened by Ireland as a competitor nation. Why was it that any attempt by the Irish over the course of the eighteenth century to develop a nascent capitalism was snuffed out? The corollary was no Irish industrial revolution or the creation of an industrial working class other than and to some extent later in the North East of the country and some other isolated sites. A further corollary of these policies was that Ireland became an *Officina Militum* for the thousands of Irish consigned to the British army and navy, or consigned as indentured slaves to colonial plantations, or to live their lives in English slums and become despised workers in *'the dark Satanic Mills'*[7] of the English industrial revolution, competing for work with their English counterparts. The alternative of remaining in Ireland was removed, or, if not, they were destined to subsist as farm labourers to provide a cheap source of food for Britain's colonial armies and the growing army of industrial workers in Great Britain displaced by land clearances. It is not well known that the first trade unions appeared in Ireland and laws prohibiting combinations were passed in Ireland decades prior to England. How did the American and French revolutions influence events in Ireland leading to a form of bourgeois unity initially which later divided along class lines into unionist and republican variants? These events led on to the 1798 Rebellion and to the introduction of the Act of Union, ultimately to the growing nationalism of O'Connell and the Irish Catholic Church, Catholic Emancipation, and the Repeal movement. The actions, or more likely inactions, of landlordism, absentee landlordism, the Protestant Ascendancy, and the British government before and after the Act of Union and their catastrophic lack of response created the circumstances where famine took hold; a million died through starvation and disease and millions more emigrated to Great Britain, the USA, Canada, Australia, and further afield. The Irish population

---

[7] Blake, William, Preface to Milton.

halved between 1840 and 1900 from eight million to four million. After the Famine three million of the labourers, cottiers, and small holders were literally dead or emigrated.[8] The landlord was no longer propped up by a social order based largely on the poor and potato-dependent labourer.

This Famine (1845-1849) wiped out in their tens of thousands the ordinary peasant class, the *'million Irish toilers'* or Irish *'sans culottes'*, potential backbone for progress in struggles similar to the struggle by the French peasantry against the Aristocratic landowners in Revolutionary France. Instead, there emerged fifty years after the Famine and Land struggles not a proletarianized tenantry but a class of landowning tenantry.[9] These went on to form a conservative backbone in Irish society and joined the petit-bourgeoisie of shopkeepers and *gombeen men* (monetary interest), reliant on a middle-class of large farmers and graziers, in turn, allied to the professional, finance, and manufacturing classes. These class divisions were to shape the future Free State after the War of Independence and Civil War in Ireland.

The foundations of Unionism and loyalism, Republicanism, democratic and physical force, and Catholic nationalism have their origins in the social history of Irish society and the social, economic, industrial, and political relationships that developed between Ireland, Great Britain, Europe, and North America. The political forces that emerged in the latter part of the nineteenth and early twentieth century have their foundations in this epoch and continue to shape and influence Irish society, even up to the present day. I trust this work will help to illuminate this history and provide a greater

---

[8] Poirteir, C., (1995), (ed.), The Great Irish Famine, p10, RTE/Mercier Press, Cork.

[9] Mathur, C., and Dix, D., (2009),*The Irish Question in Karl Marx's and Friedrich Engel's Writings on Capitalism and Empire*, Social Thought on Ireland in the Nineteenth Century, pp97-107, University College Dublin Press.

understanding of the background to present day relationships on the island of Ireland and relationships with our nearest neighbour as Ireland emerges as a European country, but arguably one that has not yet taken its place among the nations of the earth.[10]

---

[10] Robert Emmet's Speech from the Dock, 1803.

CHAPTER ONE

CLASSICAL CIVILISATION –

GREECE, ROME AND THE SLAVE

ECONOMY

In classical Greece the divorce of work from the concepts of liberty was so defined that the Greeks had no word in their language even to express the concept of labour, either as a social function or as personal conduct. For Plato, labour remained alien to any human value and, in certain respects it seems, he considered it even to be the antithesis of what is essential to life. Aristotle summed up the social principle involved in the slave economy as follows: '*the best State will not make a manual worker a citizen, for the bulk of manual labour today is slave or foreign*'. The slave mode of production which underlay Athenian civilisation found its foremost expression in the privileged social stratum of the city, whose '*intellectual heights its surplus labour in the silent depths below made possible*'.[11]

In Roman theory the agricultural slave was designated the speaking instrument, one grade away from the livestock that constituted a semi-speaking instrument, and two from the actual tools used which were designated a silent instrument. On the other hand, slavery was the most urban commercialisation of labour

---

[11] Anderson, P., Passages from Antiquity to Feudalism, NLB, London, 1974.

conceivable. It was the economic hinge that joined town and country together to the inordinate profit of the *citizenry*. It also had the paradoxical effect of promoting certain categories of slaves to responsible administrative or professional positions, which in turn facilitated manumission and subsequent integration of the sons of skilled freedmen into the citizen class. This process was not so much restorative for those concerned but another index of the radical abstention of the Roman ruling class from any form of productive labour even of an executive type. The wealth and ease of the propertied urban class of classical antiquity above all that of Athens and Rome at their zenith rested on the broad surplus yielded by the pervasive presence of this labour system underpinning their economy.[12]

Classical civilisation was in consequence inherently *colonial* in character: the city state invariably reproduced itself in phases of ascent by settlements and war. Plunder, tribute, and slaves were the central objects of aggrandisement, both means and ends to colonial expansion. Military power was more closely locked to economic growth than in perhaps any other mode of production, before or since, because the main single origin of slave labour was normally captured prisoners of war. While the raising of free urban troops for war depended on the maintenance of production at home by slaves; battle-fields provided the manpower for corn-fields, and vice-versa, captive labourers permitted the creation of citizen armies.[13]

A perspective on slavery and Empire came from Tacitus, the Roman historian. He attributed it to Galgacus, Chieftain of the Caledonian army, by way of a speech delivered in advance of the Battle of Mons Graupius in 84/85 CE. The speech describes the

---

[12] Ibid.
[13] Ibid.

exploitation of Britain by Rome and was a call to arms to rouse the troops in the upcoming battle against the Romans. It is probably the first anti-slavery and anti-imperialist speech recorded. (It has been regarded as having been written by Tacitus as it was not uncommon for the opposing argument to be presented in writings of the time.)

'... there are no tribes beyond us, nothing indeed but waves and rocks, and the yet more terrible Romans, from whose oppression escape is vainly sought by obedience and submission. Robbers of the world, having by their universal plunder exhausted the land, they rifle the deep. If the enemy be rich they are rapacious, if he be poor, they lust for dominion; neither the east nor the west has been able to satisfy them. Alone among men they covet with equal eagerness poverty and riches. To robbery, slaughter, plunder, they give the lying name of empire; they make a desert and call it peace.'[14]

For others, *'golden ages'*, whether Athens or Pericles, Augustan Rome, Spain's *siglo de oro*, or indeed Ireland's middle ages, are the accomplishment of a small artistic and intellectual cadre, supported and patronised by a much larger and powerful extractive elite that lords it over a wretched mass of toilers, some free, many slaves, all exploited, the sweated and bloodied underbelly of a profoundly unequal society. The *'privileges and the freedoms these elites arrogated to themselves were denied their inferiors, a denial that may have extended not only to the goods of this life, but to the rewards of the next'*.[15]

The Portrayal of Early Medieval Ireland

During the first part of the twentieth century, early medieval Ireland

---

[14] Tacitus, Germania, Penguin Books, 2010.

[15] O'Corrain, D., Island of Saints and Scholars: Myth or Reality, Celts, Catholicism and the Middle Ages, Irish Catholic Identities, Rafferty, O P, University Press Scholarship, 2015.

was adopted as the poster image for the new nation; it was recent enough to be emotionally accessible and it also felt sufficiently similar to the Irish Free State in the 1920s and 1930s, i.e. predominantly rural, self-sustaining, and Catholic. There was a wealth of data from the early medieval period, both documentary and archaeological, that helped feed the *'Golden Age'* myth of a Land of Saints and Scholars. This philosophical direction was credited to a conservative Irish commercial and landed bourgeois class, who, after the Easter Rebellion (1916), usurped control of the direction of the subsequent *'War of Independence'* (1919-21), and the policies of the newly founded Irish Free State.[16] In some accounts this is attributed to the loss of the radical leadership during the 1916 rebellion and the later Irish Civil War (1922-23).[17] [18]

Nineteenth and early twentieth century scholars tended to regard the years 400-800 CE as the *'Golden Age'* of the Irish Church which came to an abrupt end with the Viking invasions. However, many of the greatest works, including the sagas and some of the most iconic features of the Irish landscape, including the round tower and the Irish high cross, flourished from the ninth to the twelfth centuries. Creativity accordingly continued unabated after these invasions, albeit in different media and literary forms.[19]

Earlier approaches to Irish history also *'situated early Ireland in a nebulously defined heroic Iron Age, extending back into a romanticised Indo-European antiquity'*. The exploration of Irish-speaking communities, on both sides of the Irish Sea, has showed the limitations of treating

---

[16] Kerr, Thomas R., McCormick, F, O'Sullivan, A, The Economy of Early Medieval Ireland, EMAP Report 7.1.

[17] Kostick, C., Revolution in Ireland, Cork University Press, 2009.

[18] Greaves, Desmond, C, Liam Mellows and the Irish Revolution, Lawrence and Wishart, London, 1971.

[19] Downham, C., Medieval Ireland, Cambridge University Press, 2018.

Ireland as an *'archaic peculiarity'* untouched by the experience of its neighbours. There is the need to *'reframe conversion to Christianity as part of a broader socio-political dynamic connecting Ireland and its' neighbours, especially Roman Britain ... these open glimpses of Irish society between the second and sixth centuries, before and after the imaginary boundary of the Patrician problem'.*[20] In turn, it appears that there has been an unfortunate tendency to treat Ireland as culturally homogenous, a judgement based largely on the writings of the Christian literate elite who had established themselves at least by the sixth century.[21] Assembling the foregoing into a coherent narrative presents a task of illuminating the reasoning underlying these narratives and counter-narratives.

The Roman Influence on Ireland

Ireland's contact with the Roman Empire began as early as the first century as witnessed by archaeological finds of imported goods and references in Latin texts. Ptolemy, a geographer working in Egypt, charted a recognisable outline of Ireland's coasts and the positions of major river mouths, promontories, settlements, and islands based, it appears, on information from traders. We also learn from Ptolemy that kingdoms named for their ruling dynasties occur concurrently both in Roman Britain and Ireland: Brigantes, Corondi, Marapii, The Dumnonii, recorded by Ptolemy in Britain, southern Scotland, and in the Devon and Cornwall Peninsula are also referred to in Irish records. There the form is Domnainn and as kings of Leinster at Dun Alinne they appear in the second to fourth centuries. Elsewhere, the

---

[20] Johnston, Elva, Ireland in Late Antiquity: A Forgotten Frontier, Studies in Late Antiquity, Summer 2017.

[21] Ibid.

Domnainn appear to be very widely spread in Ireland.[22]

In a further reference to Ireland, attributed to Tacitus, it appears that an invasion of Ireland was contemplated and that there was interaction between the Romans and native clans and a healthy commerce was also in existence between Ireland, Britain, and other parts of Europe. Tacitus stated: *'In the fifth year of the war, Agricola himself … in that part of Britain which looks towards Ireland, … posted some troops, hoping for fresh conquests rather than fearing attack, inasmuch as Ireland, being between Britain and Spain and conveniently situated for the seas round Gaul, might have been the means for connecting with great mutual benefit the most powerful parts of the empire. Its extent is small when compared with Britain, but exceeds the islands of our seas. In soil and climate, in the disposition, temper and habits of its population, it differs but little from Britain. We know most of its harbours and approaches, and that through the intercourse of commerce. One of the petty kings of the nation, driven out by internal faction, had been received by Agricola, who detained him under the semblance of friendship till he could make use of him. I have often heard him say that a single legion with a few auxiliaries could conquer and occupy Ireland, and that it would have a salutary effect on Britain for the Roman arms to be seen everywhere, and for freedom, so to speak, to be banished from its sight.'*[23]

Three centuries later Ammianus Marcellinus identified the Irish (Scotti) as among the peoples who had crossed the frontiers in order to attack Roman territories in c360 CE. Ammianus's reference to previous treaties broken by the Irish suggests some level of formal political engagement.[24] Finds of Roman artefacts at Drumanagh, County Dublin, Newgrange, County Meath, and off the East Coast of Ireland at Lambay and Dalkey Islands also support evidence of

---

[22] O'Corrain, Donnchada, Orosius, Ireland and Christianity, Perita 28, (2017).

[23] Tacitus, Agricola 24, Harvard University Press, 1989.

[24] Johnston, Elva, Ireland in Late Antiquity.

trading links with Britain and the continent. Economically and politically through trading, exchange, and diplomatic intervention, even without the invasions experienced by others, Roman contact it can be said contributed to social differentiation.[25] There is evidence that Roman coins, silver spiral rings, disc brooches, and other objects were deposited at various Irish sites such as Newgrange. It is suggested that Drumanagh was a Romano-Britain emporium of some sort where the manufacture of high-class objects occurred.[26]

Ireland's early exports consisted primarily of slaves and hunting dogs, raw materials including cloth, leather goods, foodstuffs, and, it is thought, copper. Early imports consisted of manufactured goods Roman coins, glassware, pottery containing olive oil, wine, and other foodstuffs. Items of personal adornment and toiletry as already listed have been found on Irish sites. These types of objects suggest that members of the Irish elites were visually emulating Romano-British models through choices of adornment and contributing to social differentiation already mentioned.[27] This evidence points to a close relationship in dynasties, languages, and culture between southern Ireland and Britain. Irish raids on Roman Britain were also common in the fourth century and attacks continued into the fifth century. There were also Irish settlements in Wales, Devon, and Cornwall.[28]

Early Christianity – Romano-British

It is reasonable to suggest that prior to the fifth and sixth centuries

---

[25] Anderson, Perry, Passages from Antiquity to Feudalism.

[26] O'Sullivan, A & Breen, C, Maritime Ireland, An archaeology of coastal communities, The History Press, 2007.

[27] Johnston, Elva, Ireland in Late Antiquity: A Forgotten Frontier, Studies in Late Antiquity, Summer, 2017.

[28] O'Corrain, Donnchada, Orosius, Ireland and Christianity.

much of what passes for history is legend or hagiography based in the oral or clerical tradition. It is mostly the work of the fifth, sixth, and seventh century clerical elite as storytellers or hagiologists who had their own reasons for the promotion of particular agendas. It is also evident that there was domination and control of the written word amongst the clerical orders. Much of the written word during the late sixth and seventh centuries was their output and correspondingly much of it was sponsored by a quasi-dynastic elite. The Ui Neill and the Airgialla were prominent correspondents in this regard. The work was driven amongst other considerations for the benefit of the ecclesiastical centre of Armagh as it sought to establish its primacy against the other great religious centre in Kildare. Whereas, the relics of Brigid and Conlaed were said by seventh-century Cogitosus to be housed in metal-mounted shrines in the *basicalla* of Kildare, no such claims were made for Patrick. However, *Muirchu* made an exception for Patrick's relics as it related to Armagh. In his case *Muirchu* states an angel enjoins that Patrick's relics should be deeply buried *'lest the relics of your body be removed from the ground'*. The primary implication being a seventh century uncertainty as to the site of Patrick's grave.[29]

Cultural appropriation

In hagiography the numerous saints, their holy wells, and their numerous miracles can also be seen to be part of a cultural appropriation which had as its central purpose the assimilation and displacement of Druidism and its culture with Christianity. The Druidic culture of sacred wells, oral traditions, rituals, and magic were appropriated and assimilated by the Christians of the period. This

---

[29] Bourke Cormac, CORPOREAL RELICS, TENTS AND SHRINES IN EARLY MEDIEVAL IRELAND, Ulster Journal of Archaeology, Vol 74, 2017-18.

appropriation eased its passage as a dominant single deity. There are numerous examples throughout the island of Celtic-sacred sites becoming the sites for early Christian activity and sacred wells and woods becoming holy wells or sites for churches. A significant example is Brigid, *'the exalted one',* a Celtic Goddess who was the patron of poetry, healing, and metalwork. She was in due course transformed into St. Brigid of Kildare or Cill Dara; *'church of the oak'.*[30] Early Christian churches of wood or stone were assimilated onto the native pagan Celtic landscape by being incorporated into sacred paths through the terrain that continues in use even today as pilgrimage routes. These routes called *'patterns'* (after the local patron saint) are walked in a clockwise direction following the sun and comprise a circuit of sacred features including venerated rocks, sacred trees, megalithic monuments, and wayside shrines. Most common of all holy wells are converted to *'Stations of the Cross'* *(Via Crucis)*. For example Knocnadobar *'mountain of the wells'* in County Kerry was a very important pagan mountain and at its base is a sixth century holy well, St. Fursa's Well, considered to have mineral healing properties. In more recent times it is also a pilgrim trail, one of twelve which incorporate former pagan sites, and in the nineteenth century Stations of the Cross were added. Generally, the sacred features were incorporated into the story of the local saint's life and thus the *'Pattern'* incorporates the ancient pagan sites and ritual into a Christianised landscape.[31]

The success of the journey to Christianity was also enabled by a number of common practices in Celtic religion and Christianity, in particular the belief in the existence of an afterlife. Thus the new

---

[30] Kearney, Hugh, The British Isles, Canto Classics, 2012.

[31] Maguire, Martin, Churches and Symbolic Power in the Irish Landscape in LANDSCAPES, Vol 5, No 2, (Autumn 2004).

religion had a level of acceptance amongst the Celts who could retain a number of their pagan practices and superstitions without conflict with the new religion.[32] As has also been observed, *'Irish Druidism absorbed a certain amount of Christianity, and it would be a problem of considerable difficulty to fix on the period where it ceased to be Druidism, and from which onwards it could be said of Christianity in any restricted sense of that term'.*[33]

Christianity became the official religion of the Roman Empire, with the Edict of Milan in 313 CE, and, despite the fact that by 393 CE all pagan cults were banned, Pagan traditions continued long afterwards and by some arguments well into the twelfth century. The Culdees or *Ceile De* were considered by the *Venerable Bede*[34] and others as the last remaining links with the Druids. The often presented view that Christian monotheism arrived with, by, and following St. Patrick and swept all through the country is more likely part of the efforts of the clerical chroniclers. A further example of the cultural appropriation process was as to how existing legends were dealt with, for example, the story of Patrick and the legendary *Oisin,* son of *Fionn MacChumhal.* Oisin had returned from *Tir na nOg* (the land of youth) and the legend goes met with Patrick who was in the process of converting the Irish to Christianity. Oisin, having fallen from his horse and snapping the livery as he displaced a large rock, touched Irish soil which was forbidden under the conditions of his return. Aging rapidly as a result of contact with the soil he lay dying and it was at this point, the story goes, he was converted to Christianity by Patrick.

There is a similar tale in relation to the Children of Lir, they were restored to their human forms by Patrick after four hundred years as

---

[32] Grunke, KR., The Effect of Christianity on the British Celts, UW-L Journal of Undergraduate Research XI (2008).

[33] Bonwick, James, Irish Druids and Old Irish Religions, 1894.

[34] Bede, *Ecclesiastical History of the English People,* 731CE.

swans when he cast out an evil Druidic spell that had transformed them and they were also Christianised. Another tale supporting the chronology has St. Patrick raise Cuchulainn (legendary warrior) from hell to convince King Loegaire Mac Neill (fifth century) to convert to Christianity. There are other stories in similar vein suitably adapted and appropriated. Much of this cultural adaptation is considered to be part of the development of the cult of Patrick in the sixth and seventh centuries, in particular by *Muirchu*. All going to prove the powers inherent in Christianity were much more than anything the Druids could muster.

Thus, we see the merging of the legends of *Na Fianna, the Children of Lir,* and other sagas with Patrick and his conversion campaign. This hagiography laid the ground for the superior magical powers of Christianity and in the process paid homage and created Patrick the secular hero. Druids who opposed Patrick are miraculously done to death. When one reviled the faith: '*Holy Patrick … with a loud voice confidently said to the Lord 'O Lord who is most powerful … may this impious man, who blasphemes Thy name, be now raised up outside and quickly die'*. At these words, the druid was lifted up into the air and cast down headlong; he hit his head against a stone, and was smashed to pieces.[35] By the seventh century Christian secular learning and tribal sagas were incorporated into the Christian chronological framework.

The way was also open for the rise of a national myth; firstly the '*Book of Invasions' (Lebor Gabala)*, written in the twelfth century but probably based on an eighth century original [36] in which the Irish kings traced their descent to *Mil*, whose sons, on leaving Spain, settled in Ireland and thence back *to Gomer Son of Noah*.[37] The scribes

---

[35] O'Corrain, Donnchada, Island of Saints and Scholars: Myth or Reality.
[36] Hughes, Kathleen, The Church in Early Irish Society.
[37] Kearney, H., The British Isles.

put together a great mass of miscellaneous material in these three great manuscript collections: the *Book of Invasions*, *Lebor na Huidre (Book of the Dun Cow)* transcribed at Clonmacnoise and *The Book of Leinster (Lebar na Nuachongbala)* compiled by *Aedh,* Abbot of Terryglass.

Aedh included in his volume a version of the *Tain Bo Cualinge*, part of Ireland's oldest heroic cycle. He notes at the end of the tale that *'some things in it are the delusions of devils, some things are poetic images, some things are like truth, some not, and some things are for the pleasure of fools.'* This reference is an extract from a manuscript now in the Bodleian Library, *Rawl. B. 502*, the provenance of which is unknown.[38]

---

[38] Hughes, Kathleen, The Church in Early Irish Society.

CHAPTER TWO

EARLY CHRISTIANITY – THE ARRIVAL OF

PALLADIUS OR ST. PATRICK AND OTHERS

Following the collapse of the Roman Empire, the surviving conduit was Christianity. Thus, as the military and administrative structures of the Western Roman Empire collapsed, more and more responsibility passed into the hands of the Christian Bishops. They continued to expand their kingdom while the earthly kingdom around them fell to pieces.[39] As noted: *'after the collapse and confusion of the Dark Ages, one single institution spanned the whole transition from Antiquity to the middle Ages in essential continuity: the Christian Church'.*[40] Christianity's most important cultural change was the form of individualism and personal responsibility it preached which contrasted starkly with the collective responsibility of the tribe or clan.

The Arrival of Christianity – The Debate

The debate surrounding the arrival of St. Patrick raises a number of conflicting opinions. In most accounts it is presented as being in 432 CE, which coincides with the arrival of Palladius, and others in 431 CE. For some sixth century clerical writers, chronology being

---

[39] DePaor, M. and L., Early Christian Ireland, Thames and Hudson, London, 1994.
[40] Anderson, Perry, Passages from Antiquity to Feudalism.

uppermost in their minds, Palladius and Patrick became one and the same. However, as Palladius was sent by Pope Celestine in 431 *"to the Irish believing in Christ"* as a direct sequel to the visit of Germanus to Britain in 429 in order to tackle the *Peliagian* heresy there but conceivably in Ireland as well (there was a belief in some circles that *Pellagius* was Scotti [Irish] as he ate porridge) it presupposes there was already a Christian community in existence in Ireland prior to Patrick's arrival.[41]

This argument is sometimes countered by the alternative proposition that Patrick ministered to the pagan Irish as not all were Christian. However, there are contrary arguments to this proposition as well in so far as, at that point in time, Rome did not appear interested in ministering to pagans or Barbarians (this later became a name for warriors) and indeed such ministry was forbidden.[42] This line of argument also ignores the indigenous strength of Druidic influence and the evolving, almost integral, relationship which developed between Druidism and Christianity.

Furthermore, there is a persistent but uncertain tradition of Munster saints earlier than the mission of *'Patrick the Briton'* but otherwise undated. *St Ibar* of Becceriu on the north side of Wexford harbour; *St Brioc* of Rosslare also in Wexford who had links with *Germanus* of Auxerre; (in some versions St. Patrick was with *Germanus*), *St Declan* of Ardmore in Co Waterford; *St Ciaran* of Saiger in Offaly, originally linked to Corcu Loigde, and *St Ailbe* of Emly. The first three can be associated with the trade route along the south coast of Ireland, the route of Christianisation and Romanisation. More recent archaeological work provides very early, even fifth century, evidence for Munster Christianity, including artefactual

---

[41] O'Rahilly, Thomas F., The Two Patricks, DIAS, Dublin 4, 1981.
[42] Doherty, Charlie, The Problem of Patrick: History Ireland, Issue 1, Spring 1995.

evidence for direct connections with the east Mediterranean as well as with Roman Britain. All of the foregoing supports the view of a close relationship between southern Ireland and west Britain and links with the eastern Mediterranean as already outlined. [43]

There is also evidence of Irish colonists within the Irish kingdom of Dyfed in Wales, the *Ui Liathain* colony in Cornwall, and the presence of Irish missionaries SS Brychan in the former and Piran and Breaga in the latter. There is also evidence for a strong Romano-British influence for those who initially accepted Christianity by a fifth century *ogham* producing community on the Dingle Peninsula in County Kerry. This is supported by further evidence from the fourth to fifth century from the excavation of a Christian site at Reask in the same general area as Ballintaggart, also in County Kerry. [44]

Thus, it seems the two main forces for external change which ran in parallel and were interlinked were contacts between Irish groups each side of the Irish Sea from the second or third century onward, Christian missionaries either (Britons) Wales, possibly Gaul in origin as visitors or escapees from continental invasions or captured slaves. [45]

It is also significant that some other important and early sources simply don't mention Patrick. *Columbanus* makes no mention of the apostolic role of Patrick in bringing the faith to Ireland and *Bede*[46] seems to have known nothing about Patrick. Notwithstanding the widespread cult of Patrick, there is no trace of his connections with Armagh, still less of an Armagh primacy until the seventh century.

---

[43] O'Corrain, Donnchada, Orosius, Ireland and Christianity.

[44] Swift, C., Ogam Stones and the Earliest Irish Christians, Maynooth Monographs, Series Two, 1997.

[45] Mytum, Harold, The Origins of Early Christian Ireland, Routledge 1992.

[46] Bede, Ecclesiastical History of the English People. (Bede considered the Irish church close to pagan).

From that time the course of Patrick's chronology allows us to see the Patrick legend shift from a generalised cult to gain its focus on Armagh. In the same period, Armagh can be seen rising to power for reasons other than hagiological, and political alliances appear to have played an important part.[47] It is also recorded that the purpose of the Papal-sponsored visit of *Germanus* in 429 CE was to keep Roman Britain Catholic and Christianise the Barbarians in Ireland. Furthermore, by erecting an episcopate in a previously non-Christian country, Pope Celestine brought the Barbarian (non-Roman) island of Ireland within the orbit of the official Christian world.[48]

The traditions associated with Patrick include the names of two continental and non-British clerics as often misreported Bishops *Auxilius* and *Secondinus*, both of whom are represented as disciples of the saint. Far from being companions of '*Patrick the Briton*', these were in fact companions of the continental Palladius who was conveniently disposed of through martyrdom. These two assistants were later subsumed into the all-devouring Patrick legend. It is worth repeating the observation of; '*the many other and better arguments for the existence of pre-Palladian Christian communities in Ireland, but none of these were ever published.*[49]

Some texts (now considered an invention) have noted an association at this time with *Joseph of Arimathea,* whose feast day, strangely enough, was celebrated on the 17th March.

Other studies have placed Patrick's arrival in the period 460 to 490 CE.[50] So whether it was Palladius, sometimes called Patricius, sent by Rome in 431 CE, who arrived in 432 CE and was

---

[47] Sharpe, Richard, St Patrick and the See of Armagh, Cambridge Medieval Celtic Studies 4, 1982.

[48] O'Croinin, Daibhi, Early Medieval Ireland, Longman, 1995.

[49] Ibid.

[50] Charles-Edwards, T.M., Early Christian Ireland, Cambridge, 2000.

conveniently disposed of through martyrdom, or *'Patrick the Briton',* or some other all-encompassing entity, there is the undoubted influence from Rome and all that that entailed in terms of administrative structures and culture. A structure which formed the diocese (a Roman civil unit) with a bishop in overall control as the organisation subsequently evolved.

The Cult of St. Patrick and Armagh

Other than subsequent writings in the seventh century, it can be considered that Patrick's compositing with Palladius and others and the hagiographical chronology therein is more to do with the contest by Armagh for ecclesiastical supremacy in Ireland as a whole, in the sixth and seventh centuries. These clerical propagandist works can also be considered a creation of the seventh century and which went to sustain this version of events.[51] The first reference in this chronicle appears in the Book of the Angel, a composite document, the greater part of which was probably composed c.640 CE. In this Armagh attempted to define a territory within which she exercised immediate ecclesiastical overlordship. This area stretched from Slemish in County Antrim to the hills just north of Slane in County Meath. These expansive claims are likely to have arisen out of political expedience in the seventh century. In the Battle of Mag Roth in 637 CE the Ulaidh suffered a massive defeat from which they never recovered.

In the aftermath the Airgialla, a confederation of tribal groups achieved a degree of independence until their defeat by the Ui Neill in the battle of Leth Cam in 827 CE. Armagh itself was surrounded by the Airgillia and, as the Airgillia emerged from under the

---

[51] Ibid.

overlordship of their political masters, the Ulaidh, the rise of Armagh to dominance had followed their fortunes. The *Book of the Angel,* in which Patrick is given the primatial rights and prerogative of Armagh by an angel, possibly *Victor,* can be seen as Armagh's attempt to make a bid for the headship of the cult on the strength of the patronage of the Airgialla.

Tírechán and Muirchú – Gifted Propagandists

Armagh claimed to be the chief court of ecclesiastical appeal in the island, claimed jurisdiction over diocesan churches, and claimed a *'special tax'* from all churches – even monasteries – since St. Patrick, it claimed, had converted *'all the Irish tribes'.* Just before this time contact was also made with Rome in relation to Easter dates, and at the same time Armagh acquired relics of the principal martyrs of the church, as Armagh did not possess the body of its saint a requirement of the time. (This omission is dealt with earlier by *Muirchú*). By the time *Tírechán*[52] is writing in the late seventh century there is a deliberate policy of searching out churches which ought to belong to the Armagh federation and claiming back those that had been appropriated by other great churches of the period. Armagh's greatest rival for ecclesiastical headship was Kildare but by the late seventh century political circumstances dictated that she could not match the power of the Church of Patrick. *Tírechán*[53] also had Patrick meet the ancestral figures from whom the current ruling dynasties took their names. As well as protecting the weak the Armagh propagandists flattered the powerful into the cult.

---

[52] Tírechán, *Collectanea* ed. and tr. L. Bieler, The Patrician Texts in the Book of Armagh.
[53] Ibid.

Muirchú's[54] skill lay in harmonising relations among the churches and in particular in confirming Armagh as the centre of the cult. He also endowed Patrick with the attributes of the secular hero and ensured that the cult was elevated to that of a *'national apostle'*.[55]

In summary, the notion that early Irish society was archaic and immutable was a fiction peddled from the Middle Ages onwards to suit the interests of different elites. It appears that significant innovations in Irish society, culture, religion, and politics were set in train from the third century in response to climatic change and contacts with the Roman Empire.[56]

Further studies into the relationship with Britain and Gaul also support the argument that a healthy Christian community was already in existence in Ireland through visitors from Britain and Gaul from the third or fourth century onwards. British Christianity was established sometime in the third century, arising from Roman trade, raids, and other links between Britain and the continent. It made its way on an onward journey to Ireland and in some accounts was passed on through the large numbers of captured slaves or via trading routes. Patrick, the legend goes, arrived in Ireland from Britain as a slave (at one point in his attributed *Confessio* he refers to thousands of slaves). These numerous captured slaves were engaged in heavy domestic and agricultural work, either in tillage or, as suggested in Patrick's case, herding.[57] Again, the placing of the arrival of Christianity in the early fifth century seems more to do with creating a chronological proximity by clerical writers in the sixth and seventh centuries to the founding of Armagh in the middle to late fifth

---

[54] Muirchu, *Vita S Patrici*, ed. and tr. L. Bieler, *The Patrician Texts in the Book of Armagh*.

[55] Doherty, Charlie, The Problem of Patrick.

[56] Downham, Clare, Medieval Ireland, Cambridge, 2018.

[57] Charles-Edwards, T.M., Early Christian Ireland.

century. Clerical propagandising was directed to support Armagh's ecclesiastical dominance despite Armagh not being founded by Patrick as an ecclesiastical centre.[58]

In Ireland Celtic paganism, Romano-British Christianity, and classical culture all found a receptive home. The church fostered by the Papal sponsored Palladius or Patricius, or others, was the church already established elsewhere in so far as the church established in Ireland was similar in its main features to the churches of the Western provinces of the Roman Empire. It was not until later that its peculiarities hardened into a markedly different organisation. Hughes cites *Ladner* in his work, *The Idea of Reform*, as follows: '*Could the monastic organisation of the Irish Church, still rather enigmatic as to its origins, be a peculiarly inverted adaption to Celtic rural clan society of the Western Mediterranean and Gallic, originally urban, fusion of monasticism and clericate?*' A question which may well explain the subsequent adaption of monasticism to tribal society. However, Hughes goes on to say that it does not fully explain of itself the peculiarities of the later Irish system. She refers to the Romanised areas of Wales (the Briton influence on Ireland), where there were strong traditions of a territorial diocese of a continental type, whereas in the non-Romanised areas the monastic *paruchiae*[59] carried all before them. Monasticism was present from the beginning and developed in a collective form in Ireland with the creation of monasteries. It owed much of its impetus to the individual ascetic spirit. This manifested itself as withdrawal from society and dedication to spiritual matters. Its origins can be traced to the lives pursued by early Christian hermits or anchorites in the deserts of the Middle East.

---

[58] O'Rahilly, Thomas F., The Two Patricks.

[59] An area of ecclesiastical jurisdiction.

Social Change

By the seventh century the monastic *paruchaie* were flourishing and had adapted to Irish notions of overlordship and their quite different arrangement of jurisdictions.[60] The position of the tribal bishop corresponded to the position of the petty king in his *Tuath* of which there were somewhere between 150 and 180 on the island. Once a confederation of monasteries was founded the position of the abbot of the major church corresponded to the position of an over king. Other houses were founded and houses already in existence joined the confederation, recognising the overlordship of the patron saint and his heirs.[61] Ecclesiastics were given a high grade in this society, undoubtedly influenced by the fact that many prominent ecclesiastics were also members of royal families and prominence in the Church became associated with prominence in society in general.

The monastic communities, which became typical of the Irish Church, were essentially local lineage groups in a religious setting in which the Abbot, as the kinsman of the saint, founder of the monastery, enjoyed the realities of power while the Bishop played an overarching, if secondary, role. This pattern of *'coarbs'* (heirs of the saint) lasted in some areas of Ireland until the seventeenth century. It was this system contrasting so sharply with the centralising ecclesiastical structure of Rome which the Irish missionaries also introduced into parts of Britain. Its strength lay in the establishment of strong local roots. The rules of the Anglo-Saxon Kingdoms, however, expanding into Celtic-sharing areas of Britain, found episcopal organisation more appropriate as an instrument of government.[62] They were also very much opposed to the hereditary

---

[60] Hughes, Kathleen, The Church in Early Irish Society, ACLS, Cornell 1966.
[61] Ibid.
[62] Kearney, Hugh, The British Isles.

elements of the Irish church. The Council of Whitby in 663 CE marked the ending of the relationship with the Insular Celtic church and saw the adoption of Roman practices. This was a vital turning point in the development of the Church in England.

In Ireland, Romanised Christians found a wholly rural-oriented society with a barely embryonic conception of the State but a well-developed legal tradition in which law making was the special function of essentially private persons – a professional class of juriconsults and arbitrators known as the Brehon's. Law and order and the adjustment of conflicting interests were achieved through the giving of sureties rather than state-monopolised coercion. They were basically reflective of the social and legal principles, practices, and procedures of tribal Irish society and the grade, status, and *'honour price'* of individuals. The earliest Irish texts reflect the existence of several different schools of law, each producing its own particular code or tract. It also appears that a Northern and a Southern regional affinity can be detected. It was from the tenth century that the legal fiction arose that the Irish law was a unity.[63] The Roman legal system in essence comprised of two distinct sectors, civil law regulating economic transaction between citizens, and public law governing political relations between the State and its subjects. The former was *jus* the latter *lex*. The enhancement of private property from below was matched by the public authority from above.[64] The Christian church was *Romanised* in its institutional and cultural conceptions. It was urban-oriented, and thanks to St Augustine, had reconciled itself to the Roman conception of the State.[65]

---

[63] Ibid.

[64] Anderson, Perry, Lineages of the Absolutist State.

[65] Peden Joseph R., Property Rights in Celtic Irish Law.

CHAPTER THREE

CELTS, CULTURE AND SOCIAL

TRANSITION IN EARLY IRELAND

The fifth century also saw the decline of the system of independent small kingdoms and the rise of two major over-kingdoms, that of the Ui Neill in the North and Midlands of the country and that of the Eoghanachta in the South.[66] By the eight century, the political order established by the Ui Neill was based upon consent more than military power. The consent was expressed in contractual form, in treaties of *cairde* between the principal kingdom and in contracts of clientship with the base-client kingdoms. The political order therefore was one of contractual lordship, but it was also a complex pattern of lineages related by real consanguinity, by fictional consanguinity, and by the non-consanguinity kinship of foster-parents and foster-children. The political order was also the social order.[67] Later, the formation of a retinue system was mostly a decisive preliminary in the gradual transition from a tribal towards a feudal order. It constituted the critical break with a system governed by kinship relations: the retinue was always definable as an elite that cut across kin solidarity, substituting conventional for biological bonds of loyalty. This system,

---

[66] Kearney, Hugh, The British Isles.
[67] Charles-Edwards, T M , Early Christian Ireland.

when it arrived, signalled the approaching demise of the clan system.[68]

In cultural terms the arrival of Christianity marked the opening up of Ireland to the Latin language, the first signs of literacy, and to the values of Rome. During the fourth century, Christianity had become the established religion of the Roman Empire and as a consequence had modelled itself on the Roman administrative model. The church was no longer a network of sects but an organisation made up of dioceses (the secular term for the imperial administrative unit) ruled by bishops in a monarchical system in which the Emperor, as well as the Pope, exercised a great deal of power.[69]

Tribal Social Formations

There are a number of constructs in relation to societal formations around clan, sept, and tribal communities. It is arguable that early medieval Ireland was a highly stratified society and was not a monolithic social entity. In their early formation, rather than being a homogenous whole, the Celts formed a set of societies that were complex and varied in nature. Some Celtic groups depended on trade while others relied on farming and stock herding. Language and culture were possibly the only things that distinguished the Celtic peoples from the other peoples of Europe. Theirs was a linguistic group, not a racial one. However, language was not the only unifying factor. A community in religion very effectively tied the Celtic peoples together, as well an order of pagan priests – the Druids – who existed throughout the Celtic world and acted as a unifying force.[70] As tribal social organisation was inseparable from tribal

---

[68] Anderson, Perry, Passages from Antiquity to Feudalism.

[69] Kearney, Hugh, The British Isles.

[70] Grunke, KR., The Effect of Christianity Upon the British Celts.

religion, the political passage to a territorial system was equally invariably accompanied by ideological conversion to Christianity. The Christian religion concentrated the abandonment of the subjective world of the clan community, as a wider divine order was the spiritual complement of a firmer terrestrial authority[71], and introduced the concept of individual responsibility.

Monasticism and Social Attitudes to Labour

On the margins of the ecclesiastical apparatus, the growth of monasticism pointed in a different direction. In the 370s CE Basil linked ascetics, manual labour, and intellectual instruction into a coherent monastic rule for the first time. This evolution can be retrospectively seen as one of the first signs of a slow sea change in social attitudes to labour. Transplanted to the West and reformulated by Benedict of Nursia during the depths of the sixth century, monastic principles proved organisationally efficacious and ideologically influential from the later dark ages. In the Western monastic orders, intellectual and manual labour were united in the service of God.[72] From a position where manual labour was deeply associated with loss of liberty, agrarian toil now acquired the dignity of divine worship and was performed by literate monks; *labore est orare,* and with this one of the cultural barriers to technical invention and progression undoubtedly fell.

The different course of events in East and West made it clear that it was the total complex of social relations, not the Church itself, which ultimately allocated the economic and cultural roles of monasticism. (Its productive career could only start once the

---

[71] Anderson, Perry, Passages from Antiquity to Feudalism.
[72] ibid.

disintegration of classical slavery had released the elements for another dynamic, to be achieved with the formation of feudalism). The Church without doubt was also more directly responsible for a more formidable, silent transformation. The Bishops and clergy of the Western provinces of the Roman Empire, by undertaking the conversion of the mass of the rural population, durably Latinised their speech during the course of the fourth and fifth centuries. This central achievement of the early Church indicates its true place and function in the transition to feudalism. Its autonomous efficacy was not to be found in the realm of economic relations or social structures but in the cultural sphere above them.[73]

Irish Monastic Families

Early Christian Ireland developed a rich monastic culture centred not on territorial churches but on the monastic families linked by blood to a common founder. The succession to the abbacy of these monastic sites rested primarily in the family of the founding saint and secondly in the family of the original donor of the land. The network of monastic quasi-tribal federations called *paruchiae* was essentially an adaptation of monastic Christianity to tribal society.[74]

Ruling families spread into the churches and tended to rule as hereditary possessions the important churches of the local kingdoms. Wealth and power attracted ambitious superiors, royal and aristocratic ecclesiastical lineages took root in the church, and with them ambition – worldly and ecclesiastical – that led to conflict and violence in and between them.[75] Superiors of great churches often

---

[73] Ibid.

[74] Maguire, Martin, Churches and Symbolic Power in the Irish Landscape.

[75] O'Corrain, D., Island of Saints and Scholars: Myth or Reality?

behaved as did great secular lords: they engaged in conflicts over property with other churches and sometimes with the kings and secular lords. The *manaig*[76] supplied the manpower and the clergy the leadership.[77] Married clergy, lay abbots, sons succeeding their fathers in ecclesiastical appointments, offices held in plurality, all characteristics usually considered as abuses of the Viking Age were in fact all present in the Irish Church before the Viking raids began.[78] Additionally, by encouraging whole families to go over to the religious life, the church circumvented the difficulties involved in alienating land belonging to the kindred; and by extending ever wider the degrees of consanguinity within which people could not marry, the church eliminated the potential heirs to the property. The vast properties accumulated by the monastic *paruchaie* in the following centuries shows just how successful this strategy was to become.[79]

In some cases familial land was donated with the consent of all the kindred but the abbot or cleric holding the benefice had to be chosen from the kindred of the donor. For example, ten of the first eleven Abbots of Iona were kinsmen of the founder Columcille. St. Malachy of Armagh, the leading promoter of the Hildebrandine reform in Ireland, struggled to dislodge the greatest hereditary ecclesiastical lineage in Ireland, the Ui Sinaig of Armagh. Its family members had ruled Armagh in the late eighth century, but from 1001 to 1105 they held it without a break passing the office to siblings, sons, and grandsons. This lineage was also the target of St. Bernard in his *Life of Malachy*, '*for they allowed none to be bishops but members of their own tribe and*

---

[76] *Manaig, they sustained the Church by their labour and payments and also reflected the secular categories of soer-manaig and doer-manaig, (free and unfree), others were acquired with the land, (serfsfuidir and senchleite), as were slaves, O'Corrain. D, The Irish Church, Its Reform and the English Invasion, Four Courts Press, 2017.*

[77] Ibid.

[78] Hughes, Kathleen, The Church in Early Irish Society.

[79] O'Croinin, Daibhi, Early Medieval Ireland.

family ... there have been already fifteen instances of succession in this wickedness. And so far had an evil and adulterous generation established for themselves this depraved rule, a wickedness that ought to be punished by death of any kind, that though sometimes there were no clerics of that family, there were always bishops'.[80] Although, this is considered in other quarters to be part of a campaign exalting the life of Malachy who had to resign as Archbishop of Armagh for political reasons and is alongside later propaganda which provided support for the Norman Invasion.[81]

Law enforcement was not a function of the state, which didn't exist in any formal way, or of the king in an Irish *Tuath*, who was not sovereign. Certain mythological kings like Cormaic Mac Airt were reputed to be lawgivers and judges but turned out to be euhemerised Celtic deities. So Irish law was in essence Brehon's law and the state was absent in its creation and development. Law and order, and the adjustment of conflicting interests, were achieved through the giving of sureties rather than state-monopolised coercion. Outside the institutions of the state the Brehon's evolved an extremely sophisticated and flexible legal response to changing social and cultural conditions while preserving principles of equity and the protection of property rights.[82]

The general effect of Christianity upon Irish Law was to modify it without dislocating it; its rigidity was reduced and the result was a strengthening of Irish institutions.[83] The failure of the church to impose its own will upon the Irish law is best appreciated if one considers the fact that the Church was compelled to create its own legal codes in which a wide variety of criminal and moral practices were outlawed and appropriate penalties assigned. The Church did

---

[80] O'Corrain, Donnchada, Island of Saints and Scholars.
[81] O'Corrain, D., The Irish Church. 2017.
[82] Peden Joseph R., Property Rights in Celtic Irish Law.
[83] Hughes, Kathleen, The Church in Early Irish Society.

secure for itself almost total freedom from lay ownership and secular obligations and the four *Cana*[84] provided for the protection from violence of clerics, church property, and women and children. It has been suggested that the existence of two competing law systems in medieval Gaelic Ireland reflected a more subtle tendency in Irish jurisprudence and practice to conceive of *Ecclesia* and *Tuath* as separate and alternate entities with each having its own rights, and relations between the two governed by contract.[85]

Early Economy and Social Structure

There are two competing versions as to how economic activity was regulated in early medieval Ireland and which can be identified. The first suggests reciprocal rights and duties originating through bands of kinship and clientship, a form of quasi-feudalisation, while the second focuses on individual agency and social mobility. The authors in this case argue that to better understand the economic situation in early medieval Ireland, it is necessary to recognise the productive activities that were pursued at the time to identify certain aspects of commerce or trade.[86] The early medieval society that emerges, from studies on the base or dependant clientship relationship, is a strict almost pyramidal hierarchy. There is inherently a fundamental need to acquire property built in to this relationship. Economic activity had been embedded in this society with each one tied to their neighbour by the circulation of goods and services. Livestock farming was dominated by cattle, with sheep and pigs making up the balance. Arable farming was dominated by barley production and less

---

[84] O'Croinin, Daibhi, Early Medieval Ireland, p 80.

[85] Peden Joseph R., Property Rights in Celtic Irish Law.

[86] Kerr et al, The Economy of Early Medieval Ireland.

prominently by oats. This seems to reflect the property qualifications desirable for farmers in the various law tracts of the time. There is also an amount of industrial activity. Thus we have pastoral farming, arable farming, and craft working. Early medieval Ireland, it is suggested, embraced two spheres of economic activity.

The first area focused on farming and land-holding and was largely controlled by the nobility and this seems to have been dominated by various reciprocal acts and tight social contracts. The second area focused on industrial activity, and this may have been more dominated by supply and demand. It is likely that the monasteries may have been a major controlling factor in some of these activities, for example bronze-making and glass-working. However, the most widespread industries, such as iron-working or cloth-making, may have been primarily in the hands of individual craft workers known as *Nemids*, with goods being exchanged from one economic sphere to the other. This included producing a surplus for external trade and exchange, for example types of cloth-making and shoe-making. It does appear there was insufficient economic capacity at that time to support a mercantile class.

Sources are scarce as to what role was played by Irish ships or shipping in the import and export trade but it does not appear that they were passive recipients only.[87] There is at least one reference to *Breccan, 'a distinguished merchant for the Ui Neill; he had fifty currachs engaged in trade between Britain and Ireland'*. After 800 CE, no merchant of the Ui Neill is likely to have organised the sea-borne trade between Ireland and Britain on such a scale; as that was now the preserve of the *'heathens'* (Vikings) and part of their trade was selling Irish slaves their reward for their raids on Ireland itself.[88]

---

[87] Ibid.

[88] Charles-Edwards T.M., Early Christian Ireland.

Though there is some evidence of markets, it is probable that imported goods which were luxuries were sold directly to their consumers, mostly the establishment of kings and the greater monasteries. There is good reason to believe these were trading centres of some sort and by 800 CE many of them had developed into monastic towns, with populations large by medieval standards and by some sources upwards of 1,500 to 2,000 people. Monastic freedom from military imposts and secular war was important not only for religious but for commercial purposes. With their superior administration, more sophisticated agricultural work, and income from the faithful, they were in a position to develop a surplus in their economy far quicker than secular rulers. This is evident from the fact that in times of severe famine or cattle-plague the secular rulers plundered the greater monasteries with regularity. By the eighth and ninth centuries monastic towns with workshops and crafts with extensive farmland very largely given over to grain-growing and related brewing and bakeries became an important feature of the Irish economy.[89]

As in many ancient societies, in Ireland many economic transactions took place under the guise of a contractual relationship known as clientship. In Irish law clientship was of two distinct types- free and base, distinguished from one another by the type of services required by each. Free clientship – *soer-celsine* – was the grant by a king or noble to another free man of livestock in return for a payment of a "rent" of one third of the value of the livestock to be paid annually for seven years. At the end of that time, the client became sole and absolute owner of the livestock and his clientship terminated. Where a form of communal ownership existed it provided that certain lands could not be sold without the consent of the *derbfine* – all males

---

[89] O'Corrain, D., *Ireland before the Normans*, Gill and Macmillan, Dublin, 1972.

descended from a common great-grandfather to the third generation. All classes of free men were eligible to become free clients without any loss of legal status, franchise, or honour price. The only other obligations were that the free client did homage to his lord or creditor by standing in his presence and by attending him on certain ceremonial occasions. The Irish upper classes invested a large part of their assets in acquiring as many clients as they could afford. This gave them increased rank, social and legal status. It also raised the value of their honour-price, thereby increasing their capacity to act as sureties and compurgators. The base-client was also a free man, an owner of some land, but usually a commoner. He received a grant of either stock or land from a person of higher rank in return for a payment in kind (a food rent) proportionate in value to the borrowed land or stock. In addition he owed specified labour services and this is why his clientship was base.

Amongst the ranks of the unfree were a specific class – the *seanchleite* – who were legal equivalent of the English *villeins*, hereditary holders of a parcel of land in return for uncertain service and they passed as appurtences should the land be alienated or sold as they were included as part of the owners' property. Another class of the unfree were the *fuidhir* who were not *villeins* but were tenants at will and free to move subject to notice. Beneath them came the slaves who had no status at all.[90] However, slavery itself was highly important in early medieval Ireland and this was underlined by the fact that *'cumhal'*, the term for a female slave, was taken as a standard value of worth and as a land unit.[91]

---

[90] Peden Joseph R., *Property Rights in Celtic Irish Law*.
[91] Kerr et al?

Social Change

The emerging society in Ireland was one with inequalities of descent, inequality of wealth, and lines of class division developed from these relations, be it employer-labourer, landlord-tenant, and debtor-creditor as part of a transition from kinship organisation to a territorial one.[92] Engels dismissed the clan system as a *'feudal-patriarchal system'* when researching work for his *History of Ireland* (which was never completed). Alternatively, in the *Origins of the Family, Private Property and the State*, Engels refers to; *'the English jurists of the 17th century who were sent across to Ireland for the purpose of converting the clan lands into royal dominions. Up to this time the soil had been the collective property of the gens or clan.'*[93] MacNeill accepted that in relation to the property of a family or kindred group, *'communal ownership existed, in that certain land could not be sold without the consent of the derbhfine—all males descended from a common great-grandfather to the third generation'.*[94]

Clan ownership became an important feature of all subsequent attempts at plantation, dispossession, or transfer of land ownership. The Anglo-Norman invasion of Ireland in the late twelfth century, and the subsequent partial conquest of the territory, illuminates a view of what preceded it. This invasion was to have a detrimental effect upon the status and legal rights of the Irish clients, particularly those who were base. Neither form of Irish clientship was equivalent to Anglo-Norman vassalage. Free clientship was essentially a form of commercial contract in which the purchaser bought stock on a deferred time-based payment basis. This could not be mistaken for a feudal bond of vassalage or a fief, but base clientship where manual

---

[92] Jackson, T.A. , Ireland Her Own, Lawrence and Wishart, London 1976.
[93] Ellis, Beresford P., A History of the Irish Working Class, Pluto Press 1985.
[94] Peden Joseph R., Property Rights in Celtic Irish Law.
[94] Ibid.

labour services were required along with an annual food rent was more easily misunderstood as equivalent to English *villeinage* or serfdom. With the English occupation, both the base clients and the *fuidir* were reduced to serfdom under English law. Thus the English conquest meant a vast displacement and dispossession, and loss of status, for most of the Irish landholding classes and tenants as well. The English government encouraged Irish rulers to surrender their *Tuath* and its landed territory to the English Crown which would then re-grant its feudal tenure to the Irish king who thenceforth would be a feudal vassal. The result of this transaction was to transfer ownership of all lands from the allodial Irish owners to the English king and then as a fief to the new Irish vassal-dispossessing the people to the benefit of the Crown. A further result of the English conquest was the displacement of the Irish law of inheritance. Under the feudal customs of England the law of primogeniture prevailed and was also applied to Ireland. The English State was incompatible with the Irish *Tuath*; the English common law was totally incompatible with the Irish law. Ireland from the twelfth century was a single country in which two nations, two laws, and two cultures engaged in a constant struggle for dominance or survival.[95]

The social and political world of classical antiquity, the nature of the transition to the medieval world, the resultant social relations, and evolution to feudalism in Western Europe, and their sequel absolutism emerge and present central to the illumination of any further examination of early and medieval Irish social History.

---

[95] Ibid.

CHAPTER FOUR

THE VIKING INVASIONS AND CHANGE IN

IRISH SOCIETY

At the close of the eighth century, and prior to the arrival of the Vikings, Anglo-Saxon colonists controlled an area stretching from the Forth to the south coast of England, and as far east as a line stretching from the Dee to the Tamar. Irish culture had become dominant in the Western Isles of Scotland and in the area of Western Scotland north of the Clyde. Irish culture also established itself in the east of what is now Scotland, among the Picts who were introduced to Christianity by Irish missionaries from Iona led by Columcille (Columba). During this period also, Irish culture penetrated into South Wales and to the Isle of Man. There was also an influence of Irish culture in the Anglo-Saxon kingdom of Northumbria and as the Anglo-Saxon and Irish cultures rose in importance the Pictish and British cultures declined. The relationship between Anglo-Saxon and British cultures, between colonists and colonised, was permanently antagonistic.

These cultural links did not exclude political tension when the interests of the Anglo-Saxon and the Gaels clashed either, for example the battle of Degsastan in 603 CE, when Aethelfrith of Northumbria defeated Aedhan MacGabhrain, King of Dalriada. Bad relations between the Britons and the Saxons, who following Bede[96]

---

[96] Bede, Ecclesiastical History of the English People, Oxford University Press, 2008

were now called the English, continued into the eighth century and beyond. Thanks to Bede, the English found themselves provided with a Christian version of their past which obscured the realities of their Barbaric origins and which linked them with Christian Rome rather than pagan Germany. Early West Saxon law codes treated Britons, whom they called Welsh (foreigners), as second-class citizens and it was not until the ninth century that a political unit resembling Scotland emerged. Bede's stress upon the existence of an English nation is what led to an exaggeration of the degree of unity that existed in pre-Viking England.[97]

Essentially, Viking expansion was markedly commercial in character: the objects of their seaborne expeditions included not merely land for settlement but also currency and commodities in the first phase. In the second phase they sacked some towns in their path, in the Irish case monastic cities which were centres of wealth and economic development, such as Clonmacnoise, Durrow, and Kildare. But they also founded far more towns on the coast as in Dublin, Limerick, Waterford, Cork, and Wexford. Towns were the nerve centres of the Viking trade and the central traffic of this trade was slaves, captured and transported from all over Europe but above all from the Celtic West and the Slav East. It is necessary to distinguish the respective pattern of Norwegian, Danish, and Swedish expansion.

The Norwegians, on the Western flank, seem to have been impelled by land shortages in their mountainous homeland; they typically sought beyond simple booty soil for settlement no matter how inhospitable. Besides raiding Ireland and Scotland, they peopled the bleak Faroes and colonised Iceland where there was already evidence of an Irish monastic presence. This expansion led to a growing demand for labour in the new settlements of the North

---

[97] Kearney, H., The British Isles.

Atlantic. A conservative estimate puts the population of Iceland at 20,000 around 930 CE and perhaps a quarter of this population were slaves, most of them of Celtic origin.[98] The Danish expeditions to the Centre, that conquered and planted North-Eastern England, parts of Ireland, and Normandy, were much more organised assaults under disciplined quasi-royal command and created more compact and hierarchical overseas societies which extorted treasure and protection money such as *danegeld*. This booty was spent locally, building up stable territorial occupation.

Swedish expansion (*Rus*) was on the extreme Eastern flank and penetration of Russia was not concerned with land settlement but with the control of trade routes and was overwhelmingly commercial in orientation. This commercial empire was built fundamentally on the sale of slaves to the Islamic world. The generalised use of slave labour within the Scandinavian homelands themselves, the result of this predatory commerce abroad, served paradoxically to preserve much of primitive Viking society at home. The typical pattern of tribal communities in the initial phase of social differentiation was the dominance of a warrior aristocracy whose lands were tilled by captured slaves. It is the presence of this external forced labour that permitted the coexistence of a nobility with an indigenous free peasantry organised in agnatic clans. The surplus labour necessary for the emergence of a landed nobility had not yet been extracted from their impoverished kinsmen.

These Viking invasions precipitated the crystallisation of feudalism amidst the disintegration of the Carolingian Empire in the ninth century. After three centuries of overseas raids and settlements the dynamic of Viking expansion eventually came to an end with the

---

[98] Holm, Poul, The Slave Trade of Dublin, Ninth to Twelfth Centuries, Peritia, January, 1986.

last great Norwegian attack on England in 1066. The fruits of this expedition were reaped three weeks later at Hastings by the Normans, a Danish overseas community that had made its own, the new military structures of European feudalism. Heavy cavalry conquered England where long ships had been repelled. The halting of Viking expansion overseas in itself inevitably led to radical changes in Scandinavia for it meant the supply of slave labour now effectively ceased and, with this change, the old social structures increasingly broke up.[99]

The Vikings in Ireland

Bitter is the wind tonight
It tosses the ocean's white hair:
Tonight I fear not the fierce warriors of Norway
Coursing on the Irish Sea[100]

Historians have differed as to the effects of the Viking[101] raids on Ireland. Some have viewed them as agents of major change within Irish society and politics, others as merely increasing those forms of violence already endemic between the Irish themselves. The Viking threat itself developed in stages. From 794 to 807 CE the attacks were confined to islands and coastlands. In 802 CE the island of Iona was ransacked and more than sixty monks killed, as a result of which the community transferred to Kells in County Meath around 806 CE.

---

[99] Anderson, Perry, Passages from Antiquity to Feudalism.

[100] Hughes, Kathleen, The Church in Early Irish Society.

[101] Old English *wicing* was a common noun meaning 'pirate' and did not apply to all Vikings (Charles Edwards T M, Early Christian Ireland.)

After 807 CE there was more conflict on the mainland of Ireland. From 814 to 820 CE the attacks subsided. The 830s saw a major acceleration in both the frequency and range of Viking activity.

The first recorded Viking raid in Ireland took place in 795 CE and these were considered to be from Norway. Accounts of raids in the annals for the period from 795 to 820 CE is at a low but steady pace with less than five recorded between 801 and 810 CE and a similar number recorded between 810 and 820 CE. From 830 CE onwards the intensity of Viking raids increased substantially and seventy per cent of all raids by Vikings on Church settlements in the ninth century are recorded as taking place between 821 and 850 CE, with a dramatic increase between 837 and 845 CE. After this period the evidence points to an increased absorption into Irish dynastic politics. The Danish Vikings are considered to be involved from about 850 CE onwards and they clashed also with the Norwegian Vikings.

It can be said that capturing individuals for the purpose of ransoming them back to their communities was a significant objective of the Viking raids. It cannot be said to the same extent that the seizure of Irish metalwork was a significant purpose of these raids but may well have been a by-product, albeit views differs on this activity. The taking of captives on a large scale – most likely with a view to selling or using them as slaves – can be shown to be the purpose of Viking raids up to the middle of the ninth century. There are references in the annals of Ulster in 821, 831, 836 and 845 CE, which mention the taking of significant numbers of captives. The Vikings were not only on the Eastern coast: the formidable rocks of Skellig off the coast of Kerry did not protect its Abbot Eitgal (823 CE). He died of hunger and thirst as their prisoner and was probably captured for ransom a fruitless exercise where these avowed penniless, exiled, and non-materialistic aesthetes were concerned.

In 839 CE, the Vikings were on Lough Neagh and from there proceeded to destroy *'all the territories and churches of northern Ireland'*, taking captive bishops, priests, and men of learning those with the highest honour-price and putting others to death. Monasteries of the time could put armies into the field as big as those of a petty king of which there were many and alliances with churches were usually more profitable to lay princes than conflict. The political organisation of Irish society, with its numerous petty kings, had allowed endless opportunities for internecine battles – an obvious advantage to the warring Vikings. Also, it was not uncommon for such petty kings to take advantage of a neighbour's difficulty to conduct a cattle raid. There was no concept of a coordinated or common defence. The four *Cana*[102] protected clerics, church property, and women and children from the violence of laymen. Kings paid compensation for violation of sanctuary and society had recognised supernatural immunities but against the Vikings the churches were defenceless and the wrath of the saints meant nothing to these invaders.[103]

Church Wealth, Depredations and Irish Alliances

After 850 CE, raids on church settlements became more in line with the local political allegiances of the Vikings and two thirds of Viking raids on churches can be linked to their documented relations with the Irish dynasts. A case in point being the attack on the principle church of the Northern Ui Neill at Armagh in 882 CE. The Northern Ui Neill being an enemy of the Southern Ui Neill with whom the Vikings had made an alliance. Irish forces were involved in the burning, plundering, or profanation of churches on the following

---

[102] O'Croinin, Daibhi, Early Medieval Ireland, p 80.

[103] Hughes, Kathleen, The Church in Early Irish Society, pp 198-202.

occasions; 850, 851, 854, 870, 874, 891 and 896 CE.[104] Moreover, the successful depredations on church property uncompensated and unavenged could well have broken down Irish inhibitions against desecration, although historians differ on this assessment.

A notorious case was Feidlimid, King of Cashel (Munster), an anchorite and prominent Culdee described in his obituary notice as: *optimus, Scotorum, scriba et ancorita.* He was responsible during his reign (820-847 CE) for more violence towards the church than any other. In 833 CE he killed the religious family of Clonmacnoise and burned its *termon*[105] to the door of the church: in the same manner *'did he treat the family of Durrow'*. In 838 CE he entered the abbacy of Cork and also occupied the abbot's chair at Clonfert. So while most ordinary anchorites (men who withdrew from the life of the monastic city into asceticism, prayer, and preparation for the afterlife) dwelt alone in their hermit's cell, renouncing the wretched world, this ascetic held a kingdom, assumed abbacies, burned churches beyond his own borders, and slew their inhabitants.[106] The direct opposite and the most notable of the aesthetes was Aenghus, often described as the most prominent *Ceile De* or Culdee. He was considered to have been one of the influential promoters of this aspect of church organisation who were considered by Rome to be canons secular and to be under the rule of St. Augustine.[107]

In an attack on Kells in 951 CE, 3,000 persons or more were captured and a large booty of goods, horses, and gold was taken. In an attack on Armagh in 996 CE the Airgialla drove off 2,000 cows. In

---

[104] Ibid, p, 207.

[105] Areas of sanctity, up to four, including land near the monastic city. See Hughes, Kathleen, The Church.

[106] Hughes, Kathleen, The Church in Early Irish Society, pp 192-193.

[107] Healy, John, Most Rev., INSULA SANCTORUM ET DOCTORUM, Sealy, Bryers and Walker, Dublin, 1912.

1090 CE about 100 houses were burnt which indicates a dense population and the motivation for the attacks is clear: the monasteries were centres of considerable wealth and population. The process of secularisation and most of the violence towards monasteries had little to do with Viking example it appears, but was generated rather by the economic growth of the monasteries as they were the areas of concentrated economic development and wealth in Ireland.[108]

In the latter decades of the ninth century the Vikings began to concentrate their raiding activity in the central east of the country. This was where they made most of their political alliances.[109] They settled in much more limited areas than in England or Scotland and they had lost most of their independent political power by the late ninth century, becoming *just another factor in the tangled web of native Irish political alliances*.[110] In 930 CE we hear of the first united Viking-Irish action including the taking of prisoners when Ceallachan of Cashel with the Norse of Waterford plundered Meath and took many captives, among them the Abbots of Clonenagh and Killeigh. One of the Abbots was led to Dublin to be kept prisoner at Dalkey Island. Prisoners were kept there for ransom and, if the ransom was not forthcoming, taken onwards to the Dublin slave market. He drowned while trying to escape the following year.[111]

The Viking towns of Dublin, Limerick, Cork, and Waterford enjoyed no meaningful autonomy after the tenth century. The brunt of the Viking attacks was borne by the Ui Neill lands and this may well have put a stop to their dynastic interference in Leinster. However, the process of development was slowed not halted, and the

---

[108] O'Corrain, D., Ireland Before the Normans.

[109] Cox, Neville, Vikings, Undergraduate Reward Library, NUIM, 2012.

[110] O'Croinin, D., Early Medieval Ireland.

[111] Holm, Poul, The Slave Trade of Dublin.

greater kings of the eleventh and twelfth centuries' partitioned kingdoms, appointed subordinate rulers, granted away whole territories and expelled royal dynasties. They made dependant lords of their subordinate kings and developed power-based territorial lordships which bore a striking resemblance to the feudal type kingdoms of Europe. In parallel the church attempted to Christianise kingship and made efforts to introduce the ceremony of ordaining kings as was the custom in continental Europe and in Anglo-Saxon England.[112]

The internal struggles of the Ui Neill in the three decades after 945 CE did much to weaken the dynasty and gave it few opportunities to exert its old dominance. While the Ui Neill battled with one another, and the struggle for supremacy was being played out between the Northern and Southern dynasties, the kings of Leinster and Connaught grew powerful. In Munster, freed of Ui Neill intervention, the Dal Cais seized the kingship and produced in the person of Brian Boru the king who was to overthrow the Ui Neill and prepare the way for the great struggle for the kingship of Ireland. This was an event which was to dominate Irish politics until the Norman Invasion.

Viking Trading Towns and Absorption into Irish Society

In effect the Viking trading towns and their populations were gradually absorbed into the political and social system that surrounded them. The two significant defeats of Viking power in Dublin in 980 CE, and again in 1001 CE, during the kingship struggle, ensured that the Dublin kingdom remained within the orbit of Irish political affairs, while Wexford, Waterford, and Limerick

---

[112] O'Corrain, D., Ireland Before the Normans, Gill and Macmillan, Dublin, 1972.

likewise came under the control of native Irish overlords. During the last hundred years to 1054 CE in the independent kingdom of Dublin, the warrior camp was transformed into a merchant's town with a growing market and expanding economic relations with the Irish kings serving their needs for luxury products.[113]

As centres of accumulating wealth, these Norse towns came to be regarded as sources of income and power and not as the citadels of foreigners to be sacked. By the twelfth century they received the *'ultimate imprimatur'* of Irish scholarship when the mythical founder-king of Dublin was converted to Christianity by St. Patrick himself.[114] By the eleventh century Dublin became the foremost trading centre of Ireland, taking over the role of such former nuclei as the great monastic settlements. Other Norse towns like Waterford and Limerick also became renowned ports and valuable assets to any Irish king who could claim their over lordship and control the distribution of luxury items such as wine, silk, handicraft, and precious stones. To purchase these articles, Ireland would supply largely two commodities: cattle and slaves; and slaves were in demand by any aristocrats, Scandinavian, Irish, or Anglo-Saxon.[115]

The battle at Clontarf was not a struggle between the Irish and the Norse for the sovereignty of Ireland; neither was it a great national victory which broke the power of the Norse forever, long before Clontarf the Norse had become a minor force in Irish political affairs. In fact, Clontarf was part of the internal struggle for sovereignty and was essentially the revolt of the Leinster men against the dominance of Brian, a revolt in which their Norse allies played an important but secondary role. In the subsequent traditional telling of

---

[113] Holm, Poul, The Slave Trade of Dublin.
[114] O'Croinin, D., Early Medieval Ireland.
[115] Holm, Poul, The Slave Trade of Dublin.

both Irish and Norse sagas Clontarf became a heroic battle of saga and story-telling, the list of combatants was swelled by numerous additions and the contingents from the Isles and from Mann became the forces of the whole Viking world. In turn, Brian became a legend, the sovereign of Ireland, who led the forces of the nation to victory over the foreigners.[116]

Social Change

In summary, the main Viking achievement in Ireland was their introduction of towns, although proto-towns of a kind were already in existence represented by the larger monastic cities, the Viking input was its innovative character. Most of the settlements were defensive in nature at first, fortified encampments that developed into small towns, while places like Dublin, Limerick, and Waterford eventually progressed to become quasi-city-states. Viking mastery of the high seas and their control of strategic commercial land routes in Europe brought them massive wealth which was to outclass the resources of most Irish kings.

An unwelcome Viking influence was the growth of slavery and the slave-trade in the tenth and eleventh centuries. The boom of the Dublin slave market occurred in the late tenth and eleventh centuries as a result of the work of freebooters and especially the struggles of over kings for supremacy. Thus, the market expanded in response to the profound changes of internal Irish warfare and to the changing role of Dublin in the Irish power struggle. The declining importance of slavery in the twelfth century was probably caused by the Viking defeat in England, by the severance of links with Scandinavia, the rise of Bristol in Irish Sea trade, and the establishment of territorial

---

[116] O'Corrain, D., Ireland Before the Normans.

kingdoms with defined boundaries.

Between the coming of the Vikings and the Norman invasion it is clear that Irish society underwent a radical transformation. The old order of mainly two ruling federations, each resting on loosely organised networks of autonomous *Tuatha* and locally based monastic communities, gave way to new style territorial kingdoms held together by quasi-feudal ties, supported by a reformed episcopate, centralised religious orders, and subordinate towns. The overall result, it appears, was the rise to prominence of those parts of Ireland which hitherto had been of minor economic and political importance. The ports of Dublin, Wexford, and Waterford eventually brought the kingdom of Leinster and Diarmaid Mac Murrough to a leading place among the new kingdoms. The same may also be said of the effect of Cork upon the McCarthy kingdom of Desmond and of Limerick upon the O'Brien kingdom of Thomond. The economic and financial resources such centres provided became the sources of revenue which helped build territories on a much larger scale than before and provide a further explanation as to the consolidation of territory and the reduction in the numbers of *Tuath*.

Dublin enjoyed a position of unrivalled importance both as an emporium for the Atlantic trade and the base of a powerful fleet which could be hired out as a mercenary fleet most evident when the City was under the control of Irish kings. In 1165, Diarmaid Mac Murrough hired it out to King Henry II of England for a six-month campaign in Wales, a debt called in the following year. This period also witnessed the growth of an ever more powerful kingship, some, but not all of it, attributable to the Viking invasions which manifested itself in the increasing militarisation of Irish society. There was also the appearance of castles and bridges (prior to the Norman invasion), naval fleets and cavalry units, and of something akin to standing armies. There also appeared the evolution of what could be termed a military strategy and there is evidence that Anglo-Normans built their castles atop earlier Irish fortifications in the countryside.[117]

Throughout these centuries the guiding thread is the changing character and position of land ownership and its social relationship with political systems from primitive tribalism on to the eve of capitalism.[118]

---

[117] O'Croinin, D., Early Medieval Ireland.

[118] Anderson, Perry, Lineages of the Absolutist State, p 405.

CHAPTER FIVE

TWELFTH-CENTURY CHURCH REFORM

AND THE ENGLISH INVASION

Irish marital and sexual behaviour was the main and almost exclusive preoccupation of the reformers of the Irish church in the twelfth century. Other crimes and serious sins, such as parricide, murder, treachery, rapine, and theft eloquently denounced by Irish religious writers and teachers are largely ignored. These marital and sexual practices encountered by the Gregorian reformers and repeatedly condemned by them, namely, that the Irish divorce and remarry, that they exchange and sell wives, and that they do not observe the church's incest prohibitions or pay tithes, reveal a great deal about the structure of Irish society in the eleventh and twelfth centuries. They throw some light on the possible motivation of the Church reformers. Particularly, when one considers that all over Europe lineages tended to marry their close relatives in order to preserve family estates and foster the ideology of kinship on which they based their power. Equally, the church opposed the marriage of close relatives and extended the bounds of incest prohibitions to the sixth degree. Noted earlier, was one motivating factor for the church for this policy in that this would deal with inheritance difficulties and facilitate the transfer of property to the church and provide for its subsequent enrichment.

In Ireland the extension of familial degrees ruled out members of one's *gelfhine* and *derbhfhine*, the basic property-owning kin, and made it difficult to consolidate family lands by strategic marriage. This arose particularly in the case of inheriting females, in default of male heirs, who took a life-interest in family estates and could transmit an interest to their children only by marrying one of the patri-lateral heirs, usually a first or second cousin. In the case of the property owning nobility, essentially those were the ones that mattered to the reformers, the reluctance to change was closely tied in with lineage structures, strategies of heirship and significant alliances between dynasties. The rules governing their practices were clearly set out in the texts of a legal tradition that went back to the mid-seventh century, and that was studied and glossed within the church schools in the eleventh and twelfth century, that is throughout the reform period. In this regard the reformers attitude to divorce and the strange notion of selling wives may be a misunderstanding or misconstrued view of the terms governing divorce in Irish law. This law required that all the divorced wife's assets, brought into the marriage, and her share of the profits generated within the marriage, should be handed back to her.[119] Another misunderstood disputed issue was in relation to tithes as there was a long history of paying tithes in medieval Ireland. This was more about to whom these tithes were paid, namely, that they should support the new secular hierarchy and its vicars and rectors and not the traditional coarbs and erenaghs as was the custom and practice.[120]

Effectively, marriage reform meant setting aside much of the social structures of Irish lordly society. In effect, this would mean the replacement of one type of aristocratic society by another.[121] Henry

---

[119] O'Corrain, D., The Irish Church.
[120] Ibid.
[121] Ibid.

II, in whom the Pope and the Irish church reformers now placed their faith, himself was married to a divorcee, Eleanor of Aquitaine. Amongst other acts, he placed his son Geoffrey first as Chancellor, then Bishop of Lincoln and subsequently Archbishop of York. In the case of Maud Fitz Roy, her father Henry placed her as Abbess of Barking. The Irish bishops appeared oblivious, or ignored in their zeal, the bitter and protracted conflicts between the English Kings and the Church, and in particular between Henry II and Becket which ended in the Archbishop's murder. An act it is considered gave rise to the subsequent comments from the Archbishop of Cashel in response to Gerald of Wales who argued Irish saints were not willing to die for their faith, to which the Archbishop commented wryly, '*but now a people has come to our country who know how to make martyrs and have frequently done so*'.[122]

So why the push for reform? Perhaps the reformers felt threatened by Henry's reputation and menacing presence or, using reform as a flag of convenience, desired to be powerful and rich feudal bishops with a role in royal government, as chancellors, diplomats, and royal judges, like their contemporaries elsewhere in England and continental Europe. Henry's predecessor, William I, had thoroughly '*Normanised*' the English church, and rewarded his followers with its best benefices. Henry II's baronage in Ireland would soon seize more church estates than his inspired council of Cashel ever liberated.[123] Whatever the reformers motivations, they consented to the most radical departure in the history of the Irish church, since the rise of monasticism in the sixth century. More strangely, they took the decision to turn their backs on their own church and its newly reformed structure, put in place with great

---

[122] Downham, Clare, Medieval Ireland.
[123] O'Corrain, D., The Irish Church.

public ceremony and papal approval at the synod of Kells, as recently as 1152 CE.

What in effect was more significant is that these accusations supported by reformers soon brought the Irish, Scottish, and Welsh churches and peoples into disrepute in the eyes of the English racial and continental observers. They had serious consequences for the English racial and religious perception of the Irish, including the allegation of barbarism and even paganism down to the Reformation and beyond. It was used as a justification for aggression, expropriation, religious repression, and colonisation – both secular and ecclesiastical.[124]

By the time of the Council of Vivienne (1311-1312), the Irish Church were eventually making their protest known: The Irish Church stated '*before the coming of the English into Ireland it was thus free: it knew no superior in relation to temporalia, that it had and exercised jurisdiction in all ways, spiritual and temporal. A certain king of England obtained by request a licence from the lord pope (Papal Bull) to enter the said land to subjugate it to himself, saving the right of the Irish and Roman church. On the pretext of that licence that king entered that land and subjected a certain part of it to himself and in the subjugated part he and his successors, little by little and successively, usurped the estates, effects, rights, and jurisdiction of the church.*'[125]

However, Gregorian reform imposed a shallow superstructure on the pre-reform church and beneath that much of the early medieval indigenous church survived with its personnel, landholding, religious practices, and traditional pieties. In the Norman-ruled areas of the country, much church land was seized very violently by the barons who used it as castle sites and as secular estates or as endowments for

---

[124] Ibid.
[125] Ibid.

foreign religious orders.[126] (See Chapter 7 and Chapter 10 on Church Suppression for details of Orders). The Cistercian Order ultimately held in excess of 500,000 statute acres in medieval Ireland and at the time of the dissolution of the monasteries this land was 84% under arable cultivation. They maintained a presence in Ireland up to and throughout the sixteenth and seventeenth centuries.[127]

The Papal Bull Forgery and the English Invasion

From the beginning the Church was committed to the support of the Norman Conquest, although ecclesiastical historians often lose sight of this fact by isolating Church history from history at large.[128] Despite the Papal approved reforms (*Paparo*) of the Synod of Kells in 1152, within three short years there came the issuance of a Papal Bull, the *Laudabilter satis* from Pope Adrian IV. There is evidence that after the Synod of Kells there were two English missions, the first from Theobald Archbishop of Canterbury still smarting having lost three suffragans at Kells and one suffragan at Dublin who was made an Archbishop. Most importantly for him he had seen the emergence of a papally approved reformed Irish church, not only out from under the influence of Canterbury with an Irish primacy independent of itself, but with the accompanying loss of income. Theobald's agent was John of Salisbury who it appeared did not put into effect any demonstrable change from his representations. Although writing in 1159, after the death of Pope Adrian IV, he claimed that it was in acquiescence to his petition that Adrian granted and entrusted Ireland

---

[126] Ibid.

[127] Lynch, Bridget, A Monastic Landscape: The Cistercians in Medieval Leinster, Thesis, NUI, Maynooth, December, 2008.

[128] Kearney, The British Isles.

to Henry. This he indicated was by virtue of the fact that all islands were said to belong to the Roman church an ancient right based on the Donation of Constantine. This document was subsequently acknowledged to be a forgery conceived in the eighth century and exposed as such in the mid-fifteenth century.

The second mission was Henry II's own high-powered delegation which was despatched in October 1155 and was led by the Benedictine abbot Robert of St. Albans *'to promote certain difficult royal matters'*. Without waiting for Papal approval a royal council was held in Winchester in September 1155, which discussed the proposal that Henry II should invade Ireland and constitute his brother William as King. However, instead he turned his army and military equipment against Louis VII King of the French as his Irish invasion was opposed, it is said, by his mother Matilda the Empress of Germany. He was engaged in a struggle with Louis over Aquitaine, his wife's inheritance and the Irish invasion was not taken any further at that point.[129] However, within a few short years, papal endorsement was dramatically withdrawn from the Irish (Kells) church reformers and Henry II was called upon to put into effect Papal reform and mend the morals of the Irish and *'to root out from it the weeds of vice … to pay a yearly tribute to St. Peter of one penny from every house'*,[130] and *'to preserve the rights of the churches of that land whole and intact'*. Not so much it appears, as John of Salisbury's claim, that the Pope invested Henry II with the authority to rule Ireland.

The contempt for the Irish church was evidenced in the practices of the papal chancery. This reappears as a matter of fact in the letters of the subsequent pope Alexander III who was in charge of the chancery at the time. Charges of barbarism and of being outside the

---

[129] O'Corrain, D., The Irish Church.
[130] Ibid.

boundaries of the church are highlighted and thus embedded in the pope's apparent warm approval of Henry's proposals to invade. In any event, there was no attempt by Henry at invasion at this time and reforming synods in Ireland continued to meet. Had there been no Norman invasion the *Laudabilter* may have been forgotten, however, with Henry II's subsequent invasion and involvement in Irish affairs, these issues became decisive matters.[131]

The Advent of Feudalism and Henry II

It was in the last decades of the ninth century, as the Carolingian Empire crumbled away and as Viking and Magyar bands ravaged the Western European mainland, the term *feudum* – the full medieval word for fief[132] – first started to come into use. It was also at this time that the countryside of France in particular became criss-crossed with private castles and fortifications erected by rural lords without imperial permission to withstand the new barbarian attacks, and build in their local power.

The new Castellar landscape was both a protection and a prison for the rural population. The entrenchment of local landlords and landowners in the provinces through the nascent fief system, and the consolidation of their manorial estates and lordships over the peasantry, proved to be the bedrock of the feudalism that slowly solidified across Europe in the next two centuries.[133] By the late tenth and early eleventh centuries, the general French pattern was a uniquely comprehensive feudal hierarchy built from the ground

---

[131] Ibid.

[132] 'Fief' is derived from the Old German word for herds, 'Vassal' comes from the Celtic *kwas*, meaning a slave, 'Village' derives from the Roman villa, 'serf' from *servus* and manor from *mansus, (Anderson, P, Passages).*

[133] Anderson, P., Passages.

upwards, and often in multiple tiers, of sub-infeudation. There were over 50 distinct political divisions in France as a whole. It was eventually the Duchy of France which provided the nucleus for the construction of a new French monarchy. A relatively large and loyal officialdom of *baillis* and *seneschaux* was created to administer the lands under royal control. In the prolonged civil wars of the next three centuries the fabric of French feudal unity was to be repeatedly torn, without ever finally coming apart.

The parcelled out sovereignty, which was a division of public authority, distinguished the feudal mode of production in Europe. The vassal hierarchy and fief system of medieval Europe were not necessarily essential characteristics of feudalism. More so large-scale agrarian exploitation and peasant production founded on extra-economic relations of coercion and dependence. The fusion of vassalage-benefice-immunity to produce the fief system created this pattern of sovereignty and dependence. The fief was in essence an economic grant of land, conditional on performance of military service – usually a knight's fee – for the smallest fief (although these could be sub-divided) vested with judicial rights over the peasantry tilling it. It was consequently an amalgam of property and sovereignty as the division of the manorial estate into the lord's demesne and tenant's virgates or land strips emerged. Conditional property instituted the subordination of the vassal within a social hierarchy of lordship, where protection was provided and all was underpinned by strong religious sanctions. A feudal kingdom was divided amongst several magnates who were vassals of the king and these magnates had lesser barons as their vassals. A separate and universal church cross-cut all secular principalities, concentrating cultural skills and religious sanctions in its own independent clerical organisation. An estates system developed where in a tripartite assembly or feudal organisation the nobility, clergy, and burghers were represented as distinct orders.

The peasants who occupied and tilled the land were not its owners. Agrarian property was privately controlled by this class of feudal lords who extracted a surplus which took the form of labour services, rents-in-kind, or customary dues owed to the individual lord. This was exercised both on the manorial demesne and on the strip tenancies or virgates. Medieval manors varied in structure according to the relative balance between these two components within it. There were some estates entirely devoted to demesne-farming such as the Cistercian *'granges'* tilled by lay brethren; while at the other end there were some estates entirely leased out to peasant tenants. But the modal type was mostly a combination of home-farm and tenancies in varying proportions. The peasant was subject to the jurisdiction of the lord. At the same time, the property rights of the lord over his land were typically of degree only: he was invested in them by a superior noble or nobles, to whom he would owe knight service. His estates were, in other words, held as a fief. The liege lord in turn would often be the vassal of a feudal superior and the chain of such dependent tenures linked to military service would extend upwards to the highest peak of the system, usually a monarch, of whom all land in principle would be the *'eminent domain'*.

The functions of the state were disintegrated in a vertical allocation downwards whilst at each level economic and political relations were on the other hand integrated. This devolution of sovereignty was constitutive of the feudal mode of production. What emerged at the level of the village itself was a class of nobles enjoying personal rights of exploitation and jurisdiction over dependent peasants and this was consecrated in law. The feudal hierarchy excluded any *'executive'* at all in the modern sense of a permanent administrative apparatus of State. Royal rulers fulfilled their station by preserving traditional laws. Political power came for a period to be identified with the single *'judiciary'* function of interpreting and applying the existing laws. In the absence of any public bureaucracy this was what constituted power.[134]

The feudal mode of production also produced the feudal town. This dynamic created an opposition of town and country presented as an urban economy of increasing commodity exchange controlled by merchants and organised in guilds and corporations, versus, a rural economy of natural exchange controlled by nobles, and organised in manors and strips with communal and individual peasant enclaves. These towns were an autonomous development within a natural agrarian economy. Thus, and importantly, modern history was the urbanisation of the countryside and not as in antiquity the ruralisation of the cities.[135]

After his victory in England, William I proceeded to a planned and systematic distribution of some 5,000 fiefs to occupy and hold down the country and contrary to continental usages, sub-vassals had to swear allegiance not only to their immediate lords but also to the monarch —ultimate donor of all land. The traditional defence tax — the *danegeld* — continued to be collected outside the orthodox revenue system of a medieval monarchy in addition to the incomes yielded from the very large royal demesne and the exaction of feudal incidences. The most developed manorialism was established in the South and South-Centre of the English countryside with an intensification of labour services and a marked degradation of the local peasantry.

Elsewhere considerable areas were left with small holdings only

---

[134] Anderson, P., *Passages*.
[135] Ibid.

lightly burdened with feudal obligations and a rural population that escaped immediate servile status. However, in the next hundred years the trend towards a general enserfment was unmistakeable as there was a progressive levelling down of the juridical conditions of the English peasantry, until the twelfth century as *villani* and *nativi* formed a single serf class. The shire and hundred courts of the Anglo-Saxons which had survived into the new order were now dominated by royal appointees from the baronial class. Nevertheless, this system of *'public justice'* was relatively less implacable to the poor than the private seigneurial franchises which were the norm elsewhere. At the same time, Manorial courts flourished and the real economic power of the English lords was no less than their continental opposites.[136]

In England a centralised feudalism was imported from the outside by the Norman conquerors, originally Norse invaders who had settled and fused in France a century earlier. The Anglo-Saxon army was no match for the steel-laden Norman cavalry, the military spearhead of a much more developed feudal society, on the rim of the French mainland. The result was the peculiar combination of a highly centralised state and a popular justice that distinguished medieval England thereafter.[137] The Norman approach consisted of a largely military occupation with retention of much of Anglo-Saxon law, customs, and institutions while superimposing their own developed system of feudalism. In Scotland the Anglo-Normans were quickly absorbed. They had arrived by invitation of the Scottish rulers, who themselves were influenced by the French and English. By the fourteenth century, Robert Bruce, whose ancestors had come to Scotland from Brix in Normandy by way of Yorkshire, could present himself as the champion of Scottish nationhood. On the

---

[136] Ibid.

[137] Ibid.

other hand, Welsh political leadership was crushed by Edward I in the 1280s.[138]

The Advent of Feudalism and Irish Society

In contrast, the system in Ireland was very different from that existing in England in 1066. Irish society differed far more widely from the general continental pattern than that of Anglo-Saxon England. The institutions which developed subsequently in Norman Ireland were of a purely Anglo-Norman type and there was, at least theoretically, no divergence between the law of England and that of the Norman colony in Ireland.[139] In this case there was no adoption or retention of Irish laws, customs, or institutions but rather colonial occupation and the imposition of Norman feudalism. In contrast, in Wales in the years preceding the Edwardian conquest, judicial commissions appointed by the king had included Welshmen; these commissions had heard cases by common law, by the customs of the marches, or by the laws of Wales, no similar flexibility appeared in Ireland. The explanation may lie in the respective dates and circumstances of invasion. Norman intervention in Wales had occurred as early as 1067 at a time when the common law had yet to crystallise and there was no rigid scheme to which the emerging lordships there could be expected to adhere. However, in the early years of Edward I, with the encouragement of Archbishop Peckham of Canterbury, the king and his lawyers expressed hostility to Welsh law, in particular the blood-feud and compensation aspects. This hostility found its expression in the Statute of Wales 1284 where he

---

[138] Frame, R., Colonial Ireland, 1169-1369, Four Courts Press, 2012.

[139] Rutven-Otway, A.J., A History of Medieval Ireland, Ernest Benn Ltd, London, 1968.

sought to replace the criminal codes by English law. The occupation of Ireland was well advanced at that stage and so it followed that the colony would follow English common law, which was the law familiar to those lords participating in the conquest.[140]

The Norman-Irish Colony

If we view the Norman invasion of Ireland as an episode in European history, then between 1167 and about 1240 Ireland was partly colonised by a French-oriented international elite, ecclesiastical as well as secular. They had over the previous hundred year's conquered England, advanced into Wales and were still engaged in infiltrating Scotland. This Norman phenomenon was part of a wider scattering that had deposited nobles, knights, and clergy from Normandy and other parts of Northern France in Sicily, Antioch, and Palestine. The use of the term Norman for the whole of the period, from the mid-eleventh to the mid-fourteenth centuries, is an over-simplification. The followers of William the Conqueror were not exclusively Norman as many were Breton, Flemish, and Picard by background. From the mid-twelfth century the line of Norman kings was replaced by that of Henry II Plantagenet and the Angevins. The early settlers of Wales, Scotland, and Ireland included many Flemings.[141] The monarch who came to Ireland in the wake of the first invaders was Henry II of England, also Duke of Normandy, Count of Anjou, and Duke of Aquitaine; the ruler, in other words, of the greater part of Western France. It was with the intervention of Henry II in 1171 that the whole situation in Ireland was revolutionised, and it was at this point that the Norman Conquest

---

[140] Frame, R., Colonial Ireland.

[141] Kearney, H., The British Isles.

can only be really said to have begun.[142]

Social Change

The political over-lordship which Brian Boru had established had not developed after his death and by the end of the eleventh century his descendants, while they remained kings of Munster and were still the most influential of the Irish rulers, they were not supreme. In the twelfth century the O'Connor kings of Connaught were the dominant power in the South. When Turlough O'Connor died in 1156, Murchertach MacLochlainn, king of Tyrone, defeated Turlough's son and by 1161 was described by the annals as '*king without opposition*'. In this year MacLochlainn recognised his ally Dermot MacMurrough as king of Leinster.[143] When, in 1166, MacLochlainn by an act of treachery caused an uprising against himself (he took captive and blinded MacDuinnsleibe against terms agreed and noted by the Bishop of Armagh)[144] this enabled Turlough O'Connor's son Rory to seize the high kingship.

The Dublin Danes and the Irish princes of North Leinster rose against MacMurrough and Dermot was forced to submit to the new High-King, who left him in possession of Ui Cennsalaigh. But O'Rourke, still O'Connor's ally, seized the opportunity to take his revenge. Nearly twenty years previously MacMurrough had been involved with Turlough O'Connor in an attack on O'Rourke in which he had been defeated and MacMurrough had made off with his wife Derbforgilla '*with her wealth*' although she made her escape the

---

[142] Ruthven-Othway A.J., A History of Medieval Ireland, Ernest Benn, London, 1968.

[143] Ibid.

[144] O Croinin D., Early Medieval Ireland.

following year,[145] and marched on Ui Cennselaigh. On 1st August 1166 MacMurrough, seeing no hope of successful resistance, sailed for England. He first sought refuge in Bristol, one of the principal ports trading with Ireland and was entertained by Robert Fitz Harding, Reeve of Bristol, and probably at his suggestion went in search of the king, Henry. After a long pursuit he found him in Aquitaine and duly paid homage. Henry gave him letters authorising his subjects to give him aid as *'our vassal and liegeman'* in recovering his kingdom.

Dermot returned to Bristol and then made contact with Richard Fitz Gilbert de Clare, Earl of Pembroke, also known as Strongbow (not by his contemporaries as this was a name which belonged to his father). He, De Clare, was out of favour with the king as he had supported his rival Stephen, which may have given rise to his willingness to undertake such a dubious adventure having been deprived of his estates as a result. However, it was finally agreed between them that the Earl would marry Dermot's eldest daughter and succeed him in Leinster in return for which he would assist him in recovering his kingdom. This pledge was at variance with the accepted tradition of the time. The Earl was to come the following spring of 1168 but he appears to have been employed otherwise in the king's service, and did not come until Dermot sent him urgent messages in 1170. Fortified by this alliance, Dermot set out for Pembrokeshire where he enlisted the support of an important Norman-Welsh clan through Maurice Fitz Gerald, the son of Gerald of Windsor, castellan of Pembroke, and his half-brother Robert Fitz Stephen. They were promised in fee the city of Wexford and two adjoining cantreds and so undertook to come to Ireland in the spring of 1168.

MacMurrough returned from Wales in 1167 with a small force of

---

[145] Ibid.

Flemings *'only a few men, who crossed over in haste and did not remain long'* under Richard Fitz Godebert De Roche, a Pembrokeshire knight. Dermot re-established himself in Ui Cennsalaigh without apparent difficulty as O'Connor was preoccupied with an attempt to control Munster. However, in the early winter, O'Connor advanced on Ui Cennsalaigh with his allies O'Rourke and MacLochlainn. MacMurrough was defeated and forced to submit: O'Connor took hostages from him, O'Rourke accepted a compensation for the rape of his wife Derbforgilla, and MacMurrough was left in possession of ten cantreds of Ui Cennsalaigh. This probably in the hope that it would contain him. Dermot's submission, however, was only apparent.

He sent messengers to Wales and, after the lapse of more than a year, about 1st May 1169 arising from a process he had already set in train, Robert Fitz Stephen (with at least three of his nephews, Robert De Barry, Meiler Fitz Henry, and Miles Fitz David), with a force of thirty knights *'of his own kinsmen and retainers, sixty men-at-arms, and some three hundred archers and foot-soldiers'*, landed at Bannow Bay on the south coast of Wexford. These were followed the next day by Maurice Prendergast, a Fleming from Pembrokeshire, with ten men at arms and a body of archers in two ships. The arrival of this body of professional soldiers radically altered the situation.[146] The Normans were quickly joined by Dermot and proceeded immediately to reduce Wexford, which was in due course handed over to Fitz Stephen as previously agreed, while Hervey de Montmorency Strongbow's uncle, who had accompanied the invaders to watch over his nephew's interests, was given two cantreds between Wexford and Waterford. They then then proceeded to restore Dermot's supremacy. However, the invaders quarrelled among themselves as Maurice De Prendergast decided he wished to return to Wales.

---

[146] Ruthven-Otway, A. J., A History of Medieval Ireland.

Soon after these incursions O'Connor advanced with a great army against the new threat. Dermot retreated before him, and without a battle a treaty was entered into by which Leinster was left to Dermot. On his side he recognised O'Connor as high king and gave his son as hostage. He agreed he would bring in no more mercenaries and send away Stephen and his men. Whether or not he intended to keep this treaty, Maurice Fitz Gerald arrived shortly afterwards and landed at Wexford. Dermot's forces were now restored to near the level before the desertion of Prendergast. Early in 1170, Dermot with Fitz Gerald marched on Dublin and forced the Ostmen to submit. He then felt able to send a party under Fitz Stephen to the assistance of his son-in-law, Domhnail O'Brien, king of Limerick, against O'Connor. It was after this, according to Giraldus, that he began to entertain designs of seizing the high kingship, and, on the advice of Fitz Stephen and Fitz Gerald, sent messages to Strongbow urging him to come at once. Strongbow, having obtained leave from Henry II, sent ahead at the beginning of May, Raymond le Gros, another of the Fitz Geralds, who entrenched themselves at Baginbun, near Waterford. Having repulsed an attack from the Ostmen of Waterford they awaited the earl's arrival. On the 23rd August Strongbow landed near Waterford with a small army and being joined by Le Gros the army advanced to attack Waterford which was taken by storm.

Dermot McCarthy of Munster, it is said, attacked Strongbow with all the forces he could get without success. Dermot MacMurrough arrived shortly after with Fitz Stephen and Maurice Fitz Gerald, Eva was married to Strongbow and the combined force marched on Dublin, where O'Connor High King was assembling an army. Strongbow's arrival was clearly recognised as opening a new phase in what were still the wars of province kings. O'Connor, however, had troubles in Munster where the O'Brien's had rebelled against him and was not in a position to take matters too far. He guarded the passes to the south and west of Dublin, but Dermot led his army over the mountains to the city, where O'Connor did not prevent the Ostmen from negotiating. Dublin was taken by storm on the 21st September and a large body of the citizens, led by their king Asgall, fled by sea to their kinsmen in the islands. O'Connor withdrew his forces and Mac Murrough was left unhampered to reduce Offelan and Ossory after which he invaded Meath. When O'Connor protested that this was a breach of the treaty of 1169, Dermot replied by claiming the high kingship. However, Mac Murrough died at Ferns at the beginning of May 1171 leaving Strongbow as his heir, although these arrangement carried little weight in Irish traditional law.

Of MacMurrough's two legitimate sons, Connor the hostage held by O'Connor, had been executed shortly before, while the other had been blinded by the King of Ossory whose prisoner he was in 1168, and so was incapacitated from ruling. There remained the claims of his illegitimate son Domhaill Kavanagh and of his brother and other kinsmen, and Dermot's nephew Murtough who was supported by the Leinstermen. Strongbow now found himself in a position of great difficulty. In Ireland he could expect the implacable hostility of Dermot's kinsmen and in England he had the hostility of his own sovereign. Henry could not let Strongbow establish as an independent ruler and threat, but neither was he unwilling to acquire fresh lands and all that came with it, in prospect for himself.[147]

The immediate danger to the Normans came from the Irish of Leinster who were said to have risen against Strongbow. O'Connor was raising a great army and surrounded Dublin City to which Strongbow had returned, while a fleet under Gottred king of Man, blockaded the port. The siege continued for two months at which

---

[147] Ruthven-Otway A.J., A History of Medieval Ireland.

point the Normans sought to negotiate. Strongbow sent to O'Connor offering to become his man and hold Leinster of him, but O'Connor offered the cities of Dublin, Wexford, and Waterford; a lesser proposal. Also, at this point the besiegers withdrew a great part of their forces for other activities, underestimating the temper of the Normans. In a successful sortie the Normans defeated what remained and the siege was raised. Strongbow consolidated his success and persuaded his brother-in-law, the King of Limerick, to join him in an expedition against Ossory and after this Murtough Mac Murrough came to terms with and was granted Ui Censelaigh, while Domhnaill Kavanagh was granted the *'pleas'* of Leinster.

CHAPTER SIX

HENRY II AND THE NORMAN FEUDAL

CONQUEST

Hervey De Montmorency returned from the embassy on which he had been sent to by Henry II shortly before Dermot's death. Hervey had offered, on behalf of Strongbow, to surrender Dublin, Waterford, and other fortresses, and Henry, accepting this, promised to restore the earl's lands in Normandy, England, and Wales and to leave him in possession of the rest of Dermot's kingdom. Henry's projected expedition was under preparation and he was prepared for the possibility that he might have to fight Normans or Irish, or both in combination. Henry and his large army and everything necessary for an extensive campaign and siege warfare set out for Pembroke from where he embarked on the 16th October, landing the next day at Crook near Waterford. The day after he entered Waterford, Strongbow formally surrendered the city to him and paid homage for Leinster.

Gerald describes the submissions of the Mac Carthy and O'Brien kings, which took place shortly after Henry's landing: *'King Diarmait of Cork arrived. He was drawn forthwith into a firm alliance by the bond of submission, an oath of fealty and the giving of hostages; an annual tribute was imposed on his kingdom; of his own free will he submitted himself to the king of England'*.

The Synod of Cashel 1172

The king moved his army from Waterford and went first to Lismore where he stayed for two days with the papal legate Gilla Crist O Con Airge. From there he continued to Cashel to meet its archbishop and in turn to summon the bishops to council. These duly met at Cashel over the winter of 1171/1172. Having made their momentous decisions, *'nothing relative to religious dogmas, to matters of faith, or to points of essential discipline; and some of these decrees refer to matters rather of a political than of an ecclesiastical nature'*, the bishops swore an oath to Henry II. He received from the four Archbishops and the twenty nine bishops, many listed by name, *'their letters in the form of a charter with seals attached, confirming to him and his heirs the kingdom of Ireland, testifying that they had constituted him and his heirs kings and lords over them forever.'*[148]

On the next day, Domhnaill king of Limerick met him by the river Suir, where he petitioned for the king's peace; tribute was imposed on his kingdom also and he too showed his loyalty to the king by entering into the very strongest bonds of submission.[149] The classical means of acquisition was force invariably decked out in claims of religious or genealogical legitimacy.[150]

On the way, or in Dublin, the Irish Lords of Leinster submitted to him, even though Henry had already granted Leinster (their lands) to Strongbow who had paid homage for it. The other kings, O'Cerbaill king of Airgialla, O'Ruairc, king of Breifne, Donn Slebe king of Uladh and O'Maelechlainn king of Meath also submitted to Henry and gave hostages.

They took Henry as their Lord as vassals of whom they held their

---

[148] O'Corrain, D., The Irish Church.

[149] Frame, R., Colonial Ireland.

[150] Anderson, P., Lineages of the Absolutist State.

lands, and swore an oath of loyalty. The *Annals of Ulster* state that *'he took the hostages of Munster, Leinster, Meath, Breifne, Airgialla and Ulaid'.* O'Connor, who still considered himself king of Ireland, held aloof. The far northern kings McLochlain and Aed O'Neill of Aileach and the king of Cenel Conaill were too busy with a local internecine wars at that time, and made no contact with Henry.

A great wooden palace was built for Henry in Dublin on the site on what is now Dublin Castle, and here he entertained his English and Irish vassals splendidly. He issued a charter granting Dublin to his men of Bristol and made arrangements for royal land-holding in Dublin, Leinster, and Waterford. Sometime after March 1172 he granted his follower Hugh De Lacy the kingdom of Meath for the service of fifty knights. He put constables and garrisons in strategic seaport towns and he also appointed Hugh De Lacy royal governor of Ireland. He is said to have intended to remain in Ireland for the rest of the year, building castles and establishing order. In England, however, the papal legates were threatening an interdict unless he came at once to make reparations for the murder of Becket. Also, his eldest son, the young king Henry, was threatening a rebellion.[151] He sailed for England on Easter Monday 1172 to do public penance and mend his fences with the papacy over the murder of Becket and never to return.

Gerald states that the king's policy was to bring the usages of the Irish church into total conformity with those of the English churches. The bishops were now to be tenants-in-chief of the Crown part of the baronage and their recruitment and election were to be matters for royal policy and patronage as in England. The relationship of church and king, the competence of church courts, the privileges of clergy and the rights of church estates were all

---

[151] Ruthven-Otway, A.J., A History of Medieval Ireland.

assimilated to the English model without, it appears, any evidence of opposition.

In September 1172, Pope Alexander signed the Bull that ratified his agreement with a penitent Henry II in the interests of a beleaguered papacy and for reasons of political expedience, thus resolving the conflict between pope and king over Becket's murder. Less than three weeks later, the pope despatched three letters to the Irish bishops, the Irish kings, and Henry II. He ordered his papal legate and the bishops to support Henry II, *'this Catholic and most Christian king who has heard us in respect of tithes and other rights of the church and in restoring to you … those things which pertain to the liberty of the church'*. In his letter to the Irish kings, the pope ordered them to preserve their fealty to Henry II, described by the pope as *'that powerful and majestic king who is a devout son of the church'*. The most extreme statement of Irish vice was kept for Henry II himself who, *'like a pious king and magnificent prince you have wondrously triumphed over that people of Ireland, who ignoring the fear of God, in an unbridled fashion wander at random through the depths of vice and have renounced all reverence for the Christian faith and virtue and destroy themselves in mutual slaughter'*.

It begs the question as to what, if any, respect or recognition there was for the *'golden age' of Irish missionaries* or the *'land of saints and scholars'* or the papal acknowledged Irish church reform leading up to the Synod of 1152. The Angevins had no particular interest in moral reform, their episcopal appointees in Ireland were king's men before they were the pope's or the churches. The English invasion brought chronic warfare, racial conflict in the church and wider society, legal inequity, and severe social disruption that gravely affected the church. Naively the bishop's put their trust in princes, and quite misread the political landscape.[152]

---

[152] O'Corrain, D., The Irish Church.

Ruaidri O Conchobair, who did not submit to Henry II, although this is disputed by Gerald[153], held a synod at Tuam led by him and Cadla O'Dubthaig, archbishop of Connaught (who had also attended at Cashel), and three churches were consecrated by them at that synod. The papal legate, O'Con Airge, was given a lesson himself in 1173 from Henry's Chief Governor in Ireland Richard De Clare. On his return this earl came into Munster to Lismore and plundered it completely and levied a thousand marks on the legate as an amercement from the cathedral. This on the grounds that he had failed to condemn or excommunicate the Irish kings or lords who resisted the invaders as he was required to do by Pope Alexander III's letter.

In 1173, when Strongbow and other Norman lords were summoned by Henry II to France to quell a revolt by one of his sons there, the Irish kings of the South revolted against English lordship and the following year Ruadhri assisted Ui Brian, who had turned against his English allies and went on to defeat them at the Battle of Thurles. However, in 1175 he sent a delegation that included the Archbishops O'Dubtaigh and Lorcan O'Tuathail (a brother-in-law of Diarmait Mac Murrough) to negotiate terms with Henry and this resulted in the short-lived treaty of Windsor. With this treaty, Ruaidhri agreed to accept English control over Leinster and Midhe, to recognise Henry as his overlord and to pay a substantial tribute. In return he would be recognised by Henry as Irish high-king and would have his support in restraining the English adventurers. O'Connor was equally prepared to invoke the clause which entitled him to call on Norman assistance against rebels and when he had trouble with the O'Brien's in Limerick he invoked this Norman assistance.

---

[153] Gerald submits he met the English envoys Hugh De Lacy and William Fitz Audelin on the banks of the Shannon, and tendered his submission to them and one of his daughters married de Lacy, *(Expugnatio Hibernica)*.

Council of Oxford 1177

The arrangements made by Henry were settled at a council held in Oxford in 1177, which accepted the general principle of a division of Ireland between Norman and Irish Lordship (this was after the death of Strongbow in 1176). The Council was dominated by the desire to make certain that no single vassal should be able to establish an overwhelming power in Ireland. O'Connor appeared only interested in his own area of Connaught. The under-kings themselves were ready to assist the Normans against each other and thus piecemeal Norman expansion was facilitated. Henry made his son John Lord of Ireland to provide a resident ruler, albeit he was just ten years old, and so as to curb the ambitions of the resident Barons. Meanwhile, De Courcy, who it is said was granted Ulster by Henry if he could conquer it, marched northwards in 1177, and took Down and the local chieftains completely by surprise and, according to Giraldus, '*after the many conflicts of a long war, and severe struggles on every side, being raised by his victories … erected castles throughout Ulster in suitable places, and established in it a most firm peace*'.

Around this time a further Synod was held at Dublin by Cardinal Vivian papal legate. He made a public declaration of the right of the king of England to Ireland, and threatened excommunication to those who forfeited their allegiance. Soon after this Synod there occurred the first Norman incursions into Connaught. In 1177 also speculative grants were made of the kingdoms of Cork and Limerick to Robert Fitz Stephen and Miles de Cogan who were to hold them between them for the service of sixty knights. O'Connor it appears accepted these grants without protest. The grant of Limerick led to no immediate occupation and it still had to be conquered when it was granted to Philip De Braose. When De Braose, accompanied by Fitz Stephen and De Cogan, advanced on the town, the citizens set fire to it and De Braose abandoned his attempt at conquest. According to Gerald, *'it is no wonder that this expedition turned out so unfortunately, considering the number of cut-throats, and murderers, and lewd fellows, whom Philip de Braose had, by his own special choice, got together from South Wales and its marches to accompany him.'*

Cork however was successfully occupied, the Normans being assisted by Murtough O'Brien, son of Domhail. Fitz Stephen took the area east of the city and de Cogan the cantreds west of it. He was assassinated in 1182, and a general rising of the Irish under Dermot McCarthy followed, but Fitz Stephen was relieved by Raymond le Gros and their position was restored.[154]

King John's Expedition 1210

During the period 1193-94 when John was in rebellion against his brother, there seems to have been considerable disturbances amongst the Normans. After his accession in 1199 John wrote to the Justiciar in Ireland saying that John de Courcy and Walter De Lacy had destroyed his land of Ireland. They had also it seems been the heads of the faction in Ireland which supported the king against John. By the time John had been re-instated he had appointed Hamo de Valognes as justiciar and bided his time to revenge himself. By 1205, Hugh de Lacy was granted all the lands of Ulster by John, and the king belted him earl, to hold of the king in fee as John de Courcy *'had held it on the day'*. However, in due course Hugh de Lacy was used to pull down de Courcy as he himself was pulled down.

In Connaught the position of Cathal Crobhderg had been firmly established with Norman assistance and he was to hold a third of Connaught in fee as a Barony, paying an annual tribute for the rest.

---

[154] Ruthven-Otway, A.J., A History of Medieval Ireland.

His position as a vassal king was thus established. It was not until after his death in 1224 that the Norman occupation was to begin.[155] In 1203-04 large amounts of cash and bullion passed from the Irish Lordship into Normandy, and in the late summer of 1204, Meiler Fitz Henry was instructed to build a castle at Dublin, not just for the defence of the city, or administration, but because they had *'no place to deposit their treasure'*. Fitz Henry was subsequently removed from office as justiciar and replaced by De Gray, not the usual type magnate but a career royal servant and bishop of Norwich. John's involvement in Ireland grew stronger from 1205-06 onwards. Fitz Stephen and De Cogan had not left male heirs and, according to Norman law, John took possession of Cork. De Burgh and Theobald Walter had also died, leaving heirs under age and the land also passed into royal custody. In 1207 De Braose quarrelled with John and forfeited his lands in England and Wales and also returned Limerick to John's hands.

By 1206-07 a new figure appeared on the scene, William Marshall, the hereditary Marshall of England. He had been given Strongbow's heiress, Isabel de Clare, in marriage by Henry II in 1189 and had thus become lord of all Strongbow's lands in England, Wales, and Ireland as an inheritance which put him amongst the greatest of the English barons. He did not visit his Irish lands for various reasons until 1207, when he obtained a reluctant consent from John to go to Ireland out of concern for developments there. John was experiencing difficulties in Wales and Scotland until he forced a treaty on William of Scotland in 1209, and this left him free to act in Ireland.

In May 1210 John prepared his expedition to Ireland. In June he landed at Crook and was joined by the justiciar De Grey, with Irish troops from Munster and Desmond and immediately set out for

---

[155] Ruthven-Otway, A.J., *A History of Medieval Ireland*.

Dublin. In Dublin, representatives of Walter de Lacy of Meath placed all his castles and land at the king's hand, and left his brother Hugh to the king's pleasure. John was not appeased and marched through Meath taking possession of castles and turned northwards into Louth to attack Hugh de Lacy. Hugh de Lacy had his own castles burnt before him and fled to Carrickfergus, the strongest castle of the Lordship. It surrendered after a short siege but de Lacy escaped by sea. The wife of De Braoise, who had left Ireland and was also considered an enemy by John, and their son William were taken by Duncan of Carrick, one of the Galloway Scots, to whom John was shortly to grant much of Ulster. They were handed over to John and left to die subsequently of starvation in captivity. By August, John was back in Dublin and in his short sojourn had driven the de Lacys out of both Meath and Ulster.

The Marshal was the only magnate of first rank left in the country. According to an English chronicler, twenty Irish kings did homage to John in Dublin and there was a general readiness among the Irish to accept him.[156] It fell to De Grey to follow through on John's expedition and to confirm a royal presence in the spaces left by the death and destruction of so many notable figures. A new castle was begun at Athlone and a major campaign organised, with the help of the Scots, against Aed O'Neill. By 1211 the gaps in the south west had been filled by the creation of a shire organisation based on the traditional division between Cork and Limerick. John's direct grip and his push for cash are visible in the strengthening of Limerick Castle and the opening of a royal mint in the city. Throughout his reign John did not hesitate to use Irish leaders in his efforts to increase his authority, to contain magnates whom he distrusted, and

---

[156] Ibid.

raise revenue.[157]

Social Change

In the last decades of the twelfth century the richest agricultural lands in eastern and southern Ireland were seized by colonists and conquest proceeded into the more fertile lands of the north and west.[158] By this time John was coming of age where he could be expected to take up his inheritance as Lord of Ireland. It is reasonable to assume that the lands so far occupied by the Normans had been more or less thoroughly sub-infeudated by this time, although the process of forming the new manors and attracting settlers from England and Wales were in their early stages. But the preliminary work of providing fortified centres at the principal manorial sites was well advanced when De Lacy was killed in 1186, while supervising the building of a castle at Durrow the site of a Columban Abbey (he was assassinated by direction of the Sinnach Ua Catharnaigh in reparation to Colmcille while building this castle on his church).[159] Insofar as the annals tell us *'from the Shannon to the sea was full of castles and foreigners'*. From 1177 it had been Henry's intention that his youngest son John should inherit Ireland. When in 1185 John went to his lordship in Ireland, it was assumed he would have a kingly title, though remaining subordinate to his father, and eventually to an elder brother. Although John's expedition in 1185 (John was then aged twelve) was a fiasco and the kingship of Ireland failed to come into existence, he remained lord of Ireland until his death in 1216. Prior to that a sequence of deaths made John the sole

---

[157] Frame, R., Colonial Ireland.

[158] Downham, C., Medieval Ireland.

[159] Ruthven-Otway, A.J., A History of Medieval Ireland.

survivor of four brothers, making him King of England, Duke of Normandy, Count of Anjou in April 1199 and in turn leaving Ireland even more closely connected to these other Plantagenet dominions.[160]

By 1204, however, John had been deprived of his northern French possession by King Philip of France against whom he spent the next decade waging a war which finally ended in the defeat of John's forces in 1214. To finance this campaign John raised an average of up to £71,000 per year between 1207 and 1212 as compared to £24,000 per year between 1199 and 1202. It was in the aftermath of this extensive defeat that John faced the rebellion that forced him to make the concessions in the Magna Carta and reflected the changing balance of forces between the king, the barons, and the church of the time. The Charter was written in Latin and translated into French in 1215 for the benefit of the ruling class. It was not translated into English until 1300, English being the language of the peasant class. The first written versions of the Charter in English did not appear until the sixteenth century. In many cases it was the nobles who had lost land in France who were expected to pay the taxes to the king, and who led the rebellion against John. Having said that, John also confiscated the lands of all those barons in Normandy who held land in England, giving his coffers a much needed boost.

John's reign also coincided with a period of ascendancy for the church under Pope Innocent III and John's conflict with the church contributed significantly to the rebellion, prior to Magna Carta, not least because many of the richest and most powerful nobles in England at the time were ecclesiastical figures. In more recent times the Charter has been considered to reflect the progressive development to wage labour – as compared to serfdom and also to the rise of the town-dwelling merchant class and as well a weakening

---

[160] Ibid.

of the lord's ability to maintain their power over the peasants who made up 90% of the population. It also marked one of the first times that conflicting interests and rights were considered a more effective means to maintain the position of the ruling class than absolute rule.[161]

---

[161] Law and Marxism: 800 Years Since Magna Carta.

CHAPTER SEVEN

NORMAN ADMINISTRATION IN IRELAND:

STRUCTURAL AND SOCIAL IMPACT

The development of elements of the central government system in Ireland began when Henry II appointed Hugh de Lacy as Justiciar in 1172; that of the local organisation of counties had already begun before John became king in 1199. The basis for this system was the existing occupation of the land and was developed along the standard lines of Norman feudalism. Henry granted Meath to Hugh de Lacy to hold by the service of fifty knights; the grant of Leinster to Strongbow required the service of one hundred. Later grants, all made before John's death in 1216, brought the total to a maximum of 427 knights in units ranging from the large contingents of Leinster or Meath to the service of a single foot sergeant from an eight of a knight's fee as in some holdings in Co. Dublin. The manor of Lucan was held for a tabour and four pair of furred gloves annually and that of Dalkey for one hawk. Scutage appeared in England as early as 1100 and it was known in Ireland as Royal service. It was entirely at the king's discretion as to whether money or service would be required. The lands of the church in Ireland were not included in the system whereas in England the ecclesiastical tenants-in-chief all owed quotas of knights. In the larger tenancies-in-chief there was extensive sub-infeudation in Ireland as in England and it was enfeoffed considerably more than the number of knights to fulfil their bare quotas. Many of the sub-tenants had tenants of their own. A holding of perhaps sixty acres might owe anything from a twentieth to a sixtieth of a knight's fee.

The aim behind these very small military tenancies was most likely to attract the smaller tenant by giving a superior status. All military tenancies were held by exactly the same rules of law as applied in England. The work of settlement had only begun with the creation of these military tenancies and was probably not completed until the second generation of the conquest. There is not a great deal of evidence for the first period of the Norman colony but with the reign of Edward I records become abundant. This makes clear that the Norman settlement of Ireland was not just a military occupation supported by the settlement of English and French burgesses in a few towns. It was part of the great movement of peasant colonisation which dominated so much of the economic history of Europe from the eleventh to the fourteenth century arising out of a spontaneous growth of population. There was then a slackening as the growth slackened with the different problems of the fourteenth century.[162] Medieval agriculture had at the end of the thirteenth century reached a technical level equivalent to that of the years which immediately preceded the agricultural revolution. This in turn had set off a demographic boom, the total population of Western Europe more than doubled between 950 and 1348 from 20 million to 54 million.[163] The decline in population in Ireland only became acute after the Black Death and the failure to recover quickly after the Bruce invasion. This was insomuch as outlying districts of lands '*lie waste and uncultivated for lack of tenants*'. These developments can also be

---

[162] Ruthven-Otway, A.J., A History of Medieval Ireland.

[163] Anderson P., Passages.

explained in the context of the general European experience.[164]

Church Organisation

The reorganisation of the church in Ireland on the basis of territorial dioceses had been completed before the Normans came with some readjustments in their aftermath and until the eventual system of parishes based on tithes and the manor was established. The Normans added considerably to the number of foundations: nine new Cistercian houses; nine new Benedictine establishments; some sixteen houses of Augustinian canons, with four canonesses. In addition they introduced new orders: the Crutched Friars whose houses were also hospitals for the sick, the Hospitallers had two houses and the military orders the Templars were also established. By 1290, Ireland's monastic tradition was all but extinct and all of its religious houses were at least nominally affiliated to continental religious orders or canons secular under the rule of St. Augustine. Overall, there were more than twice the number of religious house in Ireland as in Wales and Scotland combined; however, whereas England may have had the greatest number of parishes, Scottish parishes were on average wealthier and Irish parishes were poorest. At the same time it should be noted that perhaps a third of the Irish were outside the Crown's jurisdiction, this according to the 1291 *Taxatio*, and based on one tenth of all ecclesiastical income.

An earlier papal tax of one tenth had yielded £156,000 – 82% from England and Wales, 11% from Scotland, and 6% from Ireland. Much of the church's 'spiritual' income derived from its substantial receipts from tithes and its own glebe lands and reflects wider patterns of agrarian and more particularly arable wealth. Grain being

---

[164] Ruthven-Otway A.J., A History of Medieval Ireland.

the single largest component and arable the single most valuable. The wealth generated from pastoral husbandry was not ignored-since tithes were payable on wool, lambs, and dairy produce but were less straightforward to collect. In relation to spiritualties and temporalities the former contributed about two thirds and the latter about one third of total ecclesiastical income.[165]

Although the church held a great deal of land, individual churches were much poorer than their English equivalent as there were a great many Irish bishoprics and income from land in Ireland was less than England.[166] In the course of the thirteenth century an unbroken succession of English bishops was established in all the dioceses of the province of Dublin, as well as Meath, Limerick, and Waterford. Most of the dioceses of Cashel had more Irish bishops than English and all of the Archbishops were Irish. The province of Tuam had Norman Archbishops from 1286 to 1312. Armagh had a Norman, a German, an Italian, and four Irish archbishops. The appointments appear more determined by loyalty to the Crown rather than purely race as is sometimes suggested.[167] The years after 1180 were characterised by the Anglicisation of the episcopate in Ireland. The spread of English settlements was reflected in the selection of prelates. After the death of Laurence O'Toole in 1181 he was replaced by an English royal nominee John Cumin. Meath, Waterford, Down, Leighlin and Ossory, Lismore and Limerick all followed in later years. Most of the bishoprics in the west of Ireland remained in Irish hands.

---

[165] Campbell Bruce, Medieval Economy.

[166] Ruthven-Otway, A.J., A History of Medieval Ireland.

[167] Ibid.

Foundation of New Towns

The secular counterpart to the great movements of monastic foundations and parish creation that dominated the twelfth and thirteenth centuries was the foundation and growth of towns and other related trading institutions.[168] Dublin became the centre of English power in Ireland. Other Viking port towns along the south, south-westm and east coast continued to flourish and new ports were also founded. Drogheda was founded by Hugh de Lacy in the 1180s, and New Ross in the south founded by William Marshall around 1200 being amongst them. Carrickfergus, Coleraine, Dungarvan, Dundalk, Galway, Sligo, and Youghal also owe their development as towns to English settlers. Along the major rivers that led inland from these ports a network of inland towns was established for the acquisition and transportation of goods and services through craftsmen, clerics, merchants, and others. Like their European counterparts the new towns were often endowed with charters, defended by castles and demarcated by ditches and walls. In addition to developing towns, many small boroughs were created by English lords in a bid to generate wealth and attract settlers. Burgess status offered freedom from some burdens of lordship and provided an incentive for English and Welsh migrants to locate in Ireland.[169]

By the late thirteenth century, where burgess tenure was used as a lure to attract settlers, there were around 330 places with some kind of borough status. Estimates vary as to activities as towns as around 56 were performing urban functions and thereby merited this designation. From other research the Lordship of Ireland had over 100 functioning towns, 80 of them small towns and 25 of them mercantile towns. Of

---

[168] Campbell Bruce, Benchmarking Medieval Economic Development, QUB, 2006.
[169] Downham, C., Medieval Ireland.

these Dublin, which conceivably rivalled Bristol, was by far the most substantial with at least 11,000 inhabitants as a port and as the seat of English administration and jurisdiction, with two cathedrals and a major concentration of religious institutions. Next in size were the cathedral cities and commercial centres of Waterford and Kilkenny. Drogheda, New Ross, Cork, and Limerick were lesser in population. However, Dublin was far outshone by New Ross, Cork, and Drogheda in the value of their dutiable overseas trade and size of their lay subsidies contributions. In terms of duty paid Dublin was the fifth port of Ireland. Trade was the lifeblood of towns and from 1275, when customs revenues were levied in England and the Lordship of Ireland upon exports of wool, woolfells, and hides, the volume and value of the dutiable export trade is one of the most measurable of economic activities. In 1290, Ireland's leading wool and hide exporting port was New Ross. [170]

European Developments

The late twelfth and early thirteenth centuries saw the formal distribution and practical occupation of Irish land that had been won by the military energies and political skills of the Anglo-Norman invaders. However, it is important to view colonisation in Ireland in a European setting. As mentioned earlier the twelfth and early thirteenth centuries were a period of rising population. This did create a favourable climate for the enterprise of lordship. On the eastern frontier of Germany new settlements were being established under the direction of ecclesiastical and secular magnates. In Spain, efforts were being made to encourage Christian re-settlements in lands re-conquered from the Moors. In France new towns and

---

[170] Campbell, Bruce, Medieval Economic Development.

villages were springing up in the countryside. In England, lords responded to the economic conditions, which included rising prices, by taking into their own hands land that had formerly been leased to tenants. Instead they exploited the land directly, drawing on a plentiful supply of cheap labour and selling on a buoyant market. It was against such a background that the colonisers in Ireland encouraged settlers to occupy the lands they were winning. Settlement in Ireland therefore took place within the controlling framework of lordship which in turn was regularly disciplined by royal authority or parcelled sovereignty which demarcated and determined spheres of influence.

What happened in Ireland was in harmony with the European experience. It was controlled by royal and aristocratic lordship and was influenced by existing patterns. However, in Leinster, Meath, and Ulster, and eventually Connaught, too most of the divisions that shaped the tenurial future were taken not by the Crown directly but by magnate/vassals including Strongbow, William Marshall, the De Lacys, John De Courcy, or Richard De Burgh.[171]

Four Countries; Two Islands

By the end of the thirteenth century, after over 100 years of economic development and demographic expansion in all four countries – England, Scotland, Wales, and Ireland – per capita, England was marked out as the most commercialised of the four countries. England supported the highest densities of people, religious houses, large towns, and per capita commanded the most money and exported the most customable goods. In Ireland the tide of English power was more or less at its height. The threat from

---

[171] Frame, R., Colonial Ireland.

resurgent Irish clans was just about contained and the Lordship was a source of modest profit to the Crown. It is matter of some debate what proportion of the Irish population acknowledged the sovereignty of the English Crown and lived within the Lordship of Ireland within whose shrinking jurisdiction the bulk of religious houses and almost all towns were located. These confined territories contributed at least two thirds of Irish taxation revenues and all the customs revenues accounted for to the Crown.

Since the advent of Norman/English rule in 1171 areas securely within the expanding Lordship had been colonised and planted with an emigrant population. Manors and parishes had been created and many additional religious houses founded. Significant numbers of towns, fairs, and markets had been chartered and the first Irish coins minted. A central administration had been established, the common law had been introduced, and commercial property rights defined and defended. A substantial export trade in cheap wool and hides had also been built up but Ireland's economic development was not on a par with England or even Scotland at that time. Relatively, it was a far less commercialised economy most pronouncedly so in the extensive areas of residual Irish control where the continuing role of cattle as a measure of wealth and store of value, along with the importance of barter in commercial exchange, and the modest contribution of foreign trade to the Irish economy were all factors. A further factor was the Lordship earned less than its counterparts either from dutiable exports due to the high cost distance to continental markets and the inferior quality of its wool. In contrast for Scotland, the export trade in wool and hides sustained its overwhelmingly agrarian economy, financed the importation of luxury and manufactured goods from overseas and fostered rapid growth of its money supply.[172]

---

[172] Campbell Bruce, Medieval Economy.

In advancing his territorial ambitions against first the Welsh, and then the Scots, Edward I enjoyed a massive demographic advantage as the English outnumbered the Welsh by at least 12 to 1, the Scots by 5 to 1 and the Irish by 3 to 1, in an overall population at somewhere between 6.0 to 6.5 million. Thanks to the Lordship of Ireland, which he had received as a wedding gift from his father (but never visited), Edward was already the acknowledged monarch of almost three quarters of those living in Britain and Ireland, even before his military annexation of Wales. By the time he declared war on Scotland this had increased to nearly four fifths. In Wales Edward I's castles symbolised the establishment of royal authority. In Scotland, Edward acting as overlord had appointed guardians to decide upon the succession to the Scottish Crown. In England the king seemed well able to cope with any opposition. The main problems seemed likely to arise in Gascony which Edward held as a vassal of the king of France.

In Ireland, the royal justiciar, John Wogan, sitting at Ardfert in County Kerry, heard a plea concerning land in Dunquin demonstrating Royal power was not confined to Dublin and the east but extended to remote areas in the south-west. However, none of the foregoing proved to be permanent. Wogan's court in 1307, the year of the death of Edward 1, was the last royal assizes to be held in Kerry for three centuries, and even in Wales the foundations were shallow.

The Bruces

In Scotland, Robert Bruce, whose father had fought with Henry III at the battle of Lewes, defeated the forces of Edward II at Bannockburn in 1314. Confusion is often caused by the use of concepts of *'English'* and *'Scottish'* in dealing with these events. Issues

of national identity were not in play in a situation that at the highest
political level was dominated by ideas of lordship and vassalage. The
contenders in the struggle, with the exception of William Wallace
(who was captured and executed in 1304), were not in a conflict
between England and Scotland but a struggle for power within the
Norman ascendancy, as the contenders in the struggle were all of
Norman extraction.

Bruce's support (from the French de Bruis) came from his fellow
Normans, although not all of them. Those who gave him their
support took their stand against a king who seemed to have shifted
his position from that of feudal overlord to one of imperial
dominance.[173] In 1314 at Bannockburn Robert Bruce the Scottish
king halted Edward II's attempt to conquer Scotland and in 1315
Edward Bruce, brother of Robert Bruce, was invited to campaign in
Ulster by an alliance of Ulster chiefs and discontented Norman
barons. They later received support from other areas of Gaelic
Ireland. For a time there was a real possibility that Ireland might
follow Scotland and become an independent kingdom with Edward
Bruce as its ruler but a combination of famine (1315-1317) and
opposition from the Anglo-Norman Lordship of Ireland and their
Irish allies led to his defeat at Faughart in 1318 and ruled this out.

The Remonstrance of the Irish Chiefs led by Donal O'Neill, king
of Cenel Eoghain (Tyrone), to Pope John XXII in 1317 against
English oppression go some way in setting out the underlying
reasons for the invitation to Bruce based on the considered perfidy of
the English. This was against[174] both those English in England and
'Englishry' in Ireland when it stated, *'on account of the injustice of the kings
of England and their wicked ministers and the constant treachery of the English*

---

[173] Ibid.

[174] Possibly the first historical reference to 'perfidious Albion'.

of mixed race, who, by the ordinance of the Roman curia, were bound to rule our nation with justice and moderation and have set themselves wickedly to destroy it … we are compelled to wage deadly war with them … And that we may be able to attain our purpose more speedily and fitly in this respect we call to our help and assistance Edward de Bruyis, illustrious earl of Carrick, brother of Robert by the grace of God most illustrious king of the Scots, who is sprung from our noblest ancestors'. The appeal to Pope John XXII (lest it be forgotten one of his predecessors had sanctioned the Norman invasion) did not succeed in transferring this kingly authority as desired.[175] The appeal had little effect on the pope, who passed it to Edward II with the recommendation that he should inquire into the complaints and put to rights if it were found true. The pope at that time was contemplating the excommunication of Robert Bruce for rebellion against the king.[176]

The Irish Anglo-Norman Feudal Magnates and Gaelic Lords

This episode in the long term went to expose the dependence of the Crown upon the feudal magnates in Ireland. By the end of the fourteenth century direct imperial rule in Ireland had been replaced by indirect influence exercised throughout the south of Ireland by three great feudal magnates. In Desmond and Kildare through the Fitzmaurices and Fitzgeralds respectively and by the Butlers in Ormond. Though they held their land in theory from the Crown as earls, they, in effect, ruled their territories as independent units. Future patterns of power in the south were already evident in the first

---

[175] Remonstrance of the Irish Chiefs to Pope John XXII, CELT, UCC.
[176] Hull, E., A History of Ireland and Her Peoples (1926), (1931), 2 vols.

half of the fourteenth century. The House of Desmond, once established, became the leading political force in Munster, and together with the Fitzgeralds earls of Kildare and the Butlers of Tipperary and Kilkenny formed an Anglo-Norman bloc. Despite internal dissensions and repeated clashes with the royal administration they remained part of the English nexus.

In the northern areas of Ireland, there was no semblance of a *'crown'* presence after the Bruce invasion. Power rested to a great extent with the rival dynasties of O'Neill and O'Donnell who claimed ancestry to the *Ui Neill*. The O'Donnells came to power and retained it thanks to Galloglasses imported from the Isles. These, the MacSweeneys, MacSheehys, the MacDowells, and other clans of *galloglass* received their reward through land and in the MacSweeneys' case the estuary of the River Moy.

Social Change

At the end of the thirteenth century the political future of the islands seemed to be directed towards a unified Norman ascendancy. However, the ascendancy dissolved into a number of independent or semi-independent units. The Norman Scots declared for a kingdom of Scotland. In Ireland their equivalents settled for a real autonomy beneath a vague royal overlordship. In Wales the great marcher lords, having met the challenge of Edward, survived for another century. All of this was made possible by the decision of *'England'* to seek an imperial future in France, a venture which turned into the Hundred Years War.[177]

---

[177] Kearney, H., The British Isles.

CHAPTER EIGHT

THE FEUDAL DYNAMIC AND SOCIETY

The technical innovations, which were the instruments for the advance of agrarian development, were essentially the use of the iron plough for tilling, the stiff harness for equine traction, the water mill for mechanical power, marling for soil improvement, and the three-field system for crop rotation. The level of organisation achieved by the feudal noble on his demesne was critical for the application of new techniques. The water mill became one of the most exploitative with the obligation of the peasantry to take their grains to be ground in the lord's mill and this activity was often the target of subsequent disputes.

The feudal mode of production afforded the peasantry the minimal space to increase the yield at its own disposal. The typical peasant had to provide labour rents often up to three days a week and numerous additional duties. Nevertheless, they were free to increase outputs on their own strips for the remainder of the time. A margin was thereby created for the results of increased productivity to accrue to the direct producer. The middle ages were marked by a steady spread of cereal cultivation and a shift within it toward the finer crop of wheat for bread as a staple food of the peasant. There was the gradual transition to the use of horses for ploughing. More and more villages came to possess forges and a scattered rural artisan cohort developed. At the same time as the population grew with the growth of the medieval economy, the average size of peasant holdings diminished because of fragmentation dropping from some 100 acres in the ninth century to 20 or 30 acres in the thirteenth century.

The normal upshot of these processes was increasing social differentiation in the villages, between families that owned plough teams and those that did not. This incipient stratum confiscated most of the benefits of rural progress within the villages and often tended to reduce the poorest peasants to the position of dependent labourers working for them. However, both prosperous and pauper peasants were opposed to the lords who battened on them and constant often silent struggles between the two were waged, occasionally erupting into warfare throughout the feudal epoch. The lords, whether lay or ecclesiastical, resorted to legal fabrication of new dues, coercive violence or seizure of disputed or communal lands. Struggles thus generated from either pole of the feudal relationship tended to stimulate productivity at both ends.[178]

It was in the midst of this conundrum that resuscitated and ever more numerous towns sprang up and prospered as intersection points as regional markets and centres for manufacture. The majority of the new towns were in origin either promoted or protected by feudal lords whose natural objective was to corner local markets, or scoop off profits from long-distance trade, by concentrating it under their aegis. Over time, and by the opening years of the fourteenth century, the progress of medieval agriculture now incurred its own penalties as the years 1315-1317 were years of European famine. The advance of cereal production had frequently been achieved at the cost of a diminution of grazing ground and with it a decline in the supply of natural manure for arable farming itself.

Clearance of forests and wastelands had not been accompanied by

---

[178] Anderson, P., Passages.

comparable care in conservation, there was little application of fertilizers so that the top soil was often exhausted. Floods and dust storms became more frequent. Lands began to be abandoned and the birth rate fell even before the cataclysms which overtook the continent later. At the same time the urban economy now reached certain critical obstacles to its development, including guild restrictions and patrician monopolies which hit petty commodity production. The shortage of metals led to repeated debasements of coinage in one country after another and hence to spiralling inflation. In France, above all the Hundred Years' War plunged the richest country in Europe into unparalleled disorder and misery. In England, the epilogue of the continental defeat in France was the baronial outlawry of the Wars of the Roses. The chivalrous vocation of the nobles war became their professional trade, knights' service increasingly gave way to mercenary captains and paid violence. Ultimately, the civil populations everywhere became the victims.

The Black Death, the Statute of Labourers, and the Statutes of Kilkenny

To complete the desolation of this structural crisis came the invasion of the Black Death, carried by rats and fleas, from Asia in 1348. The Black Death cut a fatal swathe through the population and upwards of a quarter of the inhabitants of the continent perished. Outbreaks of pestilence became endemic in many regions. Combined with famine, the plagues toll on the population by 1400 was as high as two fifths. It reached the coast of Ireland on or about early August 1348. It seems to have struck Drogheda first though both Howth and Dalkey arguably rivalled for being the ports of entry. It spread rapidly inland, hitting hardest the centres of population. Within a few weeks both Dublin, where it is estimated almost 14,000 people died before Christmas, was almost totally destroyed. It is not possible to estimate how many overall died as a result of the plague but it reoccurred at intervals right down to the end of the middle ages. There was another great outbreak in 1361 and in England it is estimated that as much as 40% of the population died as a result of the first outbreak and by the end of the century that the population might have been reduced by as much as half.

In Ireland it is estimated that, whereas it did not have as deleterious an effect amongst the Gaelic Irish population, more than two-thirds of the English nation were wiped out. It seems certain that the plague was at its worst among the Anglo-Irish, as it spread in the towns and manors and other centres of population, from which the Gaelic Irish ironically were mostly excluded. An official message from the Kilkenny Great Council of 1360 complained of the *'pestilence which is so great and so hideous among the English lieges and not among the Irish'.*

Scarcity of labour necessitated the abandonment of manors, some boroughs were wiped out, wages went spiralling upwards and prices followed. The scarcity of workers in England and high wages attracted Irish artisans and accelerated emigration from the island. A great council held in Kilkenny in November 1351 issued a series of ordinances which formed the basis subsequently for the Statutes of Kilkenny of 1366. At least 13 out of the 25 ordinances of 1351 are concerned with problems of defence and peacekeeping and the fear that the English population was more easily exposed to their Irish enemies. Interestingly the proclamation of the Statute of Labourers (there was further legislation to prevent emigration) was included in the proclamation but has not received a great deal of attention by historians in general. Nor for that matter has its inclusion in the follow-on Statutes of Kilkenny which were largely a repeat of the

1351 Rokeby ordinances in England with some additions. These were the attempt to fix the level of wages and prices as contained in the Statute of Labourers of 1361.[179]

These accumulated disasters unleashed a desperate struggle on the land. The noble class, threatened by debt and inflation, were now confronted by a diminishing workforce. Its immediate reaction was to try to recuperate its surplus by riveting the peasantry to the manor or battering down wages in both towns and countryside. The Statute of Labourers, decreed in England in 1349-1351, directly after the Black Death, was essentially a programme for exploitation. Similar decrees were passed in France, Germany, Spain, and Portugal two decades later. The ordinances provided as follows:

'Whereas it was lately ordained by our lord the king and by assent of the prelates, earls, barons, and others of his council, against the malice of servants, who were idle, and not willing to serve after the pestilence without excessive wages, that such manner of servants, as well men as women, should be bound to serve, receiving the customary salary and wages in the places where they ought to serve in the 20th year of the reign of the king that now is, or five or six years before, and that the same servants refusing to serve in such a manner should be punished by imprisonment of their bodies ... the servants, having no regard to the ordinance, but to their ease and singular covetousness, do withdraw themselves from serving great men and others, unless they have livery and wages double or treble of what they were wont to take in the 20th year or earlier, to the great damage of the great men and impoverishment of the commonalty.'

The Statute applied to all those who did not own enough land for their own subsistence, obliging them to work for lords at fixed wages: hence it struck at small-holders as such.[180] The bid to reinforce servile conditions and make the producing classes pay the costs of the crisis

---

[179] Lydon, J., Ireland in the Later Middle Ages, Gill and Macmillan, (1973), Dublin.
[180] Anderson, P., Passages.

met with violent resistance often led by better educated and more prosperous peasants.

In 1358, Northern France was aflame with the Grande Jacquerie set off by military requisitioning and pillage during the Hundred Years' War. In 1381, the Peasants Revolt in England erupted precipitated by a new poll tax while also seeking the abolition of serfdom and the abrogation of the existing legal system. All of these revolts were defeated and politically repressed. The immediate aftermath of the crisis of western feudalism however was a pervasive social alteration and, after the Peasants Revolt, wages started to rise in an ascending curve. Far from the general crisis of the feudal mode of production worsening the condition of the direct producers in the countryside, it ended by ameliorating it, and it proved the turning point in the dissolution of serfdom in the West. The presence of towns put constant pressure on the nobles to realise their income in monetary form. They could not risk driving their peasants wholesale into vagrancy or urban employment. They were compelled to accept a general relaxation of servile ties on the land. The result was a slow but steady commutation of dues into money rents.

By 1400 villeniage had passed over into copy-holding, which was insecure and temporary, permitting easier eviction from the land at a later date. In the next century the nobility reacted by increasingly switching to pasturage to supply the woollen industry that had developed in the new cloth towns, by starting a movement of enclosures; and by the complex system of paid retinues and hired violence which has been designated as the *'bastard feudalism'* of the fifteenth century. The main theatre of this operation being the Yorkist-Lancastrian wars.[181] This *'bastard feudalism'* may be seen as the final chapter in the decline and fall of the post-Norman Empire.

---

[181] Ibid.

The transformation of the Gaelic ruling classes was not unconnected with changes which were taking place elsewhere in Europe at the end of the middle ages and the beginning of the early modern period. One such change was the rise of the Irish version of '*bastard feudalism*' in which powerful Gaelic chiefs relied upon their own mercenary forces, thus Gaelic society was not completely distinctive or unaffected by change elsewhere. [182]

Hundred Years' War, the Irish, and Irish-English

Uprisings

The war between England and France was renewed at the end of 1369 which meant not much attention was left spare for Ireland. New legislation in Ireland against absentees did not help, and indeed, it had the effect of persuading a number of the more important ones to pull out of Ireland and to sell their manors to Anglo-Irish magnates already resident there. Before the war had begun the king had appointed William of Windsor (his administrations 1369-1372 and 1374-1376 coincided with one of the most costly and least successful phases of the Hundred Years' War)[183] as lieutenant of Ireland. Windsor's appointment showed that the king was prepared to continue his heavy investment in Ireland. (In the later fourteenth century we begin to find the appointment of the king's lieutenant's. Many of these were absentees who governed through deputies.) Windsor found himself immediately involved with the Irish of the mountains South of Dublin until Mac Murcada, their leader, was captured and executed. Windsor was then diverted to Munster where

---

[182] Kearney, H., The British Isles.
[183] Frame, R., Colonial Ireland.

O'Brien and Mac Namara of Thomond had led a rising, imprisoning some of the leading Anglo-Irish (including the earl of Desmond), killing others, and had burnt Limerick in their wake.

After a period of activity Windsor succeeded in procuring submissions from both O'Brien and Mac Namara before the end of 1370. The New Year saw him engaging O'Kennedy of Ormond but the sustained war was taking its toll. In 1371 there was another outbreak of the plague which exacerbated matters. Windsor could only continue by seeking lavish parliamentary subsidies and many complaints had been received by the king about his '*high handed behaviour*' as there was constant refusal by the colonists to take responsibility for the costs of the war and at this point he was ordered back to England.

In his wake and by April 1372 there were signs of panic in Government circles. This arose when a meeting of the council in Dublin was told Mac Namara, Richard Og de Burgh of Connaught, and '*almost all the Irish of Munster, Connaught and Leinster, and many English, rebels and enemies, had risen openly to war after the departure of William of Windsor ... and had confederated to make a universal conquest of the whole of Ireland before the same lieutenant should come from England.*' The increased tendency of the Irish to confederate, not only in Leinster but in Munster as well, led to the Government trying to buy off the more threatening ones. (Windsor returned in 1373 and remained until 1376.) On every side the English lost ground in Ireland. The Statutes of Kilkenny had been a failure and all further attempts to deal with the threats were a failure. The great council of 1385 stated: '*at this next season, as is likely, there will be made a conquest of the greater part of the land of Ireland that is by the Irish and Irish rebel's*'.[184]

---

[184] Lydon, J., Ireland in the Later Middle Ages.

Contracting-out wars

The last feudal array summoned on the basis of land tenure was called out in 1385 for Richard II's attack on Scotland. The Hundred Years' War was essentially fought by indentured companies, raised on the basis of cash contracts by major lords for the monarchy and owing obedience to their own captains; shire levies and foreign mercenaries provided supplementary forces. Private plunder, ransom, and land were the objects of their ambition and the most successful captains enriched themselves massively from the wars.[185] An example of this was the attempt to govern Ireland through contract by way of the grant to Robert de Vere in 1385. The king announced in October that he was going to bestow the title of marquis of Dublin on his great favourite de Vere. In December he was granted the land of Ireland for life, with writs running in his name and his arms replacing those of the king. It was anticipated that a programme of re-conquest would make Ireland once more a source of profit. De Vere's grant made Ireland more or less a palatinate for him, but he never came to Ireland. When he suffered exile and forfeiture as a result of political change in England his grant lapsed.

His successor, Sir John Stanley, who had been acting as De Vere's deputy, was appointed on more normal terms, with a retinue of 100 men at arms and 400 archers and a stipend of 8,000 marks a year. However, following complaints against him, he was removed from office in 1391. The position then worsened to the situation in 1392, the greatest single threat being Art MacMurrough Kavanagh of the Leinster Irish, who had been strong enough to threaten Dublin itself. Expeditions led against them had been largely a failure and the expedient of buying them off by means of pensions or *'black rents'*

---

[185] Anderson, P., Lineages.

were never completely successful, as the constant complaints of the English lieges demonstrated. For Richard II the real answer was armed force and this he was prepared to apply. A truce had been negotiated with France and there was nominal peace with Scotland. There was as well a domestic peace and the king now felt secure enough to leave England.[186]

Richard II in Ireland

The Westminster parliament in the spring of 1393 had ordered all absentees back to Ireland. The ordinance of 1394 in this regard was much more sweeping since it not only included holders of lands and benefices but the craftsmen, artisans, and labourers who had immigrated to England in large numbers. In effect all the *'Irish'* settlers in England. The purpose of the legislation then was not only the familiar one of getting the absentees to defend their land, it was also intended to restore a working population to areas which had previously suffered losses.

In June of 1394 Richard announced his intention of going to Ireland. He had radical plans for turning Leinster into a *'land of peace'*, and it was here the returning workers were to settle. His army was to be organised and financed by the king's household so that it was under his personal control, which gave rise to the belief that Ireland was to be the testing ground of his military strength. But magnates and their retinues were also invited to join his army for pay, especially those who were absentee landlords of great estates in Ireland, such as the Earl of March who was Lord of Ulster, Connaught, and Trim. He brought Sir Thomas Mortimer with him, the Earl of Nottingham, Lord of Carlow, the Duke of Gloucester (not a known supporter of

---

[186] Lydon, J., Ireland in the later Middle Ages.

the king) who was the greatest of the magnates, and Philip de Courtenay who had previous knowledge of Irish administration.

Towards the end of September Richard had assembled the largest army ever sent to Ireland during the middle ages. The total may have amounted to between 8,000 and 10,000 men. It was comparable to the armies which were led against France during the Hundred Years' War. Richard landed at Waterford on the 2nd October but it was not until the 28th October that he left Waterford when the Duke of Gloucester, who was delayed, joined him, and possibly because *'leaves were on the trees'* which worked against the efficacy of their archers. They attacked MacMurrough in the woods of Leighlin, which was his *'principal fortress'*, on the 30th October. MacMurrough and others submitted and O'Byrne, O'Toole, and O'Nolan, his sub chiefs, were brought to Dublin with the king, though MacMurrough was left at large for the time being.[187]

Affairs progressed rapidly and by the following January Kildare was occupied in the king's wars in Leinster, the Earl of Rutland was taking submissions in Wexford and Nottingham was now negotiating with MacMurrough. In Ulster, the Archbishop of Armagh was conducting intensive negotiations with the Irish and though the younger O'Neill held back (in February the young O'Neill wrote to the Archbishop saying that following his sage counsel and after he consulted with all the great Irish of Ulster, there were *'envoys from O'Brien, O'Connor, Mac Carthy and many more others from the south, urging me strongly not to go the king'*). However, at the end of January, his father, as proctor for his son, did homage and fealty to Richard in person at Drogheda. By February action in Munster was beginning to bring results and the king was told *'our rebels who call themselves kings and captains of Munster and Connaught'* were ready to do homage.

---

[187] Ruthven-Otway, A.J., A History of Medieval Ireland

In February Richard wrote to the Regent and council in England that there were three classes in Ireland, *'wild Irish, our enemies, Irish rebels, and obedient English ... the said Irish rebels are rebels only because of grievances and wrongs done to them on one side and lack of remedy on the other'*. This has generally been interpreted as meaning the Irish in general, the *'degenerate English'*, and the English lieges (although there is some discussion as to whether Irish rebels means Irish-born English rebels). The principal activity of February was in Leinster, here Nottingham, who as lord of the liberty of Carlow, had a special interest, had been negotiating with MacMurrough. In February 1395 Nottingham met Gerald O'Byrne and Donal O'Nolan, captain of his nation, coming from a wood where many armed Irishmen were assembled and had the letters patent of the 12th February read, first in Latin and then translated into English and Irish by a Hospitaller *'learned in the Irish tongue'*.

Then the principal Leinster chiefs, including Mac Murrough himself, successively paid homage in Irish. Following on from which MacMurrough swore to give full possession of everything to the king which he and his men had occupied in Leinster, and undertook that all his tenants and subjects in these places would swear fealty to the king. In return he was guaranteed an annual payment of 80 marks, and his wife's inheritance in the barony of Norragh. Finally, he undertook that *'all the armed men of war of his company, household or nation, should leave Leinster and go with him at the king's wages and make war on other lands occupied by the king's rebels, and he and his men should have all the lands they so acquired to hold in perpetual inheritance from the king and his successors as his true lieges and subjects'*. Letters patent were issuedm empowering Nottingham to receive the liege homage of the Irish of Leinster and Ormond, Desmond, and all other subjects were to counsel, aid, and obey Nottingham in this.

Meanwhile, negotiations were actively in progress in Ulster and the chiefs of Ulster, among whom the Archbishop of Armagh and Sir Thomas Talbot had been working indefatigably, had come in. By the 5th March the king had gone north again to Drogheda and then to Dundalk, the captains of the Irish of Meath and Breifne, and those of Ulster, including the young O'Neill, appeared doing homage and fealty in person. In February also Tadgh McCarthy *Prince of the Irish of Desmond'* had written professing that he and all his ancestors had been the king's men since the time of the conquest. In April, after defeat by Rutland, along with Mac Carthy Reagh, he did homage. During the rest of the month the remaining captains of Munster submitted as well as O'Connor Don of Connaught. Richard moved from Kilkenny to Waterford at the end of April.

When Richard had already boarded his ship, O'Connor Don, with William de Burgo (the Clanrickard Burke) and Walter de Bermingham of Athenry, formerly rebels against the king, came on board and were knighted. On the 15th May the king sailed for England. By the time Richard left Ireland every important Irish chief, with the exception of O'Donnell and some others in the north-west, had submitted to him.[188]

In 1398 Richard delegated all parliamentary power to a committee of twelve lords and six commoners chosen from his friends, making him an absolute ruler unbound by the necessity of gathering a parliament again. His kingship was thus considered to contain elements of the early modern absolute monarchy as exemplified by the Tudor dynasty later on.

---

[188] Ibid.

Social Change

The king's triumph in Ireland was very much a military one. His plan of campaign contained a ring of garrisons to pin down the Irish; an embargo on imports; a naval blockade; and the use of a large number of separate troops of light cavalry, with great mobility and great striking power. Froissart in his chronicle asks, '*How did these four kings Mac Murrough, O'Neill, O'Connor and O'Brien of Ireland come so soon to the king's obeisance ... earthly princes get little except by power and strength ... when the Irishmen saw the great number of men of war that King Richard had in Ireland this last journey, the Irishmen advised themselves and came to obeisance.*'

Richard's triumph in Ireland was a military one and while the garrisons around Leinster remained in place, Leinster remained quiet. But, as so often happens, financial expediency dictated a retreat from policy and for lack of money the garrisons were withdrawn. A report to the English Council said:

'MacMurrough is now gone to Desmond to aid the Earl of Desmond to destroy the power of the Earl of Ormond if possible, and afterwards he is to return with all the power he can get from the parts of Munster to destroy the country ... O'Neill has assembled a very great host of people without number to war upon and destroy the whole country'.

Less than three years after Richard's departure the Irish continued on as if his nothing had happened. In any event, the Dublin Government had failed in most cases to honour agreements that had been reached by Richard with the Irish chiefs who no longer felt bound as a result. In one of the engagements which was fought between the government and the Irish, Roger Mortimer, one of the protagonists and heir to the throne of England, was killed. This led to Richard's second expedition to Ireland but he failed disastrously on this occasion and was decisively defeated by Mac Murrough. At this point Richard had to deal with treachery in his own camp, where supporters of Bolingbroke (Henry IV who deposed Richard) did everything to embarrass the king.

'So Art Kavanagh, having first wrought the death of Mortimer, now by delaying Richard in the wilds of Leinster, let in usurping Bolingbroke and wrecked the unity of England for a hundred years'.

Richard's intervention was to be the last large-scale one for a hundred years. From then on Ireland was left more or less to its own devices, with the great magnates gaining an ascendancy in the governance of the Lordship which they gradually came to regard as their right.[189] After Richard II's expeditions, and the failure of his conquest, the English withdrew for the time being and created the Pale[190], an archaic English term for an area or jurisdiction and considered to be modelled on the Pale of Calais.

---

[189] Lydon J., Ireland in the Middle Ages.

[190] Lydon J., Richard II's expeditions to Ireland, Government, War, and Society in Medieval Ireland, Peter Crooks ed., Four Courts Press, 2008.

CHAPTER NINE

THE HOUSES OF LANCASTER, YORK AND

IRELAND

The Anglo-Irish had their parliament of prelates, peers, knights of the shires, burgesses, and proctors for the lesser clergy, while above parliament was the Dublin Government, the standing council headed by the lieutenant or deputy, the chancellor, treasurer, and chief justices. At one time, the council had controlled parliament in the English interest. Now a faction had grown up among the English of the Pale led by the great earls. They had many grievances in relation to the misgovernment and neglect of Ireland, the loss of great areas to the Irish, the discrimination against 'English' Irishmen in England, the rapacity of English officials, their contempt for the Anglo-Irish, and the continued absence of the king and of many of the greatest proprietors. To govern Ireland by the English Irish–born became their objective; the *'English by birth'* were held enemies of the *'English by blood'* and a handful of nobles aimed at controlling the government in the name of a limited Anglo-Irish patriotism. There was, however, a considerable faction drawn from the church, the towns, and the lesser *Englishry*, which looked to England for support and thought English-born viceroys would keep order and justice better than the feudal magnates. From 1419 to 1447, it was led by John Talbot, Earl of Shrewsbury, several times viceroy and his brother Richard, Archbishop of Dublin and chancellor till 1449, both strong

Lancastrians. On the other hand the opposing faction rallied round James fourth Earl of Ormond, called *the white earl* who was several times viceroy, from 1420 to 1446. England had its factions and so had Ireland. The Anglo-Irish faction was put in the fore by the action of Richard of York and not for another fifty years was the opposing faction to prevail. The appointment of York ended the Talbot and Lancastrian regime.[191] When the War of the Roses gripped England in the 1450s, the opposing Houses of Lancaster and York became identified in Ireland with the earls of Ormond and Kildare respectively and this Butler-Geraldine feud continued into the early modern era.

War of the Roses and Ireland

English dominance throughout most of the Hundred Year's War was a product of the far greater political integration and solidity of the English feudal monarchy, whose capacity, to exploit its patrimony and rally its nobility, was, until the very end of the war, much greater than that of the French monarchy. The French were harried by disloyal vassals in Brittany or Burgundy and weakened by its earlier inability to dislodge the English fief in Guyenne. The loyalty of the English aristocracy was cemented by the successful external campaigns into which it was led by a series of martial princes. It was not until the feudal French was itself reorganised under Charles VII on a new fiscal and military basis that the tide turned. The aftermath of the final collapse of English power in France brought about the outbreak of the War of the Roses at home. Once a victorious royal authority no longer held the higher nobility together, the late

---

[191] Curtis, E., Richard Duke of York as Viceroy of Ireland, 1447-1460, Government, War and Society in Medieval Ireland.

medieval machinery of war turned inwards, and rival usurpers clawed for succession. Brutalised retainers and indentured gangs were unleashed across the countryside by magnate feuds.[192]

As a result of the Somerset-York feud in England the authority of Richard, the Duke of York, as lieutenant of Ireland was being disputed. In May 1453 the new earl of Ormond and Wiltshire obtained a grant of the office from the English council in spite of the already existing commission of York which had still over four years to run. Ormond was too involved in English politics to come over so he appointed as his deputy John May Archbishop of Armagh. There were bitter complaints about his administration and in June 1454 a memorial from the county of Kildare related how English rebels and Irish enemies came into the county of Kildare and burnt many towns and parish churches and took prisoners of spoil, and how William Butler, cousin of the Earl, remained and did great oppression till the *daily sustenance* of the city of Dublin was destroyed.

In May 1455 the first pitched battle of the War of the Roses took place at St. Albans. Somerset was slain and in November York was made protector again. He turned the Lancastrians out of office. When York was first made protector in February 1454, after the king's imbecility was pronounced, the question as to who was the lieutenant was raised in the English council. The decision was in favour of York and it would appear the previous grant to Ormond was ignored. York also received a re-grant of the lieutenancy for ten years from December 1457, that is ten years from when the first grant was to expire. Thomas Earl of Kildare had been made justiciar by the Irish council in January 1455 and York confirmed this choice by making Kildare his deputy.

The native Irish had kept the colony in a state of siege and the

---

[192] Anderson, P., *Lineages of the Absolutist State.*

parliament of 1455 sent urgent messages to the king telling of the imminent danger to his lordship of Ireland, which *'was like to be finally destroyed'*, if a remedy were not immediately forthcoming. The *'old English'* it was said were as bad as the Irish. To the same parliament came a letter from the seneschal of the liberty of Wexford telling how Edmund Butler and seven others of his nation, with Donal Reagh McMurrough and other Irish enemies, had with *'banners displayed, ridden, burnt and destroyed the county of Wexford by time and space of four days, and four nights continually'*. So, it appears, some of the evils of the time were exemplified by the *'over-mighty'* subject and his retainers. This included the feud of the nobles and the corruption of justice. The chief justice Devereux was accused of bringing in Irish enemies and English rebels into a loyal shire and the deputy was charged with using parliament only to secure favours for another magnate Thomas of Desmond.

In Ireland unbridled feudalism prevailed, and the petty parliament and the Anglo-Irish aristocracy that ran it could not or would not do anything effective, to restore the royal power and save the pale from destruction. They were lords in their own counties and as for parliament they dominated it in order that it should serve their interests and secure them the office of state.[193]

In England, the Yorkist party issued various manifestos against the Lancastrian regime, but at the *'rout of Ludlow'* in October 1459 the Yorkist forces were scattered. York made for Ireland and his son, Edward Earl of March, and his nephew, Richard of Warwick, made for Calais the refuges chosen as the jumping off points reserved by the Yorkists for their cause in England. York viewed Ireland as a safe stronghold and was prepared to run it with local influences in mind.

---

[193] Curtis, E., *Richard Duke of York, as Viceroy of Ireland, 1447-1460, Government, War and Society.*

When he landed in Dublin in November 1459, he was welcomed as king. The English parliament attainted him but this held little sway with Irish magnates who now had *'a king of their own'*. The *'English nation in Ireland'* now proceeded to assert its legislative independence, the *'land of Ireland'* it declared *'is and at all times has been corporate of itself'*.

Richard had enlisted on his side the Irish magnates and made Ireland a stronghold for the Yorkist faction. In 1460 the Yorkist leaders resolved on an invasion of England and Warwick landed in Kent from Calais. Marching North, he defeated the Lancastrians and took the king prisoner at Northampton. When news of this victory reached York, he appointed the earl of Kildare as his deputy and left for England, accompanied by followers from Ireland. The throne of England was now within his grasp, and while Parliament, by force of circumstances, admitted his claim, they stipulated that Henry should continue to reign for the rest of his life with York as his chief Minister, heir, and successor. York did not live long enough to enjoy his triumph as in December 1460 he was killed outside his own castle of Wakefield having offered battle with his small forces to many thousands of Lancastrian supporters.

By York's side were many Irish retainers, *'those of Ulster, Clandeboy, the Glines, and the Ardes, which at that time was better inhabited with English nobility, than any part of Munster or Connaught, came over with him, [York], against Henry VI, to divers famous battles, lastly to Wakefield, where they not only lost their lives with him but also left their country naked to defence that the Irish … cast up their old Captain O'Neale, relyed themselves with their ancient neighbours the Scots and repossessed themselves of the whole country, which was the utter decay of Ulster'.*[194]

His son Edmund, Earl of Rutland and of Cork, was murdered

---

[194] From a record of a later time. Curtis, E, Richard, Duke of York, Viceroy of Ireland, 1447-1460.

after the battle and the heads of both were placed over the gate of York while Richard's head in derision was crowned with a paper crown. York's eldest son, Edward Earl of March, was soon avenged and although Warwick was defeated at St. Albans by the Queens forces, he marched from the West, entered London was crowned by his party as Edward IV, and secured his kingdom at Towton in March 1461. After the battle James Earl of Ormond and Wiltshire, one of his most determined opponents, was taken and beheaded on the 1st May. Edward was also Earl of Ulster, Lord of Trim, Leix, and Connaught. The vast de Lacy, de Burgo, and Mortimer estates now merged into the Crown. For the next forty years and longer Anglo-Ireland, under the leadership of Desmond and then Kildare, embraced the Yorkist cause.

The first real sign that Desmond would merit the attention of Edward IV, and the application of the methods of government that were so successful in England, was with the appointment of Sir John Tiptoft Earl of Worcester as deputy in 1467. The circumstances which made it easier to replace him were that in 1466, there were widespread risings against Desmond that led to his own capture and defeat in Offaly. Tiptoft was ruthless and efficient at what he did and had earned the nickname of the '*butcher of England*' for his methods in the treatment of victims and his penchant for impalement as a means of execution. Parliament was summoned on his arrival and met in Dublin in December. The next session met in Drogheda, which was an anti-Geraldine town, in February 1468. The very first act conducted was a mounted attack on Desmond and Edward Plunkett attainting them of '*horrible treasons and felonies, by allying and helping the Irish*'. Desmond was arrested and executed on the 15th February.

The removal of two earls, with Ormond already out of the way, and the confiscation of their estates, enormously enhanced the power of Edward in Ireland. However, they had miscalculated as there was a violent reaction in Ireland to the execution. The Earl of Kildare was then allowed to return to the king's peace in response. Tiptoft had come to the realisation that the goodwill and cooperation of Kildare was necessary if peace was to be secured and Kildare's attainder was then reversed. In October 1470, when Edward IV fled overseas, Henry VI was restored to rule in England. One of the first victims of the new Lancastrian government was John Tiptoft. He was tried at Westminster in October and on the following day was beheaded on Tower Hill.[195] Subsequent preoccupation with dynastic changes, French war, and the civil War of the Roses kept the English kings from paying too much attention to Ireland until after the accession of Henry VII in 1485.[196]

Ireland enjoyed a period of home rule of an oligarchic nature in which her parliament and law courts were internally supreme. When Henry VII triumphed at Bosworth in 1485, he saw Ireland as a dangerous stronghold left to the beaten faction. As a restorer of the Lancastrian regime he viewed all that had been done by York as usurpation. The return to power of the Lancastrians meant the return to favour of the Butlers and Kildare found it politic to marry his second daughter to Piers Butler, the cousin and heir of Ormond, who eventually became the ninth earl. In 1487, a boy of ten was brought to Ireland, who it was alleged was Edward Earl of Warwick (the true heir was a prisoner in the Tower). He was accepted in good faith by the majority of the Anglo-Irish as the true heir to the throne. The boy was Lambert Simnell. Only the Archbishop of Armagh, Octavian Del Palatio, and the Butler interest with the City of Waterford held out for Henry. It was not until the end of the year, and after Simnell's

---

[195] Lydon, J., Ireland in the Middle Ages.
[196] Jackson, T.A., Ireland Her Own.

supporting forces were defeated at Stoke, that Kildare and his supporters submitted. In June 1488 Sir Richard Edgecombe was sent to Ireland equipped with power to grant pardons. Henry's position was surprising to many but his position in England was still precarious, and the possibility of further continental intervention was by no means at an end. A Bull against disturbances against his right of succession, in which Ireland was specifically included, was also procured from Pope Innocent VIII. Negotiations commenced as Edgecombe had been instructed to ensure that Kildare and the Yorkist's entered into bonds by which their lands would be immediately forfeited if they ever rebelled against Henry. This they flatly refused to do, telling Edgecombe that rather than do so *'they would become Irish every of them'*.

Eventually, it was agreed that Kildare and the others would take oaths of allegiance to Henry, and they would never assist his rebels or traitors and they would resist and disclose any plots against him, amongst others the *'lourd Burke of Connaught'*, then Kildare and the others did homage. In 1490 Kildare was summoned to England. But he did not go and nearly a year later, in June 1491, he wrote that he had intended to come but had been asked by the lieges, and especially Desmond, to remain for their defence and to settle a quarrel between Desmond and Burke. He also said that if the king would send a messenger, he would cause Desmond and Burke, with all the lords temporal and spiritual of Munster, to enter into the same engagements as he himself had done.

In spite of these protestations, another Yorkist pretender, Perkin Warbeck, who was put forward as Richard Duke of York, Edward IV's second son, one of the princes murdered in the Tower, was about to appear in Ireland. He asked support from both Desmond and Kildare but nothing very much seems to have come of his visit.[197] Nevertheless, it caused concern for Henry who considered Kildare as involved in another plot. Kildare was dismissed from office in December 1491 and replaced in June 1492 by Walter Fitz Simmons, Archbishop of Dublin. Kildare supporters were also removed from office, Alexander Plunkett became chancellor and James Ormond (a son of the fifth earl) was made treasurer. By now accusations against Kildare began to reach the king, serious enough for Kildare to go over to England and answer the charges in person. It was chiefly the English colonists who were Yorkist and concerned in the episodes of Simnel and Warwick, the native Irish in general, took little or no interest in either claimant.[198]

Poynings' Law

On meeting the king, Kildare supposedly treated him on equal terms, making jokes at the expense of his main accuser, his old enemy Sherwood the Bishop of Meath. The bishop apparently retorted *'You see the sort of man he is; all Ireland cannot rule him'*. To which Henry is supposed to have replied, *'then he must be the man to rule all Ireland'*. The reality behind the story was very different as he did not re-appoint him as Deputy until August 1496, and in the meantime he sought to revolutionise the administration with the appointment of Poynings' in 1494, and all that that entailed. By means of the so-called *'Poynings' Law'*, Henry ended the independence of the medieval Irish parliament. Sir Edward Poynings was sent in 1494 with the avowed object of ending forty years of local rule, restoring royal control, and ending the domination of Kildare, the most powerful of the feudal magnates in Ireland. In the parliament of Drogheda, 1494-95, the

---

[197] Ruthven, Otway, A.J., A History.
[198] Lydon. J., Ireland in the Middle Ages.

'*home-rule*' declaration of 1460 was annulled. Nevertheless, the supremacy of the house of Kildare remained intact for another forty years, until its fall in 1534, with the orchestrated '*rebellion*' of Silken Thomas.[199]

More Irish Than the Irish Themselves?

The myth that the Normans became more Irish than the Irish themselves became deeply embedded in the Irish psyche and Irish historiography after the mid-seventeenth century. Evidence from the hearth money records and the 1659 Census are helpful in testing the validity of this long-assumed pattern of acculturation which emphasised the capacity of Gaelic Irish culture to assimilate and incorporate the culture of the descendants of the medieval settlers known as the Anglo-Normans. If the thesis or myth that the Normans became more Irish than the Irish themselves is correct, one might expect that over more than four hundred years of conflict, interaction, and assimilation between the two groups, at least some of the Old English families would come to carry first names which had been borrowed from the Gaelic naming stock, however the evidence suggests that the families of Anglo-Norman ascent stubbornly retained their own naming patterns. The descendants of the Anglo-Normans may have borrowed freely when it came to cultural matters of poetry, song, music, and indeed language but they yielded little when it came to matters of property, in land or the Church or the professions more generally. In a powerful Anglo-Norman zone of colonisation and property control, under the aegis of the Butler overlordship, the deeper feudalisation of the '*Old Irish*' population, and their naming patterns, were much more modelled on those of the

---

[199] Curtis, E., Richard of York.

Anglo-Norman lords and their principal tenants. Not only had the Normans not become more Irish than the Irish themselves; rather the cultural tide was running in the opposite direction in the sixteenth and seventeenth centuries with the adoption of Old English naming patterns by families of Gaelic descent. There is also evidence of correlation in naming patterns between the Gaelic zones, in the north, west and south, the hybrid middle zone and the much *'feudalised'* south-eastern zone. This latter region is seen to extend over much of lowland Leinster, presents a sharp frontier to the Gaelic world of Ulster and its borderlands in Leinster and Connaught, extends into Normanised Roscommon and swings south to reveal the cultural zones of high assimilation to medieval naming patterns amongst the Gaelic families of both east and north Cork and north Kerry. The long recognised frontier between Desmond North Kerry and Gaelic South Kerry is evident in this regard.

The most striking feature is the regional distinctiveness of Ulster at this time. However, it is also relevant to note the large transitional zone in the middle of the country where Gaelic and Norman cultural forms met and fused to a greater extent. The Anglo-Norman colonisation and the associated great increase in continental religious foundations had clearly a profound long-term transformational effect on culture and naming patterns on the island.[200] In 1488, when the king's ambassador Sir Richard Edgecombe was trying to impose unacceptable terms on Kildare and others who had been involved in the Simnel treason, they not only refused to accept those terms, but uttered the ultimate threat – they would rather *'become Irish'* they said, *'every one of them'*. In the middle ages, 1171 and 1541, the Anglo-Irish (and for that matter most of the Irish as well) had no real crisis of loyalty. Ireland remained a *'parcel'* of the English Crown, indeed the

---

[200] Smyth, William J., Atlas of Family Names in Ireland, UCC, Cork.

'*oldest member thereof*' as the Anglo-Irish community of the land of Ireland reminded Edward IV in 1474.[201] By 1500, Gaelic and Gaelicised Ireland was still an expansive confident world and both the Irish language and Irish surname forms predominated in such regions beyond the pale. English speech and English name forms were then concentrated on the enclave of the Pale and Dublin, a few other key port cities and a few pockets elsewhere. However, by the early eighteenth century, in contrast, the tide had turned dramatically in favour of the English language and culture and in favour of anglicised surname forms. The Tudor, Cromwellian, and Williamite conquests had oppressed Gaelic Ireland and the story of the beginnings of a linguistic conquest is chronicled with ever increasing geographical precision between the 1530s and the 1660s. For males forenames such as John, Thomas, Richard, William, and Henry are to the fore and amongst women, Elizabeth, Mary, Anne, and Katherine feature strongly

Social Change

With the foundation of the new Tudor dynasty in 1485 and the reign of Henry VII, this now prepared the emergence of '*a new monarchy*' in England. Centralised government was exercised through a small coterie of personal advisers and henchmen of the monarch. Its primary objective was the subjugation of the rampant magnate power over the preceding period, with their liveried gangs of armed retainers, systematic packing of juries, and constant private warfare.

Supreme prerogative justice was enforced over the nobility by the use of the Star Chamber, a conciliar court which now became the

---

[201] Lydon, James, Ireland and the English Crown, 1171-1541, Government, War and Medieval Society, Crooks, P, ed. Four Courts Press, Dublin 2008.

main political weapon of the monarchy, against riot or sedition. Recidivist, usurper rebellions were crushed and local administration was tightened up under royal control while liveries were banned. Regional turbulence in the North and West, where marcher lords claimed rights of conquest, not enfeoffment by the monarch, were quelled by the Special Councils delegated to control these areas. A small bodyguard was created in lieu of armed police. The royal demesne was greatly enlarged by resumption of lands whose yield to the monarchy quadrupled. Feudal incidences and customs were likewise maximally exploited. The reign of Henry VII marked the end of a period. Signs of more radical change came with the rise to power of Wolsey and with the execution, at Wolsey's instigation, of the Duke of Buckingham in 1521, the most powerful of the marcher lords. In 1531 Rhys ap Griffith, the grandson of Grys ap Thomas, was executed on charges of treason, events which anticipated events in Ireland and which involved *'Silken Thomas'*.

The Crown was clearly challenging the *'old order'* in Wales as soon it was to do in Ireland. In 1536 the decisive shift came with the passing of an Act of Union. The Act of Union completed the attack on feudalism which had been foreshadowed in 1521 with Buckingham's execution. The decline of feudalism in Ireland began with the overthrow of the House of Kildare in the 1530s. This left untouched, for the time, being the great *'pretendid palatinates'* of Ormond and Desmond, as well as the *Gaelicised* chieftaincies of the west and north. In so far as Ireland was concerned the choice facing the Crown was whether to be content with a policy of *'amiable persuasions'* exercised indirectly through a great Anglo-Irish magnate such as the Earl of Kildare, or to intervene more directly through an English Lord Deputy.[202]

---

[202] Kearney, H., The British Isles.

CHAPTER TEN

THE TUDOR DYNASTY AND ABSOLUTISM

By the end of Henry VII's rule, total royal revenues had nearly trebled and there was a reserve of between one and two million pounds in the treasury. The Tudor dynasty had thus made a promising start towards the construction of an English absolutism by the turn of the sixteenth century. Henry VIII inherited a powerful executive and a prosperous exchequer.[203]

The first twenty years of Henry VIII's rule brought little change to the secure domestic position of the Tudor monarchy. Wolsey's administration of the estate was marked by no major institutional innovation; at most the Cardinal concentrated unprecedented powers over the church in his own person as Papal legate in England, both king and minister were preoccupied with foreign affairs. The limited campaigns fought against France in 1512-14 and 1522-25 were the main events of this period. To cope with the cost of these military operations two brief spells of parliamentary convocation were necessary. An attempt at arbitrary taxation aroused sufficient propertied opposition for Henry and ultimately Wolsey the instigator to disavow it. However, it was the marriage crisis of 1527-28, caused by the king's decision to divorce and the ensuing deadlock with the papacy, that affected the domestic succession and all of a sudden altered the whole situation.

---

[203] Anderson, P., Lineages.

New and radical legislation was required and national political support had to be rallied against Pope Clement VII and Charles V the Habsburg Emperor. Wolsey posed as an arbiter of European concord with the Treaty of London and aimed for nothing less than the papacy as Henry entertained hopes of becoming Emperor in Germany. Despite the fact that their domestic power was increasing, these aspirations reflected the perpetual difficulty of English rulers to adapt themselves to the new diplomatic configuration, in which the stature of England had in real terms much diminished. These policies it can be said lay behind the miscalculation of the royal divorce.

Neither Cardinal nor King realised that the papacy was bound to submit to the superior pressure of Charles V because of the dominance of Hapsburg power in Europe. By the early sixteenth century the balance of forces between the major western states had totally altered. Spain and France, each victims of English invasion in the previous epoch, were now aggressive and dynamic monarchies, disputing the conquest of Italy between them. England had suddenly been outdistanced by both. However, at the critical juncture of the transition to a *'new monarchy'* in England, it was neither necessary nor possible for the Tudor state to build up a military machine comparable to that of French or Spanish absolutism. This continental ascendancy was not translated into any equivalent strike-capacity at sea so that England, conversely, remained relatively immune from the risk of a maritime invasion. The absence of this constraint of constant potential invasion allowed the English aristocracy to dispense with a modernised apparatus of war, as it was not endangered in the epoch of the Renaissance by feudal classes abroad. Like any nobility it was not prepared to submit to a massive build-up of royal power which was the logical consequence of a large standing army.

The Statute of Proclamations, with sweeping powers, was

neutralised by the Commons but this did not prevent Henry, alternatively, from conducting purges of ministers and magnates or creating a secret police system of delation and summary arrest. The State repressive apparatus was steadily increased throughout his reign and nine treason laws were passed by the end of it. Upwards of 70,000 people were killed during his 37-year reign apart from those considered a threat or opponents. The majority were the religious dispossessed and vagrants, respectively, casualties of the dissolution of the monasteries, and the creation of enclosures by landlords, for sheep runs and the stocking of common land.

Thomas Cromwell

The central bureaucracy was enlarged and re-organised by Thomas Cromwell, who converted the office of royal secretary into the highest ministerial post and created the beginnings of a regular privy council, which soon after his fall (he was beheaded in 1540) was formally institutionalised as the inner executive agency of the monarch and became the hub of the Tudor state machine.[204]

In 1529 Henry summoned what became the longest parliament to mobilise the landed class behind him in his dispute with the papacy and the Empire, and to secure its endorsement of his seizure of the Church by the state in England. This was also a drive to enhance the power of the Crown by way of the Reformation parliaments. Not only did they greatly increase the patronage and authority of the monarchy by transferring control of the whole ecclesiastical apparatus of the Church to it, but, under Cromwell's guidance, they also suppressed the autonomy of seigneurial franchises by depriving them of the power to designate JPs. They integrated the marcher

---

[204] Ibid.

lordships into the shires and incorporated Wales legally and administratively. More significantly, monasteries were dissolved and their vast landed wealth was expropriated by the State, amounting to somewhere between a quarter to a third of the land of the realm.

In 1536 the government's combination of political centralisation and religious reformation provoked a potentially dangerous rising in the north, the Pilgrimage of Grace. This was when the poor and the powerful raised an army of 40,000, and would have outnumbered the king's soldiers by 4 to 1, in opposition to his new taxes, his threats to the rights of landowners, and betrayal of the *old religion* and they came close to deposing Henry. The leader of the rebellion, Robert Aske, was persuaded to abandon military force and negotiate terms in London. Shortly after he was arrested, charged with treason, hanged, castrated, disembowelled, and chopped into quarters at Clifford's Tower in York.[205] The rebellion was rapidly broken and a new and permanent Council of the North established to hold down the lands beyond the Trent.[206]

The Kildare Ascendancy – Ending Feudalism – The Geraldines

It was under Thomas Cromwell, Henry's chief minister, during the 1530s that the critical decision was taken to overthrow the Kildare ascendancy in Ireland and to rule, so far as was possible, from London. His *Ordinances for the Government of Ireland* and Ossory's indenture, with the king to support it, *'passed sentence of death on bastard feudalism in the colonial area of the Lordship and decreed the resuscitation of*

---

[205] Moorhouse, G., The Pilgrimage of Grace, (2002), Weidenfeld.
[206] Anderson, P., Lineages.

crown government'. It has been noted that this particular set of ordinances was inspired by a group of Anglo-Irish reformers in 1533-34; however, what was new on this occasion was that in a bid to secure their observance, Cromwell had them printed for wider circulation, as they had been ignored in the past.[207]

Ultimately, in 1537, *'Silken Thomas'* and five of his uncles were attainted and hanged at Tyburn on a single gallows, and the whole senior line of the Geraldines became extinct except for an infant who had been overlooked in the sack of Maynooth. He, Garret, was spirited away by his tutor Fr. Leverous via various relations and locations eventually to St. Malo where he received the protection of Charles V. Later, he spent time in Italy and entered the service of Cosimo de Medici. After the death of Henry VIII he was received into favour by Edward VI, and later Queen Mary restored him to his honours and estates.[208] The Kildare virtual monopoly of office and the zeal, with which they had sought to bring Ireland under their rule, were turned into weapons against them. All the rivalries they had aroused – particularly their feud with the Ormond-Butlers – were fostered and crystallised into charges against them. With the destruction of the Geraldines, the entire *'middle-nation'*, with their Irish allies, were at the mercy of the royal power. The Pale now extended virtually to all of Ireland, save for pockets of Gaelic clan influence.[209]

The Crown then proceeded with an *'anglicising'* policy of *'surrender and re-grant'* in those areas of Ireland where the Irish system of landholding based upon the rights of kinship prevailed. It was Cromwell's policy to establish full English rule in Ireland as the overall solution and in turn set the scene for Henry to be crowned

---

[207] Ellis, S.G., (1980), Thomas Cromwell and Ireland 1532-40, Historical Journal, 23, 497-519.

[208] Hull E., A History of Ireland and its Peoples. (1926), (1931)

[209] Jackson, T.A., Ireland Her Own.

king of Ireland with an enhanced parliament in Dublin.[210]

Henry VIII was determined to reduce Ireland to submission and William Skeffington was re-appointed Deputy together with Piers Butler, who, in consideration of the territories of the former Earls of Ormond bestowed upon him, agreed to resist the usurped jurisdiction of the pope, especially in regard to appointment to benefices. The campaign opened early in 1535, but as the new deputy was physically unable to command a military expedition, Lord Leonard Grey the brother-in-law of the Earl of Kildare was entrusted with the conduct of the war, and by August of *'Silken Thomas'* who had surrendered allegedly on a promise of his life. The rebellion was suppressed and O'More of Leix, O'Carroll of Ely, O'Connor of Offaly and the other Irish adherents of the Geraldine's were reduced to submission and accordingly the work of the conquest was well begun.

In 1536, and on the basis that he would carry the work of subjugation to a conclusion, Grey was appointed Deputy. At the same time Henry VIII had separated himself from the Catholic Church and had induced a large number of English bishops, ecclesiastics, and nobles to reject the jurisdiction of the pope in favour of royal supremacy. When Henry decided to detach Ireland from its allegiance to Rome *(Henry's legal title to the Lordship of Ireland was the supposed grant of Adrian IV and such a grant would lapse on heresy and schism)* a new title needed to be sought in the conquest of the country. In pursuance of this goal he resolved to utilise the Archbishop of Dublin and the Irish Parliament. In the meantime careful steps were taken by the Deputy and the Earl of Ormond to ensure that only trustworthy men would be elected as *'knights of the shire'* to the Parliament, where no representatives attended except from the Pale and from the territories under the Earl of Ormond and

---

[210] Ellis, S.G., (1980), Thomas Cromwell and Ireland.

his adherents. Accordingly, it was in no sense an Irish parliament, as not a single Gaelic Irish lay or clerical took part in it.

The fallout from the Geraldine rebellion and the religious rebellion in England prevented the desired measures being passed. The Deputy informed Cromwell that the spirituality was still obstinate, that the spiritual peers refused to debate any bill, unless they were allowed to vote, and, as the Irish Parliament had refused to pass the bill imposing a tax of one-twentieth of their annual revenues (half of that required in England) on the holders of benefices, he was obliged to adjourn. Cromwell was warned that as the proctors and bishops had formed a combination little could be passed unless the proctors were deprived of their votes. He suggested the king should send over a special commissioner to be present at the opening of the next session. In July 1537, a royal commission was dispatched to Ireland to deliver the following acts to be passed by parliament. Acts depriving the spiritual proctors of their right to vote and against the power of the bishop of Rome, together with acts giving the king the tax of one-twentieth on benefices, enforcing the use of the English language and dress and prohibiting alliances with the *wild Irish*.

At the same time Henry wrote to the Deputy and council warning them to obey the instructions of the commissioners and wrote to the House of Lords ordering them to ratify the bills being submitted, and telling them that if any member be unwilling to do so, *'we shall look upon him with our princely eye as his ingratitude therein shall be little to his comfort'*. When parliament met again in October the spiritual proctors were deprived of their votes and it was then that the act against the bishop of Rome was carried. The threats against the Dublin assembly produced the same effects as on the English parliament.[211] In

---

[211] MacCaffrey, J., History of the Catholic Church: From the Renaissance to the French Revolution, (1915).

England, Henry VIII had turned his attention after the separation from Rome to the suppression of the monasteries and religious houses. Partly because the religious orders were the most energetic supporters of the pope, and partly because he wished to enrich the royal treasury, by the plunder of the goods and land of the monasteries.

The Church, Its Wealth, and the Suppression in Ireland

According to de Burgo there were in Ireland, at the time, two hundred and thirty one houses of the canons regular of St Augustine, thirty-six belonging to the Premonstratensians, twenty-two of the knights of St. John, fourteen to the Trinitarians or Crouched Friars, nine to the Benedictines, forty-two to the Cistercians, forty-three to the Dominicans, sixty-five to the Franciscans, twenty-six to the Hermits of St Augustine, twenty-five to the Carmelites and forty-three belonging to various communities of nuns. Many of these institutions were possessed of wealth derived from the most part from lands and church patronage. By Henry's orders steps were taken in 1536 to secure the approval of parliament for the suppression of the monasteries. In October 1537 an act was passed for the suppression of Bective, Dunbrody, Tintern, and a number of others. Their lands, house, and possessions were to be vested in the king and a pension was to be secured for the abbots and priors for those who co-operated. Together with these, eight abbeys mentioned in a special commission under the great seal were suppressed.

The other religious houses, alarmed at the course of events, began to cut down the timber on their properties, to dispose of their goods, to hide their valuables and church plate, and to lease their farms. Urgent appeals were sent from Archbishop Browne (the replacement for Allen who was killed during the later rebellion) and others requesting that a commission should be issued immediately for the suppression of the monasteries and convents. Accordingly, a royal commission was addressed to the Chancellor William Brabazon, Vice-treasurer Cowley Master of the Rolls, and Thomas Cusake, empowering them to undertake the work of suppression (April 1539). A month later Brabazon and Cowley were appointed to survey and value the rents and revenues of the dissolved monasteries, to issue leases for twenty-one years of both their spiritualties and temporalities, and to reserve for the king the plate, jewels, and ornaments. They were also to grant to the monks and nuns pensions for their maintenance on the basis that they surrendered willingly. Alternatively they were *'to apprehend and punish such as adhere to the usurped authority of the Romish pontiff'*. The superiors of most of the monasteries and convents within the Pale or in the territories dominated by the Ormond faction surrendered their houses. During the years 1539-1541 nearly all the monasteries within the jurisdiction of the king were suppressed. The priory of Conall, which boasted that though it lay among the *'wild Irish'* it never had any brethren unless they belonged *to 'the very English nation'*, petitioned against dissolution unsuccessfully. Many of the superiors and religious merely threw off the habit of their order to become secular clergymen and to accept a rectory or vicarage in some of the churches of which their community had enjoyed the rights of patronage.[212]

In England, it is estimated that the income to the Crown coffers was in the order of one and a half million pounds, most of which was dissipated subsequently in wars in England and France. Five hundred and sixty-three religious houses in England and Wales, 7,000 monks and 2,000 nuns, 35,000 lay brethren who did manual labour with an

---

[212] Ibid.

overall annual income of £165,000 were dispersed and a quarter to a third of all cultivated land was taken into ownership.[213]

Newly Acquired Wealth and Hereditary Beneficiaries

Long before the commission for Suppression arrived in Ireland, the scramble for a share in the plunder had begun. The Deputy, the Archbishop, and the principal members of the Privy Council led the way. John Allen took possession of the property of St. Wolstons and Lord Grey secured for himself the goods and possessions of the Convent of Grane. The Earl of Ormond and the Butler family generally enriched themselves out of the lands of the monasteries situated in the south-eastern portion of Ireland. As did also a host of hungry officials and gentlemen in different parts of Ireland, such as the Cowleys, Allens, St. Legers, Lutrells, Plunkets, Dillons, Nugents, Prestons, Birminghams, Townleys, Aylmers, Flemings, Wyses, Eustaces, Brabazons, and so on. In this way Anglo-Irish nobles were bribed into acquiescence to the king's policy and were enabled to transmit to their descendants immense territories over which they were to rule as hereditary landlords long after the title had been forgotten. Wealthy merchants were not slow in coming forward to secure leases and lay the foundation of a new so-called aristocracy. Large grants were made to the corporations of Dublin, Waterford, Limerick, and Clonmel. The gold and silver was sold for the benefit of the king but the officials were never particularly careful about making the proper returns. A special commission was also issued (August 1541) to the Earl of Desmond and others, '*to take inventories of, to dissolve, and to put in safe custody all religious houses in Limerick, Cork, Kerry, and Desmond*'. In return, the Earl of Desmond was rewarded

---

[213] Moorhouse, G., The Pilgrimage of Grace, (2002), Weidenfeld.

with several grants of monastic land and O'Brien of Thomond did not think it beyond him to share in the plunder.

The Irish princes from the north who rebelled against these policies, and were attempting to rally with those of the south, were defeated at Bellahoe in Co. Monaghan in 1539 by Grey, Lord Deputy. Grey was implicated in several massacres and brought a new element to Irish warfare where the killing of women and children by the Tudor English forces was seen as acceptable to the establishment.[214] One by one the Irish princes began to submit to terms, so that before Lord Grey was recalled in 1540 he had vindicated English authority in the country of those still supportive of the Geraldines and in sympathy with the pope. However, instead of being rewarded and having given credence to the stories circulating that he had connived at the escape of young Kildare, his sister's son, and had supported the cause of Rome, Henry committed him to the Tower and in July 1541 he was handed over to the executioner.

The new Deputy, Anthony St. Leger, was to profit by the successes of Grey. Previously, Allen, Master of the Rolls (1537), had called the attention of the royal commission to the fact that many of the Irish regarded the pope as temporal sovereign and Henry only as Lord of Ireland by virtue of papal authority. He advised that Henry should be proclaimed king of Ireland by an act of Parliament. This was endorsed by the Deputy and Council in a letter addressed to Henry in December 1540. This in turn was accepted by Henry who empowered St. Leger to summon a parliament to give it effect. Parliament met in June 1541 and duly proclaimed *Henry VIII, by the Grace of God, King of England, France, and Ireland, Defender of the Faith, and of the Church of England and also of Ireland, on earth the Supreme Head'.*

---

[214] Edwards, D., Age of Atrocity: Violence and Political Conflict in Early Modern Ireland, Four Courts Press Dublin, (2010).

The policy that was devised, Lord Chancellor Cusacke wrote, *'for the sending of the Earls of Desmond, Thomond, Clanrickard, and Tyrone, and the Baron of Upper Ossory, O'Carroll, Magennis and others into England was a great help of bringing those countries to order for none of them who went into England committed harm upon the King's Majesty's subjects'*. All of them, together with a host of minor chieftains and dependents renounced the authority of the pope, accepted re-grants of their lands from the king, accepted English titles and primogeniture for hereditary purposes as well as English apparel and language. Apart from the various titles including Earls and Barons, knighthoods were distributed freely among the lesser nobles.[215]

Post-Reformation

In 1542 two English Jesuits who visited Ireland in the hope of spreading the gospel of the counter-reformation concluded that their cause was lost. While the faith of the *'simple people'* was strong enough, the leading Gaelic chiefs were committed to the Reformation and had refused to even meet them. However, the English Government and the Gaelic chiefs interpreted their new alliance in different ways. For the chiefs it provided an opportunity to increase their power within their territories and not to cede it to the English. The social change envisaged by the English Government was not easily implemented because there was no clear line of hierarchy between the elite and the masses or nobility and commoner as the Gaelic social order went all the way down. The Tudor reform programme was supported by the Pale gentry, some of whom played a prominent role in the formulation of policy. The elimination of the Kildare magnate power caused few of them grief. A government commission into the state of

---

[215] MacCaffrey, J., History of the Catholic Church

the colony showed the small- to medium-sized landowners regarded Kildare and the other magnates as tyrants and were pleased to see the back of them. Some Pale gentry families went as far as offering to sponsor the children of Gaelic elite families, so that they could learn the English language, civilised values, and good manners.

There were significant differences between the social structure of the Pale and a typical English region in the sixteenth century. One of the most striking differences was the very limited development of a *'yeoman'* stratum among the peasantry of the Pale. The slow emergence of this prosperous yeoman stratum in England was a product of the development of market relations and the consolidation of peasant holdings through stable tenure closely linked to the spread of written legal documentation. In the Irish colony the same level of social differentiation within the peasantry does not appear to have occurred, nor was land enclosure commonly practiced at this time. The majority of the peasantry in the Pale were Irish-speaking by the sixteenth century, with custom rather than written law regulating relations between landowners and the peasantry. Custom and kinship continued to play a significant role, while fixed rents for plots of land gave way to share cropping, similar to England. With the effective collapse of serfdom, the gentry increasingly resorted to a system of patronage to secure their social position and now unable to prevent peasant flight, securing adequate returns on land necessitated greater compromise. The Pale was not just a frontier zone, the Gaelic Irish the necessary manual labour was inside the Pale, and surviving in this environment had induced in the Pale gentry a different mind-set from the gentry of the southern English shires. It was this vantage point which put them increasingly at odds with the English Government and the culture of the *'New English'* elite. The latter subsequently became the Protestant

Ascendancy and came to dominate the Government in Ireland following the reformation and Henry's intervention.[216]

According to Archbishop Browne in a letter sent in 1546, the Irish people were not reconciled to English methods of Government and according to the chancellor the king's writ did not run in the Irish districts. The Irishmen, who pretended to submit, they considered did not keep their promises as they still followed their own native laws regardless of English statutes.[217] The accession of Edward VI made no notable change in Irish affairs. The Deputy, St. Leger, was retained in office as were almost all of the old officials. Bellingham succeeded St. Leger in May 1548 and was soon busily engaged against the O'Connors of Offaly, the O'Carrolls, and others. He met with some success and by 1549 he had pushed forward the religious campaign. However, he was recalled in 1549 and in 1550 St. Leger was once more sent as Deputy. The Deputy was commanded to ensure that no sale or alienation be made of any church goods or lands without royal assent. On his arrival in Dublin he found affairs in a very unsatisfactory condition and wrote '*so far out of good order for in the forts there are as many harlots as soldiers*'.

Social Change

Though St. Leger pretended to be a strong supporter of the new religion, his main objective was the pacification of the country and the extension of English power, both of which he knew would be endangered by any active campaign against the Catholic mass. St. Leger was recalled and Crofts was sent in April 1551. Crofts was forced to admit that the Reformation was making little progress in

---

[216] Coakley, M., Ireland in the World Order, (2012), Pluto Press, London.
[217] MacCaffrey, J., History of the Catholic Church.

Ireland.[218] However, the mid-Tudor developments were central in shaping the eventual outcome of the Tudor Reformation in Ireland. The possibility of a rapid, officially orchestrated Protestant breakthrough in Ireland was effectively ruled out by the poverty of the ecclesiastical endowment and the inadequacies of government control. The attitude of the '*Old English*' community was particularly crucial. Their growing political alienation from government after 1547 provided the agents of the Counter-Reformation with a receptive and influential base from which to organise. Moreover, this alienation was added to by the Government policy of increasing reliance on '*New English*' officials.[219]

The pattern of religious change in Ireland's different communities did not follow the pattern of either Scotland or Wales. Neighbouring parts of Gaelic Scotland demonstrated an adaption to Calvinist doctrine and over the course of the Elizabethan-era Wales adopted the reformation. Rather than a successful implantation of the Reformation in Ireland, the sixteenth century witnessed instead a growing attachment to Catholicism on the part of the *Gaelic Irish* and the *Old English,* namely the pre-Elizabethan colony. The episcopal financial issues referred to earlier were a factor in the failure of the reformation but not the only one. The language barrier on the island or the externality of the reform, in a comparative sense to Norway and Denmark also, do not provide sufficient reasons as to Protestant failure. Rather, of critical importance in Ireland was the manner in which the change of the religious complexion of the state incurred in tandem with the expansion of English power throughout the island. This fatal confluence deeply affected the reaction of both the *Gaelic*

---

[218] Ibid.

[219] Ellis, S.G., Economic Problems of the Church: Why the Reformation Failed in Ireland, Journal of Ecclesiastical History, Vol. 41, No.2, April, 1990.

and *English* communities of the island to the reforming religious initiatives imported from Tudor England. Furthermore, the removal of the feudal magnates the Geraldine Kildare's in 1537 arising from the *'orchestrated'* rebellion, although it owed little or nothing to genuine religious dissatisfaction, attempted to legitimise itself and draw wider support, on the grounds of the king's repudiation of Rome.

This foreshadowed a critical pattern of linkage between political rebellion and religious justification for future years.[220]

Henry VIII's last major act, his alliance with the Empire and attack on France in 1543, was to have fateful consequences for the ulterior destiny of the English monarchy. The military intervention was misconducted; its cost escalated and eventually totalled ten times the first French wars of his reign. The State not only resorted to forced loans and debasement of the coinage, but it also started to unload on the market the huge fund of agrarian property it had acquired from the monasteries amounting to over a quarter of the land of the realm. The sale of the church estates multiplied as the war dragged on and until Henry's death. By the time peace was restored it is estimated that two thirds of the monastic domains had been alienated. It had momentous, if still hidden consequences, on the domestic balance of forces within English society.[221] The land was sold to *'courtiers, merchants, and groups of speculators, who sold on to small landowners and capitalist farmers, so that a large and influential class was created who had the best reasons for maintaining the reformation'.*[222] It was a bulwark established to withstand the inevitable counter-reformation.

---

[220] O'Hannrachain, T., War of Religion or Ethnic Wars? Religious Conflicts in Ireland 1500-1650, Historical Review 2009/1, (No 649)

[221] Anderson, P., Lineages.

[222] Morton, A.L., A Peoples History of England, Lawrence & Wishart, London, 1989.

CHAPTER ELEVEN

IRISH PLANTATIONS AND ENGLISH COLONIALISM

The minority of Edward VI witnessed a swift regression in the political stability and authority of the Tudor state with a predictable jockeying for position, between the largest territorial lords, Somerset and Northumberland, for control of the Court. Peasant unrest and religious crises punctuated the decade. Rural uprisings in East Anglia and the south-west were crushed with hired Italian and German mercenaries. The rivalry between the Dukes of Somerset and Northumberland, with their respective patronage of lesser nobles functionaries and men-at-arms, led to coups and counter-coups in the Privy Council. It led to nothing more as neither side had client troops at their disposal and was only cut short by the death of Edward. The upshot of the interlude of rule by Somerset and Northumberland was merely to radicalise the local Reformation. The brief passage of Mary, with its dynastic subordination to Spain, and ephemeral Catholic Restoration, left little political trace.[223] The long reign of Elizabeth largely restored the domestic status quo. The religious pendulum swung back to Protestantism with the establishment of a domestic Anglican Church. The Privy Council was concentrated and stabilised under the long secretary-ship of Burghley and the espionage and police networks – mainly concerned with suppression of Catholic

---

[223] Anderson, P., Lineages of the Absolutist State.

activity which were then extended by Walsingham. The political influence and prosperity of the gentry was now an increasing stumbling block to the royal prerogative and the House of Commons grew steadily in size from some 300 to 460 members, of whom the proportion of country gentlemen steadily increased as boroughs were captured by rural squires or their patrons.

The moral dilapidation of the church of the previous fifty years permitted the gradual spread of an oppositional Puritanism among considerable sections of this class. The military inferiority of English Absolutism continued to preclude any expansionist goals in mainland Europe. Foreign policy was confined to negative aims, prevention of Spanish re-conquest of the United Provinces, prevention of French installation in the Low Countries, prevention of the victory of the League in France. The long Spanish war after 1588 which cost the monarchy dearly in domestic wealth ended without acquisition of territory or treasure.

Elizabeth I and Irish Colonisation

However, English Absolutism achieved one major military conquest prior to Elizabeth's death as Elizabethan expansionism, incapable of frontal advance against the leading monarchies of the European mainland, directed its largest armies at the conquest of Ireland as an alternative and lucrative outlet to expansion on the continent, and to complete the Anglicisation process. There had been no full-blooded policy of conquest and colonisation, for much of the pro-English landlords of the Pale enjoyed a good deal of indirect influence at court, and their voice was raised in favour of the peaceful extension of the Anglicisation process. It was not until the 1570s, in response to the growing threat from Philip II's Spain and after the publication of the papal bull, *Regnans in Excelcis,* deposing, excommunicating and declaring Elizabeth a heretic, that the forceful policy under Henry Sidney and his followers was introduced.[224] The war of resistance in Ireland lasted nine years before all resistance was pulverised by the English commander Mountjoy.

The Imperial Navy

By 1588 Elizabeth was mistress of the most powerful Navy Europe had ever seen. The ships which it carried were floating prisons in which press-ganged labour was exploited with notorious cruelty. The navy was a dual instrument, bracketed not only on trade but also on war. The bulk of the English fleets throughout the sixteenth century still remained merchant ships temporarily converted for battle by the addition of cannon and capable of reverting to commerce afterwards. The state promoted this adaptability by premia for merchant design that conformed to it. The navy became the *'senior'* instrument of the coercive apparatus. The Spanish Armada was outshot by English *demi-culverines* and scattered into the storms and mist, thus insular security was assured and the foundations of an imperial future laid. Up to 1588 the English bourgeoisie were fighting for existence: after that they fought for power. For this reason the defeat of the Armada was a turning point in the internal history of England as well as in foreign affairs. It was the merchants with their own ships and their own money who had won the victory and they had won almost in spite of the half-heartedness and ineptitude of the Crown and council, whose enthusiasm diminished as the war assumed a more revolutionary character. This victory transformed the whole character of the class relations that existed for a century. The bourgeoisie

---

[224] Kearney, H., The British Isles.

became aware of their strength and with this awareness the long alliance between them and the monarchy began to dissolve. They might still need royal support but they no longer needed their protection. Even before the death of Elizabeth, Parliament began to show an independence previously unknown.[225]

The landowning class could now develop not in antagonism but in unison with mercantile capital in ports and shires. In the century after the dissolution of the monasteries, while the population of England doubled, the size of the nobility and gentry had trebled, and their share of national wealth increased more than proportionately. The net income of the gentry perhaps quadrupled in the century after 1530. The triadic system of landlord, farmer, and agricultural labourer was already emergent in the richer parts of rural England. At the same time the concentration of trade and manufacturers in London was seven to eight times larger in the reign of Charles I than that of Henry VIII, making it the most dominant city in Europe by the 1630s. Nor was there a compelling social danger from below so there was no need to tighten the links between the monarchy and the gentry. Because there was no need for a large permanent army the tax-level had remained remarkably low, perhaps a third to a quarter of that in France. The gathering commercial impetus in the countryside made possible and profitable an abandonment of leasing of demesne land by the aristocracy and gentry. The result was a consolidation of a well-off stratum of yeomanry and a large number of rural wage-labourers, side by side with the general peasant mass. The situation in the villages was a relatively secure one for the nobility without fear of rural insurrection and as a result they had no stake in a strong coercive central machine at the disposal of the

---

[225] Morton, A.L., A Peoples History of England.

state.[226]

The First Irish plantations – Leix and Offaly

Although it was a project some years in the making, and inspired by petition in 1550 by a number of gentlemen, mostly government officials, to undertake the plantation, including well-known names such as Aylmer, Luttrell, Travers, Barnwall, Peppard, and Cosby, supported by Lord Deputy St. Leger, it was not until the reign of Mary (1553-58) that the English Administration devised its policy to change the Irish *'course of government, apparel, and manner of holding land, language, and habit of life'*. The method chosen was plantation in the Roman *'coloni'* style. English colonists would form settlements, driving out the native Irish from their lands and creating a *'New England'*. The break-up of localised Gaelic power bases by the removal of clan standing armies was deemed critical to the success of the project. The Gaelic system of landholding and social relations was in conflict with the English institutions of single ownership, primogeniture and the common law and needed to be supplanted.[227] To this end, the counties of Leix and Offaly were chosen for the experiment. Soldiers cleared the area of its leading inhabitants – the O'Connor's and O'Moores – and their adherents and the settlers moved in. They held lands on the condition that they imported and employed only English labour. The O'Moores and their septs especially fought to retain their land from the colonists, yielding only when the families were all but exterminated. This was orchestrated through a staged parley by Sidney known as the *Massacre at*

---

[226] Anderson, P., Lineages of the Absolutist State

[227] Morrissey, J., Contours of Colonialism: Gaelic Ireland and the Early Colonial Subject, Irish Geography, Vol 37(1), 2004.

Mullaghmast in 1577. The clans were eventually transferred with their Seven Septs to Kerry and other parts of Munster and Connaught. Overall, the experiment failed as the dispossessed fought back, burning out and harassing the colonists until they left, or not enough colonists were induced to come to Ireland.[228] The Gaelic inhabitants critically declared that the land belonged to the clans and not to the chiefs who therefore could not forfeit it and could, at most, forfeit their own private domains. The Irish under these plantation policies were denied all rights under the *'New English'* administration with resistance treated as rebellion. This was to be the established pattern for all subsequent dispossession and confiscation.

By Acts in the third and fourth years of the reign of Mary and Philip, the Lord Deputy Radcliffe Earl of Sussex by way of Parliament in Dublin in 1557 was endowed with *'full power and authority … to give and to grant to all and every … their Majesties subjects, English or Irish … at his election and pleasure, such estates in fee simple, fee tail, leases for term of years, life or lives, in these two counties, as for the sure planting or strength of the counties with good subjects shall be thought unto his wisdom and discretion meet and convenient'.*[229]

Accompanying this act was another entitling the Crown to Leix and Offaly and erecting them into shire ground as Queen's county and King's county. The death of Mary and the accession of Elizabeth did not materially affect the situation and in July 1559 Radcliffe was instructed to lose no time in putting the plan into execution. Despite interventions by Shane O'Neill [230] *(in 1567 the MacDonnell's of Antrim*

---

[228] Ellis, P.B., A History of the Irish Working Class.

[229] Dunlop, R., The Plantation of Leix and Offaly, The English Historical Review, Volume VI, Issue XXI, January 1891

[230] Elizabeth I stigmatised Shane O'Neill as 'a false, perjured, seditious and pernicious conspirer, rebel and traitor', Falls, C, Elizabeth's Irish Wars, Constable, London 1996.

beheaded Shane O'Neill and sent his head 'pickled in a pipkin' to the royal administration in Dublin) and the Earl of Kildare in support of the clans, in November 1561 Radcliffe announced his intention to divide the confiscated counties into *'baronies and making estates to the inhabitants'*.

A number of grants were made to Englishmen and Irishmen, servitors who had been mainly instrumental in pressing the rebellion such as the Dempseys, who, having won their lands by the sword, could be entrusted to defend them with the sword. The objectives were to secure Ireland to England; to establish the supremacy of the English laws on the island; to reduce the Irish to one homogenous mass by substituting for the old Gaelic relations of chief and clansman the relationship of landlord and tenant. The next forty years was a continuous battle of resistance to these policies by the dispossessed Gaelic owners until eventually in April 1601 Mountjoy Lord Deputy, by force of arms and suppression, could write *'no force left in all Leinster against her Majesty but a few scattered thieves of the Mores and Connors whom I refused to take to the mercy'*.

Chichester, who succeeded Mountjoy as Lord Deputy, declared *'eighteen several times within the last sixty years had the Mores and O'Connors risen in rebellion, only to be suppressed after great loss of life and treasure to the Crown'*. His proposal (though he was predated on this by one of the O'Mores in 1585, Thomas Meagh, a prisoner in the Tower of London) was to transplant them bodily into some other parts of the kingdom where they would have no chance of combining in rebellion. Beginning first with the O'Mores and their follower septs the Kellies, Lalors, McLaughlins, Clandeboyes, Dorans, and Dowlings, together known as the Seven Septs, Mr Patrick Crosby (a *'pretend Englishman'* originally a McCrossan whose family were formerly bards to the O'Mores) had offered his services to remove them. Chichester, warmly applauding his patriotic conduct, recommended that a grant should be made to him for that purpose, of the seigneury of Tarbert in Kerry. This had been passed to Sir John Hollis, *'who was soon weary of it, so that hitherto it hath yielded no benefit to the crown'*. The plan received the approbation of James and authority was given to Chichester to *'employ force should other means fail to induce these recalcitrant rebels to transplant'*. Ultimately, the Seven Septs transferred with Crosby to Kerry, parts of Connaught and Thomond on the basis of assigned lands on a yearly rent. There was a steady trickle back up to the 1620s and they were again so numerous as to be suppressed with force by the then Lord Deputy Falkland. However, by that time the English settlers and the plantation were firmly established. The dispossessed proprietors could not restore the old order of things, the social circumstances had moved on but they hung on nevertheless in anticipation.[231]

New English – Munster Plantation – Desmond Rebellions

The decline of feudalism in Ireland had begun with the overthrow of the house of Kildare in the 1530s. This still left the great *'pretendid palatinates'* of Ormond and Desmond as well as the Gaelicised chieftaineries of the west and north. The Earls of Desmond and their extensive network of subordinate lordships, *'no less than fifty lords and barons paid them tribute and were ever ready to march under their banners'*[232] throughout Munster, had consistently resisted the *New English* presence and were progressively mistrusted to oversee Government policy. This was a process which saw them revolt against Crown

---

[231] Ibid.

[232] Mac Curtain, M., The Fall of the House of Desmond, Journal of the Kerry Archaeological and History Society, 8, 1975.

control initially in the late 1560s and early 1570s, and again in the late 1570s and early 1580s. The Desmond earldom was an imposing super-structure upon older Gaelic holdings and was semi-autonomous. Sidney, in an earlier report on the Earl of Desmond, to Elizabeth wrote *'he enjoyeth under his rule, or rather tyranny, the third part of this great country, which I assure your majesty to be greater than Yorkshire. In all which his limits neither your name reverenced, nor your laws obeyed. Neither dare my Sheriff execute any part of his office therein'*.

The Desmond rental book, it was stated, *'was greater than any other subject in Her Majesty's dominions'* and the earls were probably the wealthiest landowners in Ireland. His exactions on the freeholders of his own palatinate were sharp and cruel and his system of taxation unremitting and harsh. It was a desirable prize for the Queen's officials to capture for the crown. Desmond was twice imprisoned by the Queen and more than a third of his life-time as earl 1559-83 was spent in prison.

Sidney established lord presidencies in Munster and Connaught on similar lines to the Council of the North in England, each with a military force at their disposal, with a view to replacing the authority of the magnates. Sidney had mentored Sir Humphrey Gilbert and it was his actions which were believed to have played a major part in the cause of the first Desmond rebellion. Along with Carew, who was pursuing a far-fetched claim to the inheritance of lands within the Butler territories, these conflicts were proving extremely disruptive. Gilbert was an eager participant, and after Carew's success in 1569, he advanced with his forces through Leinster and on into Munster where James Fitzmaurice Fitzgerald reacted to the incursion.

Gilbert was created a colonel by Carew and charged with pursuit of Fitzgerald. Gilbert, *'saying always that he thought his dog's ears too good to hear the speech of the greatest nobleman amongst them, so long as he was a Rebel'*.

Gilbert, during the succeeding campaign, gave no quarter and all Irish including women and children were treated as combatants and put to the sword. He considered *'the men of war could not be maintained without their churls and calliackes, old women and those women who milked their creaghts and provided their victuals and other necessaries. So the killing of them by the sword was the way to kill the men of war by famine, who by flight oftentimes saved themselves from the dint of the sword.'*[233]

An even more gruesome spectacle was devised by Gilbert to menace the rebels by the use of the decapitated heads of his enemies; *'the heads of all those, whosoever they were, which were killed in the day should be cut off from their bodies and brought to the place where he encamped at night, and should be laid on the ground by the side of the way leading into his own tent so that none could come into his tent for any cause but commonly he must pass through a lane of heads, which he used ad terrorem … and yet did it bring great terror to the people when they saw the heads of their dead fathers, brothers, children, kinsfolk, and friend lie on the ground before their faces, as they came to speak with the said colonel'*[234] Prior to his return to England in 1570, Gilbert was knighted by Sidney in the ruined Fitzmaurice camp amongst the bodies of the Galloglasses for his part in suppressing the rebellion.

The ineptitude of the New English administration in dealing with the Desmond *'rebellions',* which Ormond was ultimately to suppress, confirmed Ormond as the most effective defender of the Crown's interests. It was Ormond who negotiated with the Earl of Desmond near Adare before the latter was proclaimed a traitor. The proclamation asserted that Desmond had treated with foreign princes for the subduing of Ireland and that he had entertained James

---

[233] Churchyard Thomas, A General Rehearsal of Warres, (1579), Edward White, London.
[234] Kearney, H., The British Isles

Fitzmaurice. The latter had landed at Smerwick, near Dingle, with a papal force of some 700 troops, Spanish and Italian, who took over the fort at Dun an Oir. Some went to the Fitzmaurice castles at Ardfert and Fenit, later besieged by La Zouche, while the 600 at Dun an Oir were subsequently massacred after surrender to Lord Grey. Any native Irish men and women present in this fort had their arms and legs broken by a blacksmith's hammer before being hung from the fort walls. Also amongst them, Dr Sanders (a Catholic recusant despised by Elizabeth) and the Spaniards, who were accused that they had displayed the Pope's ensign against the Queen and that he (Dr Sanders) had brought strangers into the kingdom.

Critically, as a consequence of this invasion Ireland was considered to be moving into the realm of international politics and was becoming a factor in counter-reformation papal strategy.

By 1580, the Geraldine war was a curtain raiser for a decade of international war which England embarked on against her greatest enemy Spain. Correspondence between Desmond and Pope Gregory XIII indicated a religious element to the war and a turning to Europe for help. By 1580 Ormond felt sufficiently strong to put into effect his systematic conquest of the Desmond palatinate. Below the level of ostensible religiosity was the reality that the Desmond palatinate was capable of being smashed once and for all. In March 1580 Sir William Pelham and the Earl of Ormond marched with their armies into Kerry, *'burning, spoiling, and preying'* as they went. Their policy was simple: to kill all who resisted or who might resist them, and to destroy all buildings, cattle, and goods which were likely to be of use to the rebels. In the winter of 1580 Lord Grey, who had replaced Pelham, carried on the campaign with *'relentless barbarity'* and within two years Munster, which had been the richest and most prosperous province, was in the words of the Four Masters, *'reduced to a desert'*, and the *'lowing of a cow or the voice of a ploughman could scarcely be heard from Dunquin in Kerry to Cashel in Tipperary'*. In the words of one of the planted landowners and poet Edmund Spencer (his abode at Kilcolman Castle was plundered and burned to the ground in the rebellion of 1598): *'Out of every corner of the woods and glens they came creeping forth upon their hands, for their legs could not bear them, they looked like anatomies of death, they spoke like ghosts crying out of their graves ... a most populous and plentiful countryside left void of man and beast'*.

Lecky in the Preface to his 'History of Ireland' wrote, *'the suppression of the native race was carried on with a ferocity which surpasses that of Alva in the Netherlands, and which has seldom been exceeded in the pages of history'*.

The Provincial President Warham St. Leger reported in April 1582 that up to 30,000 people had died of famine as a result of the scorched-earth tactics that had been used.[235] Grey was recalled by Elizabeth in 1582 and it was Ormond who finished the war in the beginning of July 1583. By then all of Desmond's supporters had submitted; the Earl of Clancarthy, Viscounts Barry and Roche, the Baron of Lixnaw, Sir Thomas of Desmond, Sir Owen O'Sullivan, Edmund McGibbon, and a host of others.[236] Desmond, who was then hiding out in the woods at Gleannaginty, between Tralee and Castleisland, County Kerry, was betrayed by his foster-brother, Owen Moriarty, who informed the garrison at Castlemaine where he was to be found. The soldiers surrounded Desmond, took him out, and beheaded him in November 1583. In some accounts the beheading was by one Daniel O'Kelly who was rewarded for the act but later executed for highway robbery. Fifteen years later Moriarty was

---

[235] Dorney, J., The Munster Plantation and the MacCarthys, 1583-1597, The Irish Story.
[236] MacCurtin, M., The Fall of the House of Desmond.

hanged on a gibbet at his own door by the Lord of Lixnaw.

Social Change

All the Desmond lands were declared forfeited to the Crown and with the end of this rebellion the feudal history of Munster came to a close under the imprint of Tudor absolutism.[237] The plantation which followed brought in the St. Legers to Doneraile, the Fentons to the inheritance of the White Knights, the Herberts to Castleisland, the Greenvilles and the Raleighs, the Carews, and the Thorntons and later the Boyles, Earls of Cork. Later still the Lansdownes by the union of the Petty heiress with the Fitzmaurices of Lixnaw.[238]

By 1583 the power of Desmond was overthrown and in 1585 the Crown arrived at a *'composition'* with the lords of Connaught whereby they agreed to pay a rent to the Crown, provide military service, and introduce the common law.[239] More important for the ordinary people of Munster than a change of landowner was the devastation of much of the province.[240]

The Plantation proper began with the vast confiscations which followed on the Act of Attainder at the close of the Desmond rebellion in 1586, when 574,628 acres of land in Munster were forfeited and vested in the Crown. (*The Desmond Survey Roll of 1584 put the vast estates of the Earl of Desmond, together with 140 of his adherents, at nearly a million acres*).[241] Each *'undertaker'*, as the purchasers of these properties were called, who had taken up to 12,000 acres, were

---

[237] Hul,l E., A History of Ireland and Her People.

[238] Mac Curtain M., The Fall of the House of Desmond.

[239] Kearney, H., The British Isles.

[240] Dorney, J., The Munster Plantation.

[241] Pierse, J.H., The Pierse Family, Eltham, London, 1950, ed. Richard G Pierse, (2006).

required to place eighty-six English families on these estates. Great inducements were held out to suitable planters to take up land. Letters were written to every county in England to encourage younger brothers to become undertakers. Estates were to be held in fee at two pence per acre in the counties of Cork and Waterford and to be rent free until March 1590, and then to pay just half-rent for the following three years. Their product was to be transported duty free to any country in friendship with England and they could import necessaries free of custom.

It was intended that no Irish should reside on the lands but this idea was soon given up as the planters found it more profitable to keep the Irish on the estates. For their part, the Irish were ready to give the same services in labour that they had hitherto given to their chiefs, besides the fourth sheaf of all their corn and sixpence yearly for a beast's grass, so that *'many planters cared not although they never placed any Englishman on their estates'*. In that context, and under English law, they were made the possessors of their own holdings. However, it was considered that the men of *'best quality'* who were favoured and who purchased estates never came over and that of the two thousand able men, who, according to agreement, ought to have been in the province, two hundred could not be found. Most of the men of *'best quality'* turned over their *'knockdown'* priced estates at enhanced rates in London towards their further better quality of life.

The largest planters, or *'seignories'*, in the south were the two Herberts with over 17,000 acres and Denny and Brown with 6,000 acres each in Kerry. Lord Treasurer, Edward Fitton, got 16,000 acres in Cork and the generals and officials such as St. Leger, Norris, Grenfell, and Walter Raleigh each received a large share. Even though 12,000 acres was the maximum anyone was to get, Raleigh, who, along with Mackworth, was associated with the *'fell to slaughter'* of the Spaniards and Irish at Smerwick, received 42,000 acres as two other names were associated with him. (Mackworth later died at the hands of the O'Connors in Offaly and Raleigh was executed in 1618). This land was later sold on to Boyle, it is reckoned, at one penny an acre, the price of an acre in Cork at the time.[242] Boyle, later created Earl of Cork, was among the *'adventurers'* who built up the largest fortunes out of the escheated lands along with Sir Valentine Browne who bought up large slices of the Mac Carthy estates from the spendthrift Earl of Clancar who had sided with the English in the Desmond rebellion. Ormond wrote to Cecil in 1601: *'One Crosby and Boyle have been the only means of overthrowing many of her Majesty's good subjects by finding false titles to their lands, and turning them out'.*[243]

Throughout the whole of the Desmond wars the Irish gentry were divided into two great and powerful factions – one siding with the *New English* the other with the Irish. In Munster, not only several of the Lords of Anglo-Norman descent, such as Ormond, Barrymore, Buttevant, Dunboyne and Castleconnell stood on the Queen's side, but several of the Irish including the Baron of Upper Ossory, the Earl of Thomond, Chief of the O'Brien's, Mac Carthy Reagh Lord of Carberry, Sir Cormac McCarthy Lord Of Muskerry, and Morrough O'Brien Lord of Inchiquin were all open supporters of the Crown.

The fact that Catholic Ireland was at war with another large section of Catholic Ireland questions the ostensible religiosity and counter reformatory cause of the rebellions as opposed to resistance, support, or benefit from the *'New English'* policy of confiscation and occupation. A further matter of note on the religious question was the minor level, though more was promised, of military support from

---

[242] Hull E., A History of Ireland and Her People.
[243] Ibid.

Spain and the Pope, in the struggle against the 'New English' invasions and in support of the Counter Reformation. Spain's involvement in the whole affair, according to some reports, was considered only a diversionary tactic arising from the war with Elizabeth's England, rather than any attempt to support a de-Anglicised or counter-reformatory Ireland.

Broadly, in English minds it was hoped that the 'settlement' would attract 15,000 colonists, but by 1589 the 'undertakers' had imported no more than 700 English tenants between them at best, including families of some 2,000 to 3,000. The native lords, whether descended from Anglo-Irish or Gaelic, who had foreswore allegiance remained as landlords but not in their previous capacity as magnates or chieftains. The Protestant reformation did have some further influence and consideration. Herbert in Kerry voiced the hope that by the 'planters good example, direction, and industry, both the true religion, sincere justice, and perfect civility might be planted'. At the same time he described some of his fellow undertakers as 'lewd, indiscreet and insufficient men, who measure conscience by commodity and law by lust'. Herbert 'urged the impartial jurisdiction of common law ... and the use of the Irish language to instruct the natives in 'civility' and the Protestant religion'.

In practice, the Common Law was set aside when it got in the way of land confiscation. The Solicitor General Wilbraham reported that he had suspended judicial hearings on land confiscation because 'the Irishry have practiced many fraudulent shifts to prevent their lands from forfeiture ... and albeit their evidence be very law-like without exception, yet because fraud is secret and seldom found for her Majesty by jury, we have put undertakers in possession'. Another Kerry planter, Edward Denny, took a dim view of Herbert's soft attitude. For Denny only a complete conquest of the Irish would pacify the province, 'no persuasion will ever win the Irish to God and her Majesty, but justice without mercy must first tame *and command them*. At the same time the dispersion of Irish loyalties among hundreds of lordships, not to mention all the feuding kin-groups within them, meant it was never a straightforward battle between the *'New English'*, *Old English,* and the *'Irishry'*.

The conflict at the end of the sixteenth century was in the final analysis between rival groups of armed landowners, *Irish*, *Old English,* and *New English* for control over land, tenants, and resources.[244]

---

[244] Dorney, J., The Munster Plantation.

CHAPTER TWELVE

ELIZABETH'S WARS IN IRELAND

In theory, between 1583 and 1598, when the Nine Years' War arrived in Munster, there was peace of sorts. The reality however was that native lords were being squeezed by English settlers and the English military presence, whose treatment of the natives was often brutal. Donal McCarthy's war against the Brownes was one example of the ongoing resistance to the plantation. Attacks by natives on planters escalated from 1594 onwards. James Fitzthomas (*the Sugan Earl*), leader of the rebels in Munster in 1598-1601, claimed to Ormond that he was going into rebellion because of the many unjust killings by the English of Irish lords and gentlemen; '*Englishmen were not contented to have our lands and livings, but were unmercifully to seek our lives*'.[245]

There were thousands still in Munster, swordsmen, displaced aristocrats, and Catholic priests who had never reconciled themselves to the English plantation. There were those, other than the English, who sought to exploit war to their own advantage, such as the McCarthys, both Florence and Donal seeking the McCarthy Mor title. Donal called his rival a '*counterfeit Englishman who would betray all the Irishmen of Ireland*'. Florence, who had been arrested by St. Leger, was sent to the Tower after he married the daughter of Donal Mor for fear of him becoming too powerful and a threat to the English settlement. In 1589 he was released from the Tower in London and

---

[245] Ibid.

allowed to return to his estates, albeit these estates were much lesser now in size than anticipated. Ultimately, many had to weigh up who to side with: Hugh O'Neill or the English Crown.

O'Neill, O'Donnell, Ormond – Second Desmond Rebellion

The aftermath of the defeat of Bagenal and the English by Tyrone (Hugh O'Neill) at the Battle of the Yellow Ford in 1598 was far reaching. Ormond seized the opportunity to let the Queen and her Privy Council have his views on the enormity of taking men from the plough and the counter and putting them into uniform, herding them to a port, shipping them over the water, and then expecting them to defeat a foe as tireless and savage as the wolves still lurking in the forests of Ireland. A contingent of 1,472 men which had landed at Dublin previous to the battle misbehaved itself in the capital, *'brabbling with one another, selling their clothes and arms, and running away'.* Over half of them were sent to Kells, County Meath, to keep them out of mischief. Elizabeth, however, reproached Ormond, saying, *'it was strange to us, when almost the whole forces of our Kingdom were drawn to a head … for our honour against the capital rebel, that you, whose person would have better daunted the traitors … should employ yourself in an action of less importance'.* Ormond had decided to take on the O'Moores in Leinster.

Burghley was now dead and Hugh O'Neill (Tyrone) was established in Ulster. O'Donnell (Tyrconnell) had established himself in almost complete control of Connaught and he had set up Theobald Burke as the Mac William or overall leader. In Leinster, the O'Moores flung themselves upon the estates of the settlers in King's county and Queens's county (Leix and Offaly) despite the exertions of Ormond.

In Munster the case was more pronounced. The province was already seething when Owney O'Moore, and Richard Tyrell (Tyrone's commander) went in with over 2,000 men by way of Limerick. Tyrone had decided to start a new *Desmond Rebellion* with James Fitz Thomas Fitzgerald, nephew of the late Earl of Desmond, and later designated the *Sugan Earl* (straw-rope) to the forefront. Gathering strength as they went, the Ulster and Leinster invaders carried their fire and sword through Munster. The settlers on the escheated Desmond estates were the main targets. Those who could fled in the most part to Cork, Youghal, and Waterford, but many were intercepted and killed along the way. Castle after castle fell into the hands of the Irish to be garrisoned or demolished. Irish loyalists to the Crown that remained were not spared. The *'rebels'* burnt fifty-four *'towns'* or native hamlets on the Barry lands and took nearly 10,000 cows, 5,000 horses, and 60,000 sheep and hogs. The whole elaborate structure of the Munster plantation collapsed in their wake.[246]

Ormond was persistent in his response to the *'rebels'* and sought to garrison and protect the Pale at least until a response from Elizabeth was forthcoming. She set about a muster and raising troops by way of levy. In a message to the Lieutenants and Commissioners for the Muster, the Privy Council wrote, *'how sparingly her Majesty hath always proceeded to make any levies of men but in causes of great necessity',* and *'both for the honour of her princely calling and of the realm, is to apply these speedy and effectual remedies that may be able to cure so grievous a disease'.*

Earl of Essex – Irish Campaign and Downfall

An army of 12,000 to 14,000 foot and 1,000 horse was raised and the Earl of Essex was placed in charge. He left London on the 27th March

---

[246] Falls, C., *Elizabeth's Irish Wars,* Constable, London, (1996).

1590, riding through a double lane of citizens four miles long who called down the blessings of heaven upon him. Delayed by a contrary wind he did not reach Dublin until the 15th April. Following his arrival, his establishment now stood at 16,000 foot and 1,300 horse, it was the greatest army ever sent to Ireland. 2,000 experienced troops were sent over before him and landed in Ireland from the Low Countries. His instructions were to proceed direct to the north and engage with Tyrone, however, in the words of Essex himself he decided to *'shake and sway the branches'* before attempting to cut the root.

On his arrival he had been beseeched with tidings of risings all over the country, including the O'Byrnes in Wicklow, Fitzpierce in Kildare, the Kavanaghs in Carlow, and the O'Moores in Meath and Kilkenny. Sir William Nugent and Viscount Baltinglass were assisting the insurgents in the north. Munster was in rebellion, and Connaught, after the experience of Bingham, was seething with discontent. It was estimated that the *'rebel'* forces totalled over 20,000 men. Essex, rather than proceeding directly to confront Tyrone, proceeded into Munster and Leinster, his main object being the reduction of the castles there, especially the strong castle of Cahir held for Desmond by Thomas Butler. The President of Munster, John Norris, was endeavouring to stem the rebellion and Essex set out from Dublin with an army of 7,000 only to encounter defeat by Owney O'Moore at Maryborough at a battle to become known as the *Pass of the Plumes*.

The only result of the expedition was the capture of Cahir castle, which Elizabeth reproved as taking *'an Irish hold from a rabble of rogues'*. She urged that *'he put the axe to the root of that tree which hath been the treasonable stock from which so many poisoned plants and grafts have been derived'*.[247] By the end of July Essex had returned to Dublin, *'his soldiers being weary, sick, and incredibly diminished in number'*. A further defeat of

---

[247] Ibid.

Sir Conyers Clifford in the Curlews in Connaught reduced a large part of the army while the remaining regiments were secretly returning to England, revolting to the *'rebels'* side or feigning sick. Essex eventually made his way north and concluded a truce with Tyrone. Elizabeth ordered that none should have been signed and she also forbade the grant of a pardon to Tyrone.

The expedition was to be the downfall of Essex and after he fell Elizabeth said she would have none other than Mountjoy to finish the Irish wars as he alone *'would cut the thread of that fatal rebellion and bring her in peace to her grave'*.

Mountjoy, Carew, Spain – The Battle of Kinsale

Meanwhile, Tyrone was in Munster, camped between the Lee and Bandon, and from all hands the nobility and gentry came in to offer their adhesion and to leave hostages in his hands for their fidelity. He was signing proclamations as O'Neill (an outlawed title) and had addressed a letter to Philip III of Spain which he signed *'Your Majesty's most faithful subject'*. At the same time there arrived on the scene two of the most formidable Englishmen of the time; Charles Blount, Lord Mountjoy the new Lord Deputy of Ireland, and Sir George Carew, the new President of Munster. They landed at the Head of Howth on the north side of Dublin Bay on the 26th February 1600.

In Munster, several of the Lords of Anglo-Irish descent, namely Ormond, Barrymore, Viscount Buttevant, Dunboyne, and Castleconnell, stood at least outwardly on the Queens's side and several of Irish blood – the Baron of Upper Ossory, the Earl of Thomond chief of the O'Briens, MacCarthy Reagh Lord of Carbery, Sir Cormac MacCarthy Lord of Muskerry, and Morrough O'Brien Lord of Inchiquin – were open supporters of the Crown. In both north and south of the country the internecine strife continued. In the north there was a *'Queen's'* Maguire and an independent Maguire and a *'Queen's'* O'Rourke, opposed by Brien O'Rourke and his son. Hugh O'Neill was confronted by Turlough O'Neill and the sons of Shane; and O'Donnell had to fight Neill Garbh O'Donnell. In the south, Owen O'Sullivan Beare was out against his cousin O'Sullivan Beare and Fineen MacCarthy spent a large amount of his time struggling with his cousins for the title of Earl of Clancar.

The English Government avowedly and industriously fomented family dissensions within the clan system. Scattering promises and offering rewards to those who would turn the arms of their followers against members of their house who were in *'rebellion'*, or who would, by force or guile, bring in their heads. Carew worked covertly when other means failed and adopted a policy, in his words, of *'setting one rogue to ruin another'*. In the seizure of Fineen MacCarthy, while under the Queen's safeguard, he probably stooped to the basest act of perfidy against the customs of the time.[248] Desmond and Tyrone in all their efforts were hampered by the knowledge that they were surrounded by spies and so-called allies who would not hesitate to betray them if it were to their advantage.

During the fifteen years' war between 1588 and 1603, the towns of Ireland stood solid for the Crown albeit they mostly continued Catholic in religion. They were largely English in descent as a matter of Crown policy. All they desired was to carry on their now flourishing trade with France and Spain or to attend to their municipal duties. Additionally, in the towns the priests for the most part *'gave an opinion that it was not only lawful to assist the Queen, but even to resist the 'Irish' party and to draw the sword upon it'*. A special ecclesiastical Council held at Salamanca in 1602 recognised the right of Queen

---

[248] Hull, E., A History of Ireland.

Elizabeth to command the obedience of the Irish soldiers in fighting the Queen's rebels, but the troops were also exhorted not to use this obedience against the spread of the Catholic faith. A distinction great in theory but beyond reason in practice. To confuse matters further the Pope offered indulgences equal to those bestowed for the crusades to those who joined the armies of the O'Neill, however, none of this served to weld the Catholics into a solid body.[249] These incidences were further examples undermining the theory that religiosity was to the forefront of these campaigns.

In September 1601 a fleet of Spanish ships was spotted off the Old Head of Kinsale, heading towards Cork harbour, but when the wind dropped the ships tacked about and headed into Kinsale. Commanded by Admiral Don Diego Brochero, the fleet had originally consisted of 33 vessels carrying 4,464 foot, six pieces of artillery to be employed ashore and arms and munitions for the Irish onshore. The flagship and eight other vessels of the fleet were separated by a gale, put into Coruna, and did not arrive until some weeks later. This was serious matter as in the nine ships were Pedro de Zubiar, 650 troops, and a large proportion of the stores. Del Aquila landed with 3,814 troops. The wisdom of Tyrone's advice that they should land at Carlingford was for whatever reason not taken. Messages to O'Neill and O'Donnell in the north from the Spanish Commander Don Juan Del Aguila got no reply for nine days. Many of these messages were intercepted by Carew.

Aquila was now in a precarious position unless the Ulster leaders hastened to his support and substantial reinforcements reached him from Spain at an early date. Mountjoy in the meantime had moved to Trim in Co Meath and in mid-September reached Kilkenny. On the 22[nd,] when Carew had joined him, he heard from the Mayor of Cork

---

[249] Ibid.

of the Spanish fleet off Kinsale. On the 27th Mounjoy reached Cork and on the 29th reconnoitred Kinsale. His troops began arriving in early October and by the 27th the field army assembled, numbered 6,900 foot and 611 horse.

The speed with which Mountjoy had closed on Kinsale was in contrast to Tyrone's tardy progress. O'Donnell was the first to move; he left his base in Sligo and marched south through Roscommon in September. For three weeks he camped at Templemore in Tipperary with an army of some 3,000. However, he did not close on Kinsale as he waited the arrival of Tyrone. By mid-November, with reinforcements in new companies and the new drafts for old, Mountjoy's strength was now up to 11,800 foot and 857 horse. In early December a force of 2,000 Spaniards sallied forth from the gates of Kinsale but were repelled by Mountjoy.

Zubiar managed to arrive in December with some 700 troops and stores which raised the spirits of the Spaniards. Tyrone did not start out until the early part of November and it was at least six weeks from the arrival of the Spaniards at Kinsale before he arrived in early December. The combined Irish forces now stood at around 6,500, including some Munster allies, 200 further Spaniards, as well as the contingent of Spaniards in Kinsale, now at 2,000 fit men. This garrison was in the meantime being battered with English cannon with no sign of relief or direct co-operation from their Irish allies. Eventually, it was agreed between them that the Irish would advance and attack at a designated point and simultaneously the Spaniards would issue forth from Kinsale with all possible strength.

Treachery in the Irish camp gave Mountjoy warning of the plan when Brian McMahon, whose son had been in service with Carew in England, warned him of the planned attack. Mountjoy promptly strengthened the guard and put the army in readiness. The delay in the Irish attack made it impossible to launch at the designated time agreed with the Spaniards. Mountjoy, in any event, had left 4,000 foot to face the Spanish garrison and had cut off communications or intercepted them. With a series of successful charges and engagements from Mounjoy, Carew, Clanrickarde, Danvers, and Wingfield, the Irish were defeated and eventually took flight. O'Donnell boarded a Spanish ship at Castlehaven and made his way to Spain to seek further aid from Philip III and he died shortly thereafter[250] (poisoned, it appeared, from State papers). Clanricarde, who had been foremost in the fight, shouted to the troops *'to spare no rebels'* and after the battle Mountjoy knighted him amid the dead bodies.[251]

Aguila offered a parley on the basis that he would deliver Kinsale and the other places captured by the Spanish on the basis that the force should be allowed to depart on honourable conditions. Mountjoy and his Council deliberated and after withdrawing some unacceptable conditions agreed to the terms. In January 1602 articles were drawn up and in February the first of the Spanish departed, ultimately some 3,500 left.

Negotiations with Tyrone were soon begun as the day after the defeat Tyrone had reported to the Lord Deputy that he *'was willing and desirous to become a subject'*. The victory at Kinsale was probably the greatest military achievement of the reign of Elizabeth and also marked in particular the beginning of the end of the Gaelic stronghold in the north and northwest of the island. It also paved the way for the subsequent plantation of Ulster.

The further tactics used by Mountjoy and Carew were devastating and included the burning of grain in field or barn, a pronounced

---

[250] Hul,l E., A History of Ireland.
[251] Falls, C., Elizabeth's Irish Wars.

'*scorch the earth policy*' which more often than not inflicted more hardship and death on the people as a whole. They stationed garrisons throughout Ulster, Munster, and Connaught as a deterrent and encouraged the defection and cajoling of subjects and followers. Where the Irish were weakest of all in arms, they used artillery as they continued to pursue Tyrone and his supporters into Ulster. The towns of Galway, Limerick, Cork, Waterford, Wexford, Drogheda, Newry, and some of the smaller inland towns of Leinster and Munster were the strongholds and foundations of English support and left alone. Outside these towns the wars were merciless. Ulster was reduced to a desert, Mountjoy and his army saw everywhere as they moved along the results of their own deliberate action. He writes, '*we have seen no one man in all Tyrone of late but dead carcasses merely hunger-starved ... between Tullahogue and Toom I believe there lay unburied a thousand dead ... and there were about three thousand starved in Tyrone. Tomorrow, by the grace of God, I am going into the field, as near as I possibly can to waste the County Tyrone*'.

Flight of the Earls – James I and the New Plantation of Ulster

At that point Tyrone himself felt it time to end the conflict and made his submission to Mountjoy at Mellifont in 1603, agreeing to all the conditions imposed. Unbeknownst to him Elizabeth had died, a fact kept from him by Mountjoy. To Elizabeth, '*the cost of £100,000 and the best army in Europe had not been able to subdue*' Tyrone and these apparently were thoughts that played on her mind in her dying days and who knows whether or not she went peacefully to her grave as she desired.[252] Of the Crown's overall expenditure on wars of £5 million during her reign, it is estimated that half of it was spent on the successive Irish *'rebellions'* from Desmond to the O'Neills.[253]

After a period, Tyrone was pardoned by King James who had replaced Elizabeth on the throne and the restitution of his lands were confirmed. Rory O'Donnell was created Earl of Tyrconnell and not Neil Garbh, although he had supported the English against Tyrone, as he was considered a danger to English rule after participating in the O'Doherty revolt. He was committed to the Tower and ended his life in confinement. The experiment of setting up Tyrone and Tyrconnell as landlords came to an end with the Flight of the Earls in 1607 and there was no further rebellion until 1608. This rebellion was organised by Sir Cahir O'Doherty, tricked into it by Chichester for land acquisition purposes, and was short lived. There was a further *'plot'* in 1615 which the government got wind of and it came to nothing.[254] It was the activities of Sir John Davies, Attorney General, and Sir Arthur Chichester, the new Deputy (Mountjoy departed in June 1604), during their visit to Ulster in 1606, that possibly was the last act in Tyrone's decision to depart the country. Both of these officials were determined to execute the forfeit of Tyrone's lands out of which they planned to reap their share.

Quietly, Tyrone made his plans and in the company of ninety-nine persons, including Rory O'Donnell and his brother Caffar and other senior supporters and their families, they sailed for Spain in 1607. It was an ignominious end for a man who in 1594 had written to the Queen complaining of mismanagement by the Lord Deputy and declaring, *'there was never a man bred in these parts who hath done your*

---

[252] Hull, E., A History.
[253] Morton, A.L., A Peoples History of England,
[254] Ibid.

majesty greater service than he, with often loss of his blood upon the Queen's enemies'. With the flight of the earls, in effect medieval Ireland came to an end and with it the old clan system and the displacement of the *Old English* with the rise of the Elizabethan sponsored *New English*. It was Lord Burghley, ironically, who remarked, '*the Flemings had not such cause to rebel against the oppression of the Spaniards as the Irish against the tyranny of England'*.

When James I came to the throne he looked to a new plantation in Ulster as a means of rewarding his Scottish adherents and of increasing his own revenues. Officers and soldiers who had fought in the war were pressing for the lands that had been promised as their reward. The departure of the Earls afforded the opportunity for which all had been impatiently waiting. Since the days of De Courcy, parts of the north had been settled by Anglo-Norman families in County Down (Lecale). Old planters such as Savage, Russell, Fitzsimons, the Jordans, and Bensons had remained on their lands in close proximity to Magennis and the O'Neills of Clannaboy. Sir Arthur Magennis had, in English terms, become the most *'civil'*. The Scots had a strong hold in Antrim and the Queens' re-instatement of the MacConnells/McDonnells had established their claims to the Glens of Antrim. Other Scots occupied the north-east coast of Antrim, such as the Mac Gills and Mac Auleys. No part of the vast stretch of country lying between Lough Neagh and the Atlantic, including Derry, Tyrone, Fermanagh, and Donegal, had been in English possession. Among those who lands were declared forfeited were several who had fought on the English side during the recent wars. In the scramble for land that followed they were forgotten and had to be content with much smaller plots. O'Reilly, who had fought on the English side at the Battle of the Yellow Ford, received only a small portion of his lands in Co. Cavan and Maguire, who had also fought on the English side, had to be content with a portion of his previous estate. They became in effect *'undertakers'* like any other applicants. A similar fate became the Mac Sweeneys on Lough Swilly and the O'Boyles and O'Gallaghers in Donegal.

Amongst others who claimed indisputable rights in the land were merchants of the Pale to whom Tyrconnell had mortgaged *'great scopes of land for small sums of money'* which were subsequently voided by English law as they had come from O'Donnell. For legal casuistry, Sir John Davies (solicitor-general for Ireland) relied on the sweeping act of confiscation passed by Elizabeth on the downfall of Shane O'Neill. It was Davies who made the iniquitous suggestion that by this act, at the conclusion of the war with Shane O'Neill, all lands were vested in the Crown and consequently all the old freeholders' possessions in Tyrone *'are actually and really in his Majesty's hands and the tenants are for the most part intruders upon his Majesty's possessions'*. Catholics from Scotland also came flocking into Ulster, fleeing from the penal laws *'which gave them no rest'* in their own country. They settled on the estates of the Earl of Abercorn and Sirs William and Richard Hamilton and other Scottish nobles who welcomed them on their properties in accordance with the planter's desire to encourage English and Scottish tenants. To James his Catholic subjects were only *'half-subjects'* and entitled to *'half-privileges'*. To the English, the spread of the Roman faith meant the expansion of Roman power and *'papish'* anti-English sentiment, a belief strongly embedded in English minds.[255]

With Mountjoy's departure, Chichester wrote in 1602, '*I have often said and written that it is famine must consume them; our swords and other endeavours work not that speedy effect which is expected'*. He became Lord Deputy in February 1605, and wrote to the king *'that all will now be his*

---

[255] Ibid.

Majesty's' and followed that up with a proposal of driving out all the inhabitants of Tyrone, Tyrconnell, and Fermanagh with their goods and cattle to inhabit waste lands across the Bann, the Blackwater, and Lough Erne. His dictum, not uncommon for the time for the ills of Ireland, was *'famine to consume them; English manners to reform them'*. It was the known parlance of imperialists who would denigrate the enemy so they could subsequently civilise them. Sir Thomas Philips, an old *'servitor'*, put a claim in for *'a good share of Tyrone's land'* near Coleraine to plant with English. James approved of the forfeiture of Tyrone's estates, adding that Scottish were to be admitted with the English.

The lands for disposal not only included that of the two earls but large portions of Fermanagh vacated by Cuconnaught Maguire and O'Kane (O'Cathain), whose lands stretched from the eastern side of Lough Foyle to the Bann. The latter had accompanied the Earls and those lands of Sir Cahir O'Doherty forfeited after his brief revolt. Chichester himself was an early applicant for Doherty's lands with its valuable *'fishing's'* lands which brought him his large income. Chichester also secured for himself lands he got from *'defective titles'* with a revenue of £10,000, Inishowen, and an extensive tract around the city of Belfast based on the original castle there since Norman times. The castle and lands were granted to him in 1612 and he brought over immigrants from Devon to people the district; in 1613 it received its charter of incorporation with the right to send two members to parliament.

Social Change

In 1605 the law of Tánaiste (election of chiefs) and gavelkind (the Gaelic process by which land descended but not by primogeniture) was abolished by a judgement of the King's Bench. The Brehon Laws were described as *'a lewd custom'* and not laws at all. Previously, two Scottish Lairds, Montgomery and Hamilton in 1603, had devised a plantation scheme which had received James's blessing. Con O'Neill, who was in prison, was a chief whose clan lands in Down and Antrim was offered by Montgomery and Hamilton to effect his rescue, if he would sign over two thirds of his land for their use as a private plantation. James threw in a knighthood and he signed over the other third. This settlement by Montgomery and Hamilton had an estimated 16,000 people on it by 1614.[256]

The Estates of the Earls of Tyrone and Tyrconnell and their chief adherents, comprising over half a million acres, were escheated and the lands confiscated after their departure. The six counties that were escheated – Donegal, Derry, Tyrone, Armagh, Cavan, and Fermanagh – contained a total of 3,785,057 acres. Much of this land was considered unworkable from a colonisation point of view and it was estimated that only a seventh was available for settlement. The land was divided into lots of 2,000, 1,500, and 1,000 acres and these were assigned to be occupied by persons of three classes. The *Undertakers* on whom the largest lots were bestowed were ordinary English colonists or Scots and they were forbidden to take Irish tenants. The *Servitors*, those who had held office under Government in Ireland, who might if they chose let a portion of their land to the Irish, but if they did so their rent would be increased from £5 6s 8d to £8 per 1,000 acres. The third class, the *Natives,* could not receive as tenants anyone but their own countrymen and as a rule only small estates were given to the Irish. The total they received was less than a tenth of the whole, some 55,000 acres and not of the best land. They were required to pay £10 13s 4d per 1,000 acres. From the limited size of the holdings and the fixed rents stipulated, it is clear that the

---

[256] Ellis, P.B., A History.

object of this plantation differed from its predecessors in that the Crown's greed for revenue was subordinated to its imperial need for a reliable garrison of planted colonists, who would hold the native Irish in check.

To get around the difficulty of finding suitable colonists, part of the responsibility was shifted to the Corporation of London which was asked to undertake the planting of Coleraine (Derry) and the restoration of the cities of Derry and Coleraine. In some ways it is a fallacy to attribute to this Plantation the characteristics of the current political *'Ulster'* (Northern Ireland) as four out of the six counties planted were never part of *'unionist'* Ulster until Partition (1920) and the two most *'Protestant'* counties of Antrim and Down were never included in the plantation. In any case the difficulty of finding tenants caused even the London Corporation to ignore the terms of their grant. By 1624 they had 4,000 Irish tenants when they should have none. (This issue was used by Charles I in 1637, when he cancelled this Charter hungry for funds and the sum of £70,000 was extorted from the owners, and despite the efforts of the City of London the judgement remained outstanding until the Restoration.) With the new plantation of Ulster, and the Irish clans having being ejected on nefarious legal reasoning, Anglicisation policy was allowed to march on.[257] However, when it came to the point where new settlers didn't come over, or when they did, often without the workmen, stipulated they needed the local people for building, for service, or because the locals were willing to pay high rents in order to be left where they were. As a result and over time many settled down to be the tenants of the new settlers.

The old Irish method of loaning cattle was still in use during this period and tenants who held by this system from the chiefs and who

---

[257] Jackson, T.A., Ireland Her Own.

were now unable to enforce their rights took advantage and declined to pay their dues, They drove the cattle away to *'creaghts'* or lonely places.

Chichester's scheme was based on settling the surviving peasants upon the land as freeholders and paying rent to the Crown, thus setting them apart from the authority and exactions of the chiefs, whose lands had been confiscated. There gradually grew up a loose system of contract between the cottiers and the proprietors which became known as the *'Ulster Custom'* and which gave some protections to the rent payer.

Much of the reign of James was taken up in additional projects of plantation in Wexford, Wicklow, Monaghan, Fermanagh, and Leitrim. Settlements were also projected in Connaught but were postponed. The Wexford Commissioners reported in 1613 that a tract of land containing 66,800 acres, chiefly belonging to the sept of the Kavanaghs, was claimed by the King as having passed to the Crown on the settlement of Art MacMurrough. Whereas policy was for the surrender of one fourth of the land to new settlers from existing patent holders and they retaining the balance as freeholders in practice, one half in many cases was taken and only about one in ten got any land at all. Many were turned into *'wood-kernes'* or *'gone to the fern'* as outlaws. Others turned up in Dublin in their multitudes seeking sustenance. The countryside was scattered with smaller gentry who had lived off tenants and fighting their neighbours. The passing of the clan system changed society as a whole. One report in 1619 stated that the country was full of the younger sons of gentlemen *'who have no means of living and will not work'*. As Carew had long ago foretold; *'events were marching towards an explosion'*.[258]

---

[258] Hull, E., A History.

CHAPTER THIRTEEN

CHARLES I AND THE END OF ABSOLUTISM

The Stuart drive for a developed absolutism did not make great progress. In 1625 Charles I took up the work of constructing a more advanced absolutism with the unpromising materials he had available. The combination of Jacobean corruption and Caroline censoriousness – from Buckingham to Laud – proved itself jarring to many of the gentry. The vagaries of foreign policy also weakened him at the outset of the regime: English failure to intervene in the Thirty Years' War was compounded by an unnecessary and unsuccessful war with France based on the confused inspiration of Buckingham. Parliament, which had vigorously denounced the conduct of the war and the minister responsible, was dissolved indefinitely. In the succeeding decade of *'personal rule'*, the general direction of dynastic policy became relatively coherent and the monarchy tended to draw closer to the higher nobility once again. They reinvigorated the formal hierarchy of birth and rank by conferring privileges on the peerage in the safe knowledge that the era of magnate militarism was passed. In the cities monopolies and benefits were reserved for the top stratum of the urban merchants, the bulk of the gentry and the newer mercantile interests were excluded. The same preoccupations were evident in episcopal reorganisation at the cost of widening the religious distance between local ministers and squires.

The successes of Stuart absolutism were largely confined to the ideological/clerical apparatus of the state, which under both James I and Charles I began to inculcate divine right and hieratic ritual but the economic and bureaucratic apparatus remained subject to acute fiscal difficulties while parliament controlled the right to taxation proper. Charles I resorted to every possible feudal and neo-feudal device in the quest for tax revenue to sustain an enlarged state machine beyond parliamentary control. With this in mind Sir Thomas Wentworth was appointed Lord Deputy of Ireland in 1632 (he became Earl of Strafford in 1640, the year before his execution) with the express purpose to rule Ireland well in order to supply men and money to the King. His task was to make the country prosperous in order to wring from it abundant taxes for his sovereign; its entire submission, and the transference of what remained of Irish soil to English owners. Wentworth did not arrive in Ireland until 1633, a year after his appointment, and was considered *'a star of exceeding brightness but sinister influence'*. The difficulties he faced were carried in a pamphlet in 1623, possibly by a member of the Commission appointed in 1622 to look into the conditions in Ireland with reference to the recent plantations. The state of things, he revealed, was that of almost universal corruption in all departments of government. The state, he continued, was preyed upon by a host of insatiable *'sharks'* of obscure birth who sacrificed alike the revenue of the King and the public good by *'ingressing'* most of the wealth of the kingdom to themselves.

Defective Titles – The Graces – Land Forfeiture

The fees exacted for compositions of land often amounted to half the purchase money and frauds of all sorts were committed upon the owners and the Crown in the passing of estates by the Commission upon Defective Titles. The policy supposedly was to settle the owners with more secure titles at an enhanced rent. Wentworth also blamed the comparative failure of the new plantations to the problem of getting the undertakers to go over and undertake the development of their own properties. The *'gentlemen of England'*, he stated, *'give away their lands to footmen and others, who now live in the houses of the principal natives and overtop them with more sway and authority than their lord and master would do were he here in person'*. The displaced *'principal natives'*, mostly referred to as *'outlaws'*, were to form the seeds of the *'rebellion'* in 1641 and the transplanted cottiers were to form their band of followers.[259]

Wentworth's opinion of the Council was that they were in league to keep him in the dark about everything, Sir William Parsons in Wexford and Lord Cork chief amongst them. Lord Cork had substantial reason for hating Wentworth, he said subsequently in 1640 that he was *'worse for him by £40,000 in his personal estate and £1,200 a year in his income'*. Wentworth found that the vaults under Christchurch Cathedral, which the Deputy and Council attended every Sunday, were let for *'tippling houses for beer, wine, and tobacco, of which the fumes could be perceived in the church above'*. In the words of Sir Edward Denny in July 1633, *'the Lord Viscount Wentworth came to Ireland to governe the kingdom. Manie men feare'*.

Wentworth made no attempt to be conciliatory and he prepared for the great struggle against the *'Graces'* by an attempt to make both the parliament and council subservient to his will. His first demand was that a voluntary contribution made in 1628 should be continued for another year to meet the urgent costs of the army and the government. The earlier contribution had been made by the Catholics for *the Graces* but on this occasion he warned the gentry the appeal would be to Protestants and advised them to save themselves by offering the

---

[259] Ibid.

contribution with a request for a parliament in return. For the expediting of the second project he proposed to re-establish the Commission upon Defective Titles to give full rein to the discovery of flaws in titles to ownership of lands, which had proved so lucrative as a means of ousting landowners in all parts of the kingdom.

For his plans two obstacles were in his way; first *the Graces,* designed to put a stop to the process, he now planned to revive and, secondly, the promise of a parliament could now no longer be ignored as it was urgently required for the passing of money bills. Wentworth's Parliament of 1634 was largely tactical and divided into two sessions as he put it to the King; ' *the former session for yourself, the latter for enacting of all such profitable and wholesome laws as a moderate and good people may expect from a wise and gracious king'*. His next step was to balance the parties by the free use of his power as Deputy to name proxies for absentees and so secure a majority of subservient members he could sway any way he pleased. With the threat of abolition hanging over them and, as Charles preferred option, parliament passed the grant of six subsidies by a unanimous vote. In the next session the question of *the Graces* could no longer be deferred, as the Irish parliament pointed to the immense gifts and loans amounting to £310,000 raised in the previous two years, exclusive of the last large grant, and they pressed in return for the carrying out of the royal promises, especially the confirmation of their titles.

But *the Graces* as transmitted by Wentworth to the King were accompanied by his recommendations, dividing them into three parts – those not at all to be granted, those which might well be granted, and those which may be accepted by way of instruction but not passed into law. Among those '*not all to be transmitted'* were the two *Graces* 24 and 25, so coveted by the gentry. By these instruments, the act of perfidy was complete and the plantation of Connaught ready to proceed. A Commission was sent down to the west, mock courts were set up and by intimidating juries, inflicting heavy fines on recalcitrant jurors, and brow-beating by the Deputy himself who presided verdicts were found for the King over the large part of Connaught.

In Galway they moved on Lord Clanrickarde's property while he was absent in London, but only a packed jury and fines to the amount of £1,000 imposed on the sheriff and £4,000 on each of the jurors, with the still more effective threat of the Star Chamber, brought them to compliance. Wentworth complained that there were no people but Irish tenants on this estate and considered that the opportunity should be taken to plant them with English, but these plans were not put into effect as Wentworth was recalled in 1640.

The discovery of false titles to land touched the new planters far more than the Irish. There were no Irish titles to land under the clan system of inheritance in the Tower or patent rolls. It was the English who had built up vast estates on very insecure legal foundations who were the most under threat. Lord Cork with his 42,000 acres and his manors in Cork and Waterford (the latter bought for very little from Walter Raleigh) found his possessions claimed by the King. In the case of the Earl of Clanrickarde the King hoped to gain £55,000 by his forfeitures. Smaller owners were threatened in proportion and, though they remained loyal to the King, this sense of unsettlement affected large numbers of the gentry who had found their complaints treated with levity or indifference by the two Stuarts.[260]

---

[260] Ibid.

Rebellions in Scotland 1640 and Ireland 1641

Wentworth had crushed the wool trade during his period in Ireland because it interfered with the trade of England, and because he found a new means of profit by the double customs arising from the export of raw wool into England and its return as manufactured goods. He is credited with having promoted the linen industry; but this is an error and one of the myths which are repeated amongst others throughout Irish history. What he did was to sell a Charter of Monopoly to a linen company which would have ruined all the domestic spinners and weavers already extant in Ireland if the company had not gone bankrupt. This was part of the so-called *'thorough'* plan to establish monopolies for every industry in England as well as in Ireland.[261] The spinning of linen yarn both for home consumption and export was one of the oldest industries in the country and it was not until the great influx of skilled operatives from France and the Low Countries under William III that the industry became one of the staples of Irish commerce and a main source of the wealth and prosperity of Ulster.

The loss of the wool industry was a great blow to the prosperity of the country, both to those who grew and sold the wool and to the ports where it was shipped, Waterford and Limerick especially. Among the exports at this time to Spain and Portugal were butter, pipe staves, tallow, pilchards, salmon, skins and meat, cod and hake, beans, iron, linen-cloth, friezes, and stockings. However, industrial employment was confined to towns and was in the hands of the *Old English* families who had created it. Those who were turned loose from the plantation lands still took to the mountains or abroad and

---

[261] Jackson, T.A., *Ireland Her Own.*

had formed a nucleus of discontent.[262] They watched for opportunities of ousting the planters and recovering the clan lands. Wentworth paid particular attention to the raising, training, and equipping of an army. Its rank and file was almost exclusively Catholic while its officers were mostly English Protestant aristocrats. By ambiguously worded letters a rumour was circulated that as soon as he had reduced the English Commons to reason, the King would grant liberal concessions to the Irish Catholics. At this stage, however, Strafford was summoned post haste to England as Laud had upset matters by trying to impose the English liturgy on the Scottish Kirk and it was this revolt Strafford was sent to repress.

Charles I's final bid to create a serious fiscal base was an attempt to extend the one traditional defence tax which existed in England: the payment of ship money by ports for the maintenance of the navy. This plan was however sabotaged by the refusal of unpaid local J.Ps. to operate it. Parliament alone could provide the resources for a standing army upon which continental absolutism had been built but Parliament, if convened, was certain to start dismantling Stuart authority. For the same historical reasons the rising political revolt against the monarchy in England possessed no ready instrument for an armed insurrection. This deadlock was broken in Scotland, when, in 1638, Caroline clericalism, which had already threatened the Scottish nobility with resumption of secularised church lands and tithes, finally provoked a religious upheaval by the imposition of an Anglicised liturgy. The Scottish Estates united to reject this and their Covenant against it acquired immediate material force. In Scotland the aristocracy and gentry were not demilitarised and the more archaic social structure preserved the late medieval warlike armoury. The Covenant was able to field a formidable army to confront

---

[262] Ibid.

Charles I within a few months. Magnates and lairds rallied their tenants in arms, burghs provided funds for the cause, and mercenary veterans of the Thirty Years' War provided officers. No comparable force could be raised by the monarchy in England. It was the Scottish invasion of 1640 and the clan-led rebellion in Ireland which put an end to Charles I's personal rule. English absolutism paid the penalty for its lack of a standing army. Parliament now convoked by the King to deal with military defeat by the Scots proceeded to erase every gain registered by the Stuart monarchy, proclaiming a return to a more constitutional framework. The rebellion a year later in Ireland and the struggle to seize control over the English army that had to be raised to suppress the Irish insurrection drove Parliament and King into the Civil War. English absolutism was defeated at its centre by a commercialised gentry, a capitalist city and commoner artisans and yeomanry. Before it could reach an age of maturity English absolutism was cut off by a bourgeois revolution.[263]

In Ireland, it was on November 1st 1641, the day set apart in the English House of Commons for the consideration of a Remonstrance brought over by Irish gentlemen appointed by their peers, that the news reached London that the rebellion had begun. In the north the rebellion had taken place on the appointed day. Within a fortnight Sir Phelim O'Neill had made himself master of Tyrone and Armagh, had captured Dungannon and the fort of Charlemont and made his headquarters at Newry. He captured Dundalk and then set down at Drogheda.

Great caution has to be exercised in accepting reports as to the atrocities on both sides. There is a view that the numbers massacred were intentionally exaggerated by those who hoped to gain lands for themselves through the future forfeiture of rebel properties.

---

[263] Anderson, P., Lineages.

However, as the insurrection spread to the centre and south of Ireland the area of conflict and fatalities grew wider. Sir William Petty later estimated that out of a population of 1,466,000 before the rising about a third was wiped out and was mostly attributable to plague and famine created by the war and about a third of that figure was attributable to casualties, a large number of whom were civilians.[264] The view, however, is untenable that the numbers of Protestant casualties were small, the evidence supports higher numbers. However, the massacre numbers continued to be used later by the English revolutionaries in their campaign in Ireland and as a justification by Cromwell for his massacres even though there were not as many as 300,000 Protestants in the whole of Ireland in 1641 and the succeeding years showed the Protestant community in Ireland being without noticeable diminution. The contemporary estimates of the *'massacre in cold blood'* of *'300,000 to 400,000 Protestants'* was misused by Charles as an *'atrocity story'* for English affairs when reporting the rebellion to Parliament as he sought a supply and Parliamentary authority to raise an army for the suppression of the rebels. This request was received with deep suspicion by the Commons as they believed providing an army he could rely upon was the one thing he could not be trusted with. Indeed, the Irish rebels had issued a manifesto which avowed they were not hostile to the King or his authority but were only seeking a remedy for intolerable grievances and the putting in place of the *Graces* which contained in their minds the resolution of the land-ownership questions.

The Commons passed an act authorising the raising of an army but they inserted into the act the names of those alone who were empowered to recruit soldiers, to appoint officers, and to dismiss. These names were all those upon whom the revolutionary chiefs

---

[264] Hull, E., A History.

believed they could rely. There was a further suspicion that Charles had engineered the Irish rebellion with the pretext of raising the army he desired. Indeed, the Queen Henrietta Maria wondered before the General Assembly in Kilkenny, *'that the Irish do not give themselves to some foreign king; you will force them to it in the end, when they see themselves offered as a sacrifice'*. On foot of Parliament's rejection, Charles left London for Oxford and there raised his Royal Standard and summoned the nobility and gentry to aid him against his *'rebellious Parliament'*. The English Revolution had passed into the phase of civil war which ended the absolutist ambitions of Charles.[265]

In Ireland though they remained persistently attached to the King's interest; the sense of unsettlement affected large numbers of the gentry, especially those Catholic lords who were also harassed for their religious differences. This general dissatisfaction led them to take part in a rising with loyalist landlords of the Pale and Munster with whom they had little in common. But the methods of Wentworth and Parsons, the *'discovery of false titles'*, and the threat to vast estates built up under unresolved security titles (the *Graces* issue) was at the core of their unrest. The instruction by English officials to Clanrickard at the height of the rebellion, that no submission was to be accepted and *'that the more that were in rebellion, the more lands would be forfeit,'* was self-evident. The Ulster rebellion was essentially concerned with the restoration of clan lands and independence similar to the Scots and merged itself into the Wars of the Confederation and those who wished to preserve their estates and restore lands to the Catholic Church. However, not all of the gentry favoured restoration and generally were anti-Parliament in their support for the King other than Inchiquin who changed sides at will. At the meeting of the Confederate gentry in Trim on March 17th

---

[265] Jackson, T.A., Ireland Her Own.

1642, they protested that they had been necessitated to take up arms only to *'prevent the extirpation of their nation and religion'*. They styled themselves *'your Majesty's most dutiful and loyal subjects'*. The whole land they claimed was filled with *'escheators and pursuivants, carrying on illegal practices under the protection of the Lord Justices and the oppressive Court of Wards'*.

The union with the rebels of the north was an uneasy one for the Confederates as, throughout the years of the rising, they were a Catholic Royalist stronghold upheld by the belief that they were warring for the King against the Puritan parliament and his cause was identical with their own. At the same time in London Parliament was forcing through the nefarious *Adventurers Bill* as a means of raising a loan to pay the English garrison in Ireland. By this Bill, passed through in a week, lands in Ireland to the extent of 10,000,000 acres were *'to be confiscated'* in consequence of the rebellion and were offered for sale of which, 2,500,000 acres were to be offered to subscribers to the loan. On March 19th 1642, five months after the outbreak of the rebellion, the Act was signed by the King. Money for the lands *'to be forfeited'* poured in though little of it was used for purpose for which it was subscribed. (*The confiscations under Cromwell subsequently were largely founded on this Act*). For the Irish gentry this Act turned the war into a struggle for existence and so to secure their estates they threw their lot in with the rebels.[266]

Social title at this time was decided by the designation and ownership of property and property was also the most important productive resource. The guiding thread for future societal development was the changing character and position of this land ownership. The interdependent relationship with the political system that emerged from the eclipsed clan system progressed on through

---

[266] Hull, E., A History.

the transitionary absolutism phase until the impending eve of capitalism.[267]

Confederation – Owen Roe O'Neill – Ormond – Rinucini – General Monk

While the civil war raged in England (1641-1649) Ireland was the theatre for a succession of political combinations, divisions, and re-combinations. There were from the outset primarily three operational parties with armies in the field. The English parliamentary party held Derry city and part of the counties of Derry, Antrim, and Down. The King's party, led by Ormond, held Dublin, Louth, part of Meath, and, through Lord Inchiquin (Murrough O'Brien), part of Cork. The Catholic Confederation formed in Kilkenny in May 1642 held the rest of the country. The only common settled purpose, namely restoration of clan lands and independence, was that of the clans of Owen Roe O'Neill. He had promised those of like mind in Ulster that if they could get an army together he would come from Spain where he served as a distinguished soldier to lead it. The Confederation set up a Supreme Council with representatives from each province but from the start it disavowed separatism. It affirmed its allegiance to Charles but it courted trouble from the Ormond royalists when it decreed the restoration of church lands to the Catholic hierarchy. The Confederation took as its basic standpoint the landlordism which the New English had introduced and only tolerated O'Neill and his clansmen insofar as they were necessary for their resistance to the parliamentarians led by Coote and Munro in the north, to the royalist Ormond in the Pale, and to the considered turncoat Inchiquin. The

---

[267] Anderson, P., Lineages.

latter had changed sides a number of times and now supported the parliamentarians. At the outset Inchiquin earned the name of *'Murrough of the Burnings'* for the desolation he caused in East Munster and South Leinster.[268]

Meanwhile, the King's transactions throughout the conflict were a web of duplicity so that Puritans, Catholic gentry, Ormond's party, and Irish rebels alternatively claimed him as approving their policy and showed documents said to be executed with his own hand for their support. Early in 1643 the King, pressed by necessity, empowered Ormond to negotiate a truce with the Confederation for a year and as soon as this was done he was to bring over an Irish army to Chester. This brought about a change in affairs as it ended the rebellion. Future Acts of Settlement differentiated all lands possessed at that date as being left undisturbed and in the hands of the owners. Its immediate result was the sending over of troops and money to the aid of the king in return for rather illusory concessions. While Royalists, Ormond, and Inchiquin were campaigning against the Confederate Catholics, an emissary of Charles was negotiating a secret treaty (Glamorgan) with the Council of the Confederation. Charles' aim was the provision of an Irish army but he dare not let this be known in England because of potential desertion from his English army. When this secret treaty, apparently found later in the pocket of Archbishop Queally of Tuam, who had fallen in battle, was discovered, Charles repudiated it. Ormond imprisoned Glamorgan who had negotiated it on the King's behalf. (He was freed not too long after).

Meanwhile, Ormond for the Anglo-Irish Protestants was negotiating a peace of his own with the majority support of the Confederate Council, after the King had suffered crushing defeats at

---

[268] Jackson, T.A., *Ireland Her Own*.

Marston Moor (1644) and Naseby (1645). In 1646, into the midst of all this, the Pope launched two emissaries; Scarampi, who arrived in 1643, and Rinuccini, who came over as Papal Nuncio in October 1645.

Rinuccini landed in West Kerry and made his way to Kilkenny where he declared he had come to keep the Catholics in union among themselves, and to cherish in them the allegiance due to their lawful sovereign. He steadily opposed every effort for peace and set himself up to build up a clerical rule above the law and outside the confederacy, looking to Rome as its head and gradually ousting all lay rule from the Council. He insisted on the restitution of confiscated church and abbey lands. This met resistance from the Catholic gentry, albeit they were good Catholics they had no intention of resigning lands they lived upon, and upon which their rank and fortune depended. The Confederates believed this treaty was more tenable than the conditions set by the Nuncio Rinuccini, which required the delivery of all royal towns, Dublin included, into the hands of the Catholics and the restoration of all ecclesiastical property as in pre-reformation days. The Nuncio's proposed treaty was directed against the power and influence of the Protestant Ormond, who was unaware of Glamorgan's commission from the King to the Nuncio. Rinuccini looked on his mission to Ireland as a crusade to restore the pre-reformation position. He also looked on his mission as a first step in the recovery of England for Catholicism and Ireland would be the gateway in this regard; the church position, it appears, and not the nation was the object he had in mind.[269] However, he did supply Owen Roe O'Neill with muskets, ammunition, and money to pay his soldiers and this allowed him to put an army of 5,000 and 800 horse into the field which defeated a larger force of 6,000 Scottish Covenanters and British settlers under

---

[269] Hull, E., A History.

Monroe and Stewart at the Battle of Benburb in 1646, the only real victory of the Irish campaign.

Social Change

O'Neill took his army south to become involved in the politics of the Confederation and to make sure that the treaty the Council had signed with Ormond would not be ratified. Meanwhile, the Nuncio summoned a meeting of prelates, clergy, and heads of religious orders to Waterford and solemnly denounced the peace, backing up his condemnation with threats of excommunication against all who adhered to it. Preston[270], the Confederate general, at a later date was to obey the Nuncio's commands because he said *'his army was not excommunications proof'*. When Preston and Owen Roe marched on Kilkenny they scattered the old Council and appointed a new one which repudiated the treaty. Ormond at this point withdrew, surrendered Dublin to the Parliamentarian General Jones (1647), and retired to France. The departure of Ormond had the effect of eliminating the royalists as a separate force. Some of his followers joined the Confederation and some joined Inchquin and the Parliament. When Inchquin, who had over-run Munster, opened up negotiations with the Confederation and made offers for peace and an alliance, Owen Roe broke with the council and took to the field with an independent army. The Nuncio excommunicated everyone who had signed the treaty with Inchquin but Ormond at that point came forward with fresh offers and the second Ormond peace was concluded in January 1649. The Nuncio at this point left Ireland in

---

[270] Colonel Preston had served in Spain with Owen Roe and had been appointed General of the Leinster army by the Confederation. By all accounts not considered as good a military strategist or soldier as Owen Roe and an ongoing rivalry was said to exist between them. (Hull, E, A History).

disgust at this turn of affairs. Rinuccini could not comprehend the Irish devotion to the King. His view was that *'nothing is treated of, nothing concluded, without introducing this question of fealty to the king and on this point it appears the Ulstermen of Owen Roe were no different'.*[271] Not long after Charles I was executed at Whitehall, Ormond, returning to Ireland as the representative of Charles II, dissolved the Confederation and converted its followers into a royalist party. He had hopes of Scottish assistance as the Scots had broken with the English Parliamentarians and a Scottish army was besieging the Parliamentarian Coote at Derry. Owen Roe would have nothing to do with Ormond, Preston, Inchiquin, or any of the Irish and Anglo-Irish gentry. He drove the Scots away from Derry and entered into negotiations with the English Parliamentarian General Monk who it was said had Leveller sympathies. However, the English Parliament issued peremptory orders to Monk to break off all negotiations instantly.

As a result, Owen Roe agreed to a treaty with Ormond and prepared to march to his aid, however Ormond was roundly defeated at Rathmines by Jones, the Parliamentary general, as he laid siege to the city. In August, Cromwell, with twenty-eight regiments and his new model army of redcoats, arrived in Dublin having heard of this victory before his departure from Milford Haven. Owen Roe, whose health was now failing, lived long enough to hear of the sacking of Drogheda (Ormond's army had been close by but did not intervene) and the storming of Wexford by Cromwell's Puritan armies. He lingered till November 1649 when he died and was buried at the old abbey at Cavan. In his last letter to Ormond he wrote; *'his intention … was the preservation of his religion, the advancement of his Majesty's' service, and the just liberties of this nation.'* At the same time it has been conjectured that in his discussions with Monk, Owen Roe had discussed the

---

[271] Ibid.

restoration or re-distribution of royalist-held land in Ireland to the original owners – the clans, a position not dissimilar to the Levellers demand in England for a restoration of the common lands there which the landlords had taken. The promptness with which Monk was told to break off all negotiations with the *'rebels'* was equalled only by parliament and Cromwell's crushing of the incipient mutiny of the Levellers at Burford in May of 1649. Their resultant deployment to Ireland included the distraction and promise to the Leveller regiments of the reward of a share of the land confiscated from the Irish Royalists rather than and conveniently the distribution of the land of the English gentry or royalists. At that point, through Ormond's manoeuvres, this included virtually all the land of Ireland.[272] It may have served Owen Roe O'Neill one of the most respected of the *'old Irish'* leaders better had he paid heed to the King James Version (1611) of Psalm 146, *'Put not your trust in princes, nor in the son of man, in whom there is no help'*. An appropriate soliloquy in turn for Charles I.

---

[272] Jackson, T.A., *Ireland Her Own.*

CHAPTER FOURTEEN

THE LEVELLERS, CROMWELL AND IRELAND

The New Model Army and its supporters were only a minority of the population but at the same time they were the strongest political force and the only united and organised body. It was they who had brought the King to trial and insisted upon their parliamentary representatives exacting justice upon him. The real weakness of their position was that, even though their support was necessary to carry through the fight against feudalism and the absolutist monarchy, they were at odds with the ultimate interests of the progressive bourgeoisie. The latter wished to bring the revolution to an end and begin the work of conserving the victory won. The former rank and file wished to go further and complete the revolution by breaking the power of the squirearchy and the parson. Their demand was for the confiscation of the estates of the King and the royalist landowners and their distribution among the land-hungry in the army and the countryside. With this went the demand for the restoration of the people's rights to the common land which the landlords had stolen. The Levellers, it is thought, strongly opposed the invasion and conquest of Ireland.[273] The Parliamentary leaders in the main were Presbyterians, and by the Solemn League and Covenant with the Scots, they had promised to introduce Presbyterian Church

---

[273] Morton, A.L., A Peoples' History.

organisation throughout the land. They visualised a settlement with the King and a new constitution on much more conservative lines than did the army and from 1647 to 1660 military power decided the making or unmaking of regimes and constitutions.[274]

For Cromwell, abstract principles were always less important than the practical necessity of maintaining power, whereas the Levellers were committed by their principles to the advocacy of a social programme, which they had not the means to put through. This programme was embodied in *the Agreement of the People,* and only took final shape after the execution of Charles I. It was, however, the tragedy of the situation, as could be said of most bourgeois revolutions, that it was the narrow legalism of the defenders of property and not the vision of those for whom the revolution had aroused a vision to contend for human liberty and the rights of the exploited, which was the immediate practical reality. In the words of General Ireton, *'all the main thing that I speak for is because I would have an eye to property ... For here is the case of the most fundamental part of the constitution of the kingdom, which if you take away, you take away all by that'.* Cromwell's comments are even more revealing; *'What',* he asks, *'is the purport of the levelling principle but to make the tenant as liberal a fortune as the landlord. I was by birth a gentleman. You must cut these people in pieces or they will cut you in pieces'.* Despite his apologists and his flirtations with the Left of the period, Cromwell was, and remained, a landlord with the landowner's outlook and interests. So far as the army was concerned the Levellers were unable to make any headway after their defeat at Burford and Cromwell's departure in August 1649 to reconquer Ireland gave their movement its death blow.

The Diggers attempted to set up a model community on St. Georges Hill in Surrey in 1649 with a form of primitive communism

---

[274] Barnett, C., Britain and Her Army, 1509-1970, Penguin, 1974.

but were soon ejected. The movement never became strong but it was important as a diffused influence representing the aspirations of the Levellers.

All the most disaffected Leveller regiments were sent to Ireland where a large proportion of the mutineers perished, remained as settlers, or returned as poor as they had been to England, having sold their limited holdings to Officers and others who were accumulating vast estates. The war in Ireland was most beneficial for Cromwell, since it not only removed one set of opponents to a safe distance but it also gave him the means to recompense a second, the merchants and landowners who profited by the huge confiscations of land which followed the defeat of the clans and royalists in Ireland. As early as 1641 the financial magnates in the City of London had begun to buy up the as of yet unconquered lands of the 'rebels' as a speculation, estates being sold at a rate of £100 for 1,000 acres in Ulster or 600 acres in Munster. When Cromwell landed in August 1649, it was not alone to reconquer the country for the Commonwealth, but also to reimburse the speculators of the City of London who had financed his wars. To cover these costs, and the arrears of pay for his army, estimated to be in the order of £2 million all told, this was to be a charge upon Ireland. William Petty, the Cromwellian official who carried out an extensive mapping of the country in the 1650s (the *Down Survey*), concluded that Ireland lost around a third of its population over the course of the rebellion and conquest through wars, plagues, and transportation to the Carolinas and West Indies plantations. He estimated in the order of 100,000 men, women, and children were transported. This activity only became prohibited when the trafficker's became so bold as to start kidnapping and transporting Englishmen in England as the profits were so great for indentured labour.[275] In 1600 more than 80 per cent of Irish land was owned by Catholic Irish or old English, by 1641 Catholics owned 59 per cent, the figure had fallen to 22 per cent in 1688 and to 14 per cent in 1703.[276]

Absolutism and Transition to Private Property

The age in which *'Absolutist'* public authority was imposed was also simultaneously the age in which *'absolute'* private property was progressively consolidated. Thus, while capital was slowly accumulated beneath the superstructure of *Absolutism* and a gradually rising urban bourgeoisie, the noble landowners retained their historical predominance and social privilege. They still ruled as an aristocracy and continued to own the land which formed the bulk of the fundamental means of production in the economy.

With the transition from conditional to absolute private property in land in the epoch of the Renaissance, it was essentially the classical heritage of Roman law which facilitated and codified this decisive advance. Quiritary ownership, the highest legal expression of the commodity economy of *Classical Antiquity* (Roman), remained waiting to be re-found and set to work. The security of ownership and fixity of contract, the protection and predictability of economic transactions between individual parties assured by a written civil law were the indispensable preparation for the advent of capitalism. Engels observed, *'Roman law is so much the classical expression ... of a society dominated by pure private property, that all subsequent legislation was*

---

[275] Petty, W., The Political Anatomy of Ireland, Irish University Press, Shannon, (1970).

[276] Oakley, M., Ireland in the World Order, Pluto Press, (2012).

unable to improve on it in any essential way'.[277] However, there developed in England a dislike of the study of Civil Law – with its Roman influence and the reformed Church also became concerned with the development of secular jurisprudence. But as is often the case in the duplicitous approach to history by the empire builders it was more *'honoured in the breach than in the observance.*[278] An *'insular patriotism'* which affected English historians was how it was put charitably by Palmer but less charitably by Burdick who observed that some of the conclusions depended upon the prejudices and sympathies of the different writers and, he suggested, the conclusions were affected by the *'great conservatism of some English writers'* and *'pride in the alleged indigenous laws of their own country and prejudice against foreign influence'.* Indeed, the hostility against *'foreign laws'* was especially aimed at the canon law – *'that ecclesiastical offshoot of Roman law'.* As a result soon both became regarded with suspicion as instruments to enslave the English people to both popes and emperors.[279] Furthermore, *'the only real test of its character and extent is afforded by the development of juridical ideas; and in this respect, the initial influence of Roman teaching will be found to be considerable'.*[280]

Magna Carta

This *'insular'* approach ignores conveniently, amongst other matters, the influence of Lanfranc who had studied and taught Roman law at Pavia in Northern Italy, and who became Archbishop of Canterbury.

---

[277] Anderson, P., Lineages.

[278] *Hamlet,* William Shakespeare.

[279] DeRe, E., The Roman Contribution to the Common Law, Fordham Law Review, Vol 29, Issue 3, (1961).

[280] Vinogradoff P., ed G Pacillo, Roman Law in Medieval Europe, Ampere Publishing, 2015, (1909).

He ably assisted William the Conqueror during the Norman invasion and occupation. (The Normans along with the Romans were considered to be the other great law-givers). Furthermore, Pope Innocent compelled King John to accept Cardinal Stephen Langton, a Doctor of Laws from the University of Bologna. It is accepted that Langton joined with the Barons in drafting in Latin the celebrated Magna Carta in 1215. Many scholars believe he was the original draftsman and that the Charters source and inspiration were not the English feudalistic institutions but the universality of the law proclaimed by the Roman legal tradition. Latin was for a time the language of official documents in England and it is considered that in the context of land law, the grants of lands to private individuals *'unclogged'* by the native *'folkwright'* can be linked to Roman concepts of ownership and that the law of wills probably had a Roman origin by way of ecclesiastical law. Also, in this context the concept of trial by jury long regarded as of Anglo-Saxon origin is in fact of Roman origin. Other more specific contributions attributed to the home of English common law, for example *Habeas Corpus* and several principles of the law of torts are of Roman origin. The fundamental *'everyman's house is his castle'*, although claimed to be Anglo-Saxon in origin, is of Roman origin. The influences of the civil and canon law on the English doctrines of equity are manifest as the Doctrines of uses, trusts, and the equity of redemption in the law of mortgages may be traced to canonical and Roman concepts.

The same principles applied to the construction of legacies. The Law of Admiralty in Britain was closely aligned with *lex mercatoria*, thus the principles of Roman law equally applied to this branch of the law, and was *'engrafted into and made part of'* the common law. The Law Merchant was held to be part of English law and ultimately governed all commercial transactions in Britain.[281] Ultimately, Re submitted that the concepts, the terminology, the universality, and the jurisprudential principles of the Roman law system were transmitted and infused into the body of English law throughout its development. Re also noted that the *ius gentium* of merchants ultimately governed all commercial transactions in Britain.[282]

(The Acts of Union 1800 united the kingdom of Great Britain with the kingdom of Ireland to create the United Kingdom and Article 73 of the 1922 constitution of Ireland provided for the continuance in the new Irish Free State (subject to the 1922 constitution) of laws immediately in force prior to the enactment of the 1922 constitution. Article 50 of the Constitution of Ireland 1937 provided similarly and thus the law in force in the United Kingdom of Great Britain and Ireland immediately in force before the enactment of the 1922 constitution – with all its Roman law influences – became part of the law of Ireland).[283]

Cromwell in Ireland

When Cromwell landed[284] in Dublin, he acted with a speed and ferocity that gave a measure of what he believed to be the urgency of the situation before any perceived or threatened continental intervention would arise. He attacked Drogheda first and gave no quarter even though the garrison consisted mostly or largely of English Royalists who would have expected some rules of engagement from the new model army. When Cromwell's soldiers

---

[281] Hall, E.G., An Introduction to Roman Law and its Contribution to the World, The Faculty of Notaries Public in Ireland, (2014).

[282] Re, E.D., The Roman Contribution.

[283] Hall, E.G., An Introduction.

[284] Jackson, T.A., Ireland Her Own.

protested against the killing of prisoners who had surrendered on quarter promised, Cromwell unheeding insisted on their slaughter. The cream of Ormond's army and men, women, and children to the number of 3,000 were put to death; *'thirty persons only remained unslaughtered ... and these were instantly transported as slaves to Barbados'*. According to Leland; *'the favourite idea of both the Irish Government and the English Parliament (from 1642 onwards) was the utter extermination of all the Catholics in Ireland'*, justified by and largely based on the exaggerated numbers of massacred Protestants in 1641.[285] This event also provided the ongoing justification for the utter severity of the response by Cromwell. The same process was repeated in Wexford where civilians were also treated the same as combatants. Particular enmity was shown to friars and priests who *'were knocked on the head as soon as seen'*. In some accounts the behaviour was compared to the ruthlessness and barbarity of Alva in the Netherlands or Tilly and Wallenstein in the religious wars of Germany. The Bishop of Clogher, Heber MacMahon, was appointed general of the Northern army in place of Owen Roe with fatal results. In July the following year (1650) Coote's army encountered him near Letterkenny and completely crushed the Irish forces. The Bishop and other officers were taken and hanged. Ormond, on hearing this news, deplored *'the fatal itch the clergy have to govern people and command armies'*.

The ruthless Coote added to his severities the death of Colonel Henry O'Neill, son of Owen Roe, and this after quarter had been given. Some of the towns, notably Waterford and Limerick, put up a stout resistance, but the only real check on the new model army was when they met and were repulsed by Colonel Hugh O'Neill, a nephew of Owen Roe, and his fellow clansmen in the breaches of Clonmel. The siege of Clonmel was the great triumph of the

---

[285] Leland, T., A History of Ireland Vol III, London.

campaign for the Irish troops. Writing to Broghill, Cromwell had to confess himself twice beaten and that he had thought about lifting the siege a number of times. Between two and two and a half thousand of his army it was noted died at Clonmel. The Irish garrison fought on until their ammunition ran out and they then slipped silently away in the night. Hugh O'Neill fell back on Limerick which held out for another three months and was then lost by treachery. When General Ireton's troops entered the pestilence-stricken city, it having surrendered in October, they found it in a state of horror; '*the living seemed like walking skeletons*' too few and weak to bury the dead. Conditions in Galway were equally deplorable and it also was almost depopulated by plague. Munster defected to Cromwell and Kilkenny, Youghal, Kinsale and Cork declared for him chiefly through the services of Roger Boyle of Broghill, later made Lord Orrery. He exerted his great influence to bring over the south to the parliamentary side. This proved '*a godsend*' to Cromwell whose army was weakened by plague and warfare. Ireton, appointed to command the parliamentary armies on Cromwell's sudden departure, to put down a Scottish rebellion, caught the plague after the siege of Limerick and died of it in November 1651. Of the sixty thousand English and Scottish soldiers sent to Ireland the great majority died of plague and distemper; in a few months Cromwell's army of 12,000 was reduced to less than half. Galway was the last town to enter the conflict in 1641 and the last to surrender when taken by Coote in April 1652. In May 1652 the war ended when the last Irish armies, mostly-clansmen, accepted the Articles of Kilkenny. Petty calculated that thirty-four thousand Irish '*swordsmen*' led by the Irish nobles departed between 1651 and 1654 to take service in the armies of continental kings, particularly in Spain and France.[286] This Treaty created a further '*flight*' from the island and left

---

[286] Hull, E., A History.

the mass of the Irish people vulnerable and without the support or defence of a trained army.

The Settlement – Transplantation and Restoration

Parliament, in 1641, had in effect decided in principle what it intended to do after the subjugation and conquest. By 1652 Ireland had been in a state of war for 11 years and with the addition of plague, pestilence, and famine it was estimated that 504,000 Irish and 112,000 British had died during this period, mostly from the plague.[287] The principle of the Settlement was simple. The Parliament was in debt to sundry creditors the *Adventurers* and to its soldiers for arrears of pay. Ireland was considered to be a property to bear the whole of the burden and the whole of Ireland on this occasion was deemed to be confiscated from its owners and then a scale of criminality was drawn up. Under the first Act of Settlement, August 1652, *'those who had shown good affection'* to the parliament and its cause, which meant those who had fought for the parliament, or who had aided those who fought, were adjudged to be entitled to the acres they then held. Those who had organised the rising of 1641 were to lose all the acres they possessed; and if they were guilty of murder were to be hanged. Those whose criminality was considered less were to lose two acres in every three and lesser acts than this were to lose one acre in three and receive the equivalent on paper in Connaught or Clare.

In September 1653 the Act of Settlement was supplemented by the Act of Satisfaction which prescribed the forcible resettlement of the Irish and those whose property had been confiscated to the province of Connaught and Clare which were set aside for the

---

[287] Petty, W., The Political Anatomy.

habitation of those who were to transplant themselves, their families, dependents, livestock, and goods before the 1st May 1654. This area was chosen as it was surrounded by water via the river Shannon, the Erne, and the bogs of Leitrim, except for a ten-mile stretch which was to be protected by a series of forts and a one-mile strip a *cordon sanitiere*, around the perimeter of Connaught and Clare which was reserved for military settlers, to '*confine the transplanted and to cut them off from relief from sea*'. The Irish were also forbidden to live in the towns of Connaught.[288] There was also a general prohibition not to come within three miles of any of the seaport towns, which were now designated as Protestant-only, thus cutting off the Irish from any corporation or political involvement. The penalty for not transplanting was death by hanging. The resident landowners of Connaught and Clare also came within the category of transplanted and they too had their holdings reduced and were often transplanted from one parish to another. Some Clare landowners were transplanted to Galway, Roscommon, and Mayo.[289]

Overall, 44,210 names were recorded in certificates of transplantation by 1st May 1654. Members of the army were the first to be settled on the land vacated by the Irish, followed by the *Adventurers* the last of whom was settled on the 1st May 1659. According to Petty, soldiers debentures in lieu of pay were sold at four to five shillings in the pound, so that with the price nominal being 20 shillings for two acres, and there being eight million '*good*' acres accounted for, many of these '*tickets*' were later sold on for far less than their worth. The majority of privates were too poor to take up their holdings, even though it was intended to replace the Irish

---

[288] Ibid.

[289] O'Donovan, C., The Cromwellian Settlement, Clare Local Studies Project (1995-2006), Clare County Library.

with English settlers, these *'tickets'* were bought at low prices by officers and others who thus became possessed of large estates and many a *'nobles'* estate was accumulated in this way.[290] The Irish peasants remained as tenants or rack-rented small holders. Many of the English and Scotch settlers were also smallholders who sank within a generation or two to the common level of misery of the Irish around them.[291] The expected English settlers did not materialise and many of the adventurers sought simply to monetise their investment and sold them on for less than 10s per acre, as they had no intention of becoming landowners or farmers as many of them were shopkeepers or merchants from London or the West of England. The poorer Irish, if they had no real or personal estate to the value of £10, could, by submitting to the Commonwealth and living peacefully and obediently, obtain pardon. Husbandmen, ploughmen, artificers, and labourers fared better than the nobles dispossessed as they were more in demand and were needed by the new proprietors in a situation where many of the latter were ignorant of farming life.[292] The legislation enacted defined procedures for allotting the confiscated lands to the creditors of Parliament, to the officers and men of the English army and consolidated and extended the economic foundations of English landlordism in Ireland.[293]

All Ireland nominally was purchasable for one million pounds although in 1641 it was valued at £8 million. Additionally, Petty estimates the value of livestock which in 1641 was £4 million, was in 1652 valued at less than £500,000 so that Dublin had to get meat from Wales. Corn was 12s a barrel in 1641 and 50s in 1652, while the

---

[290] Jackson, T.A., Ireland Her Own

[291] Morton, A.L., A Peoples History.

[292] Hull, E., A History.

[293] Engels, F., History of Ireland, Preparatory Work, Varia on the History of the Irish Confiscations, Progress Publishers (1974).

number of houses in Ireland worth £2 million in 1641 were worth less than £500,000 in 1653. To cap it all and to add to the confusion over title, 121 plantation (Irish) acres were equivalent to 191 English statute acres and in many cases were converted advantageously, the Commissioners in Dublin and Athlone keeping considerable domains for themselves.[294] Many of the dispossessed joined the *Toraidh* (Gaelic word for the pursued) and fled to the woods and hills and became a serious menace to the new planters raiding the land and attacking and killing them. The Government offered large rewards for their capture and Tory hunting and Tory murder became a common pursuit. In many cases the same reward was available for a wolf a *toraidh* or a member of the Catholic clergy.

In May 1660 Charles II was restored to the throne of the three kingdoms England, Scotland, and Ireland. This was followed by the Acts of Settlement and Explanation whereby the confiscation under the Adventurers Act was confirmed but those who could prove innocence under the *eleven tests* of their part in the rebellion were to have lands restored. A Court of Claims was set up to hear the pleas and a small number mostly *Old English* succeeded in restoration. Very few Irish had their lands restored because the courts were abolished before their cases could be heard and the Courts in the end heard only 829 of the 8,000 claims.

Social change

A new Ireland emerged after the Cromwellian and Charles II plantations. Land ownership and political authority passed from the *old English* and *Irish* to the newly arrived colonists. These were the *new English,* a landed ascendancy of mostly English Protestants who were

---

[294] Petty, W., the political anatomy of Ireland.

to remain in control of the island until the early part of the twentieth century.

As a result of the confiscations under Cromwell and Charles II, by 1675 the profitable lands of Ireland estimated at 12,500,000 English statute acres were distributed and considerable tracts were occupied by soldiers and adventurers without title.

Granted to English Protestants of profitable land:
Forfeited under the Commonwealth: 4,560,037
Previously possessed by English Protestant colonists and the Church: 3,900,000
Granted to the Irish: 2,323,809
Previously possessed by 'good affectioned Irish' : 600,000
Unappropriated: 824,391
Total : 12,208,327

The 4,560,037 acres were distributed to *Englishmen* as follows:
Adventurers: 787,326
Soldiers: 2,385,915
'Forty Nine' Officers : 450,380
Duke of York: 169,431
Provisors: 477,873
Duke of Ormond and Colonel Butler : 257,516
Bishop's Augmentations : 31,596

The 2,323,809 acres were distributed to *Irishmen* as follows:
Decrees of Innocence: 1,176,520
Provisors; 491,001
King's letters of Restitution: 46,398
Nominees in possession: 68,360
Transplantation: 541,530

The unappropriated 824,392 acres were mostly a part of towns or land possessed by English or Irish without title or doubtful.

The Duke of York, brother of Charles II, later to be James II, received a grant of all the lands held by the regicides who had been attainted. *Provisors* were persons in whose favour provision had been made by the Acts of Settlement and Explanation. Nominees were Catholics named by the King and restored to their mansions and 2,000 acres contiguous. Distribution of land was limited to soldiers who had served under Cromwell from 1649. In 1660, at the outset of the Stuart restoration, a declaration stated that *'the adventurers'*, the officers and men of the parliamentary army retained their possessions in Ireland, while officers of Ormond's Royalist army, who had served under him up to 1649 (hence the term *'49 officers'*; in that year the majority of the defeated English Royalist officers had left Ireland and the resistance to Cromwell's troops was continued mainly by the Irish), received compensation out of the same fund of confiscated Irish lands. The indigenous Irish who had fought under the King's banner during the Civil War and had been deprived of their possessions because of it received practically no compensation. The Act of Settlement passed by the restored Stuart monarchy in 1662 instituted a complicated procedure of enquiry into complaints and petitions for the return of lands to Irish Catholics who had fought in the Civil War on the Royalist side. The satisfaction of complaints was encumbered by a whole system of casuistic objections and provisos. As a result only a small part was considered and still smaller number satisfied. Those who received compensation were designated as provisors.

The Act of Explanation passed in 1665 under pressure from the Protestant colonists, cancelled all complaints not hitherto considered, and was referred to as the *'Black Act'* by those dispossessed in

Ireland.[295] Charles II was short of money and Lord Boyle, recently created Earl of Orrery, Sir Charles Coote, and Sir John Clotworthy created Viscount Masserene, all of whom had been strong parliamentary supporters and beneficiaries, had self-servingly welcomed the King back. Of these, two had purchased the King's pardon for a sum of between £20,000 and £30,000 and spared no pains to prejudice Charles against the original owners of their newly acquired estates. The Cromwellian settlement by which they had gained was to be upheld at all costs and the planters left undisturbed in their possessions. The great estates of Clanrickarde in Galway and Ormond in Tipperary had been appropriated by the family of Cromwell for their own use and these were now restored to their owners and so Ormond returned with the title of Duke. The King had reserved to himself the right to make large grants to special person and in this way several of the loyalist nobles – both Catholic and Protestant – received back their estates. The Court which tried the claims of *'innocent papists'* sat only for six months. Clotworthy and his companions who drew up the *eleven tests* which any applicant who desired to prove innocence must fulfil, *'did believe there could not be found a man in all Ireland that should pass untouched through so many pikes'.* Despite this, of the first six-hundred claimants seven-eighths were restored as innocents and the colonists complained that the fund for reprisals would be insufficient. The Irish Court of Claims, having been prorogued for a time, was never re-opened.[296] Charles, not wishing to upset the wealthy who were quite capable of deciding that he was *'to go on his travels again',* gave the Irish his blessing and let it go at that.[297]

---

[295] Engels, F., History of Ireland, Preparatory Work.

[296] Hull, E., A History.

[297] Jackson, T.A., Ireland Her Own.

CHAPTER FIFTEEN

COLONIAL EXPANSION AND WARS OF EMPIRE

The bourgeois revolutions in Britain and Holland unleashed tremendous socio-economic power. The medieval economy had been harnessed to feudalism which in effect siphoned any surplus into waste expenditure on crusades, on knights jousting, castles, extravagant lordly displays, and on State feudalism. Spain and France spent their surplus on royal standing armies, frontier fortifications, and court pageantry. The Dutch victory over Spain in 1566-1609 and the English Parliament victory over the English king in 1637-1660 changed the face of these economies to become ones dominated by the market, the profit motive, and a class of gentry and merchants eager to accumulate capital through productive investment. The Dutch reclaimed land and developed new farming methods and a series of Dutch trading stations linked South Africa, India, and the Far East. The pace of development and commercial rivalry between the English and Dutch led to three naval wars between 1652 and 1674, the introduction of Navigation Acts by the English prohibiting Dutch trade, up until a common alliance in resisting Louis XIV's France brought the two bourgeois states into an alliance.

In the sixteenth century the discovery of gold and silver in South America led to *'the extirpation, enslavement, and entombment in mines of the indigenous population'*.[298] The spoils were then carved up between Spain and Portugal by Pope Alexander VI in 1494 to the exclusion of all others. These had been the richest of Imperial prizes but during the late seventeenth and eighteenth century it was the turn of the sugar plantations of the West Indies which then came to the fore.[299]

The indentured servants, many of them Irish, imported in their thousands as labourers and servants, as well as the native populations, were exposed to tropical or European diseases respectively, and suffered significant fatalities. What was now required, the merchants believed, was a new labour force resistant to malaria, yellow fever, and other diseases. The solution developed was to import slaves from Africa and around 12 million Africans were enslaved, transported, and worked to death between the late seventeenth and early nineteenth centuries. Of these around 1.5 million died on the voyage. Compared with these 12 million Africans around two million Europeans in one capacity or another travelled to the New World in this period and yet the white population was roughly twice that of the black population by 1820. The annihilation of the native peoples of the New World and the despicable slave trade were some of the greatest crimes against humanity.

Racism and Slavery

In this imperial phase the use of military and naval forces to seize territory, resources, and manpower of other peoples was easier to justify if the victims were portrayed as culturally or racially inferior. In this subjugation imperialism could be justified as a *'civilising'* mission. The native population of the imperial powers were enrolled in the

---

[298] Marx, K., Capital Volume I, Penguin Classics, (1990).
[299] Faulkner, N., A Marxist History of the World, Pluto Press, London, (2013).

enterprise through networks of patronage and encouraged to despise the conquered as foreigners and slaves.

The new racism was developed in the context of the triangular trade whereby ships carried trade goods to West Africa, which were then exchanged for black slaves as local chiefs waged wars of enslavement to supply the markets and gain access to imported prestige goods. The slaves were then transported across the Atlantic and sold to plantation-owners in the slave markets. The ships returned to Europe with cargoes of sugar, tobacco, and later cotton. The merchants of London, Liverpool, Bristol, and Glasgow were enriched on the back of this triangular trade. Racism justified colonies and slavery on the grounds that the native people were inferior, sub-human, fit only for heavy work, and in need of this assistance to become civilised and Christian.[300] The often used quote of Cromwell's treatment of the Irish dispossessed, *'Now therefore, you are cursed, and there shall none of you be freed from being bondmen, and hewers of wood and drawers of water'* (Joshua 9:23, KJV), can summarise the commonly held beliefs of these empire builders in their pursuit of their own wealth and happiness whatever about their missionary zeal.

The treatment of the indigenous population was also at its most frightful in the plantation-colonies set up exclusively for the export trade. In these colonies the Christian character of primitive accumulation was not any different. In 1703, the Puritans of New England by decrees of their assembly set a premium of £40 on every Native American scalp and every captured Native American; in 1720 a premium of £100 was set on every scalp; in 1744, after Massachusetts Bay Trading had proclaimed a certain tribe as rebels, a male scalp of 12 years and upwards paid £100 and £50 for scalps of women and children. Some decades later the colonial system took its

---

[300] Petty, W., A Political Economy of Ireland, 1691.

revenge on the descendants of the Pilgrim Fathers, who were now considered to have had grown seditious by their native Parliament and at English instigation were tomahawked by the Native Americans for English money. The British Parliament proclaimed bloodhounds and scalping as *'means that God and Nature had given into its hand.'*[301]

The Irish Economy Post-Restoration

After the Cromwellian conquest and the Restoration, trade and industry in Ireland were virtually at a standstill. Under James I the Revenue of the Crown in Ireland had doubled, shipping had increased, and exports and imports had grown considerably. During the reign of Charles I the prosperity of the country had continued and commerce was in no way restricted. Waterford and Limerick were *'towns of traffic'*, while the inhabitants of Galway *'do greatly trade with other countries, especially to Spain from whence they used to fetch great stores of wine and other wares every year'*. But after this war there was little commerce and the linen industry was as if it never existed. The native woollen manufacture had decayed and as late as 1672 Petty wrote that *'the clothing trade is not arrived to what it was before the late rebellion ... and seems to be lost and not yet recovered'*. Although the commercial policy of the Restoration period was unfavourable to Ireland with regard to trade with England and the plantations, it did not interfere at this point with foreign trade. The Duke of Ormond did attempt to restore the economy after his efforts to prevent the Cattle Acts had failed. Part of the problem being opposition to his potential income by his contemporaries in England who didn't hide their envy of his wealth.

In 1661 the Irish Parliament appointed a committee to consider how best Irish trade might be advanced. In 1662 its Bill *'for encouraging*

---

[301] Marx, K., Capital Volume I, Penguin Classics, London, (1990).

Protestant strangers and others to inhabit and plant in the kingdom of Ireland' had some effect in promoting woollen and linen manufacture. It should of course be noted that for the vast majority of the Irish population poverty was the order of the day. Many of the French refugees who landed in England were sent over to Ireland and naturalised. Ormond planted French colonies at Dublin, Cork, Waterford, Kilkenny, Lisburn, and Portarlington. They set about glove-making, lace-making, silk-weaving, and woollen and linen manufacturing. Despite the challenges Ireland recovered to a great extent from the effects of the plague and wars. Although England's trade wars with the Dutch prevented Ireland from trading with the continent, a trade in cattle, sheep, and related products developed and was conducted with England. Petty estimated that the total population in 1672 was at about 1,100,000 of whom 780,000 were *'fit for trade'*. He found that nearly one-eighth of the working population were engaged in tillage, over one-sixth in cattle and sheep rearing and nearly one tenth in the making up of wool. He found a significant cohort of the remainder were engaged in crafts of various types; smiths, carpenters, masons, tanners, tailors, shoemakers, millers, and significant numbers in brewing and alehouses. Many of the latter he proposed to deploy (120,000), along with another significant number of *'spare hands'* (220,000) as he described them, in a programme of economic reconstruction. This was one of the first plans put down on paper for the development of an economy and the creation of employment. His proposed plan of works was set out in detail for the creation of wealth both local and universal, through construction and upgrading of much needed housing stock, the planting of forestry, rivers and navigation works, ship building, tanning, mining, mills, and other related activities.

Overall, his plan was progressive for the time albeit it never appears to have seen the light of day other than his suggestions for the building of the Vice Regal Lodge (*Aras an Uachtarain* – now home of the Irish President), the construction of the Port of Dublin, and a micro version of his plan he carried on from his own acquired estate of 96,000 acres in Kerry. In a further policy, not far short of political xeno-centrism, he proposed the transfer of 200,000 Irish to England and their replacement with a similar number of British so that the numbers of each resident population would be of equal strength. Except, in this proposal and for the English their *'political and artificial'* strength would be three times as great relatively and so keep the Irish in check.

Petty also observed astutely: *'The people of Ireland are all in factions and parties, called English and Irish, Protestants and Papists; though, indeed, the real distinction is vested and divested of the land'.*

Woollen manufacturing was mainly a domestic industry as there was practically no exports from Ireland. It was prohibited and seen as being a challenge to English manufacturers and as a result the staple export trade was provisions. Few commodities were imported with the exception of tobacco. Petty reckoned two-sevenths of income of the ordinary person was spent on this. The Irish villages were more or less self-sufficient and made most things they needed for themselves. Of the 1.1 million population, 800,000 were considered Irish and 300,000 English or Scotch. Six out of every eight of the Irish lived in abject poverty in chimneyless, windowless dwellings as the English and the Scotch possessed three-quarters of the land, five-sixths of the housing, and two-thirds of what foreign trade there was. It was this land that provided the new settlers with the ability to become sheep and cattle breeders. In 1663 exports from Ireland included one-third more oxen, sheep, butter and beef than in 1641, in spite of the high duties imposed in Ireland on the exportation of livestock. The export trade in livestock was so flourishing that it was scarcely worthwhile to spend money in fattening in order to procure good meat and dairy produce for sale abroad. Three years after the Restoration the English breeders began to raise an outcry as, in those years, 61,000 head of cattle had been brought over from Ireland every year. The breeders complained that land in Ireland was so plentiful and cheap that livestock could be bred practically for nothing. An acre cost four shillings in Ireland as against forty shillings in England, and in addition they complained of the low cost of living and the cheapness of Irish labour.[302]

This led to an English Act of Parliament for the banning of the importation of cattle from Ireland (Scotland was included initially but later dropped), under penalty of a heavy forfeiture. The Act was passed into law in November 1666 and by statutes was later extended to cover sheep, swine and mutton, lamb, butter, and cheese. Farmers now found themselves with livestock they could not sell and oxen which had previously sold for 50s a head were now sold for 10s. In 1667 matters got worse as the Scotch, who had hitherto allowed Irish cattle to be imported on duty of half-a-crown a head, prohibited their importation altogether. There were attempts at a clandestine trade and trade with Rotterdam but neither of these were successful. The outstanding debt on Ireland, as it continued to pay for the army, albeit it had returned to England and with other levies, now had to be paid from any goods that could be sold to other countries. In this process they had to obtain goods wanted by England and sell them to England to meet these various claims. However, the acute and immediate distress suffered from the Cattle Acts had unintended consequences. The price of meat rose in England and rates of wages

---

[302] Murray, A.E., History of the Commercial and Financial Relations between England and Ireland from the Period of the Restoration, P S King & Son, Westminster, (1903).

had to increase proportionate to the price increase in provisions. This further impacted as the English landlords who had pasture lands for fattening could no longer import lean and cheap Irish cattle and were at the mercy of Welsh and Scotch cattle breeders who took advantage of the situation to their profit. In Ireland all that the cattle breeders could now do was turn their attention to fattening cattle and in the process produce good meat and dairy products for export. Irish beef now became in great demand abroad while Irish butter sold for more than English butter. Ireland now began to rival England in the provision trade with other countries, especially for butter, hides, and tallow. As sheep were also prohibited from export, their meat was now provided for the export trade and the wool was retained and developed into a home industry. It was observed at this time the Irish were now becoming better clothed than their English counterparts.

Social Change

In the fifteen years following the Cattle Acts Ireland began to provide the English plantations with butter, cheese, and salted beef. One of the most important results of the Cattle Acts was to give Ireland a comparatively large provision trade with foreign countries and this led in turn to an increase and benefit for Irish shipping. In 1680 it was observed that for the previous five years there were seldom less than twenty Irish ships at Dunkirk laden with beef, tallow, hides, leather, and some wool. Irish ships were also seen at Ostend, Nantes, and La Rochelle.

The establishment of this trade in provisions had another interesting outcome, a noticeable falling off in the amount of trade between Ireland and England. Before the Cattle Acts three-quarters of Irish foreign trade was with England, as Irish cattle exported to

England purchased all the commodities Ireland needed, and made up two-thirds of the Irish economy. Before 1663, Ireland had imported, on average, English manufactured goods and produce to the amount of £210,000 per year, but from that time on goods imported steadily decreased, until in 1675 it had fallen to £20,000 a year. By 1672 only one-quarter of Ireland's trade was with England. A further consequence was that the Irish cattle breeders, instead of only breeding large cattle, began to breed sheep in great numbers and an Act of Parliament which made it a felony to export wool to anywhere other than England soon began to drive a growing trade with England in raw wool. However, the importation of Irish wool dragged down the price of English wool and complaints again arose from the English producers. This large volume of exports was allowed to continue for fear that such a policy might lead alternatively to a large clandestine export of wool to foreign parts or to an increase in the Irish woollen manufactured.[303]

However, abroad Ireland was beginning to undersell England and this was not acceptable as the plantations were considered to be the exclusive domain of the *'Mother'* country. This new concept of the Irish being outside the privilege of English subjects and to be treated as foreigners had been hinted at in the Navigation Act of 1663, but it was not until seven years later, in the Acts of 1670 and 1671, that a serious number of commodities were prohibited from being carried to Ireland unless first landed in England, a continuation of colonial policy.

As a result Ireland was now unable to import any plantation goods direct in return for the provisions exported. This prohibition led to the redirection of Irish trade to other foreign plantations as in the French West Indies. This led to another outcry as these plantations could now get their provisions cheaper than the English

---

[303] Ibid.

could get their supplies from England. As time went on Ireland was to find her foreign trade more and more restricted by the establishment in England of exclusive companies such as the East Indies Company maintained by English capital and trading through chosen English ports. After the Williamite Wars, when Ireland had gone through another period of devastation followed by further wholesale confiscations, the further restrictive policies of England did lasting damage to Ireland's progress to becoming an industrial nation while in parallel the penal laws crushed the life and spirit out of the majority of the people.[304]

Marx later concluded: '*England has destroyed the conditions of Irish society. First of all, she has confiscated the lands of the Irish; then by parliamentary decrees, she has suppressed Irish industry; finally, by armed force she has broken the activity and energy of the Irish people. In this way England has created the 'social conditions' which allow a small caste of robber landlords to dictate to the Irish people the conditions in which they are allowed to hold the land and live on it*'.[305]

---

[304] Ibid.

[305] Fox, R, Marx Engels and Lenin on the Irish Revolution, Cork Workers Club, Modern Books Ltd London, (1932).

CHAPTER SIXTEEN

THE GLORIOUS REVOLUTION TO THE

WILLIAMITE WARS

The period between 1660 and 1688 had been one of rapid commercial expansion in England. The social basis of the Whigs[306] – the class of prosperous merchants – was stronger than ever before. The alliance with Portugal and the establishment of closer relations with Spain and her colonies had opened up new markets for English goods. The plantations in the American colonies and the West Indies grew steadily and provided both markets and raw materials, while the East India Company not only became an important trading concern, but also a force in English internal politics. The exploitation of the colonies had placed a great accumulation of capital in the hands of the Whig merchants.[307] Though Charles had managed to attract considerable forces behind him in his bid for absolutism, they were not the disposers of considerable amounts of capital and Tory parliaments were not prepared to grant revenue adequate to maintain a standing army. James II's accession in 1685 opened favourably enough with generous votes from a parliament packed with Tories through the earlier manipulation of the borough corporations. It also

---

[306] Whig and Tory came into use around 1680 as denoting respectively those who wished to restrict the Crown by specific constitutional law and those who considered it a curtailment of royal prerogatives. They represented clearly defined interests in a very restricted electorate.

[307] Morton A.L., A People's History.

coincided with the revocation of the Edict of Nantes in France under which the French Huguenot's had enjoyed a limited toleration. The revocation was followed by intense persecution and the flight of hundreds of thousands of Huguenot's who dispersed all over Western Europe. Fifty to sixty thousand settled in England, almost all of them skilled artisans, weavers, hat-makers, paper-makers, and glass-blowers. Arising from this rumours were soon abroad that a plot was being hatched to destroy Protestantism all over Europe. These events added to the opposition to James and his counter-revolution to restore Catholicism further and faster than his Tory supporters were prepared to go and this in turn played into the hands of the Whigs. The first blow came from the left forces of the period as plans were mounted both in England and Holland for a rising headed by the Duke of Monmouth (a son of Charles) with a proposed simultaneous landing in Scotland. On this rising were centred the hopes of those classes who had supported the Levellers and who had learnt in the last generation to regard the Crown as the instrument of popery and social reaction. Monmouth, with a banner that was symbolically of the old Leveller green, landed at Lyme Regis in June and moved inland, gathering supporters from the labourers, smallholders, and weavers of the West Country.

It was soon apparent that, unlike the previous revolution, the supporters were of one kind. None of the Whig lords and very few of the gentry declared in his favour and their lack of enthusiasm could be put down as the opposite to the popular support for the rising. The rebels marched towards Bristol but were headed off by a powerful government army and retired to Bridgewater. Here they attempted a surprise attack by night on the enemy camp at Sedgemoor which failed. The untrained and ill-armed peasants and weavers had no real chance against an army that included amongst its leaders distinguished soldiers such as John Churchill and Patrick Sarsfield. In the manhunt, hundreds were executed and many more transported to the West Indies plantations from the *'Bloody Assizes'* that followed, overseen by the *'hanging judge'* Jeffreys. Many of the remains of those hanged were displayed around the county as a salutary lesson to those who rebelled against the King. Monmouth himself was captured and beheaded. In the end it was the Whigs and not the Government who profited from Monmouth's defeat. This defeat, viciously put down by James, alienated many from him and, by crushing the popular elements, made it possible to stage in safety the revolution against him. Afterwards this revolution would be hailed as *'glorious'*, precisely because the popular masses had no part in it. It was now safe to overthrow James without the chance that his departure would open the way for the return of a republic, under which the poor might again inconveniently make demands upon the rich. James had added to his difficulties when he appointed the Earl of Tyrconnell, Richard Talbot (a survivor of Cromwell's siege of Drogheda when he escaped dressed as a woman), as his Lord Lieutenant in Ireland and Talbot set about raising a Catholic army. In 1687 and 1688 James issued A Declaration of Indulgence, suspending all laws by which Catholics were barred from military and civil office and in an attempt to win new allies, the Dissenters were also included. But to his detriment his break with the Church of England was also breaking with the Tory squire class, the one class upon whose support an absolute monarch could still possibly rely on.

At this juncture Whigs and Tories joined to open negotiations with William of Orange. On the 30th June a definitive invitation was sent by a group of leading peers promising active support in a rebellion against James. All that summer William gathered a fleet and an army waiting anxiously in case Louis might make an attack on the

Netherlands. James and his allies hesitated and William was able to land unopposed at Torbay on November 5th. One by one James's supporters escaped abroad or deserted to William; a decisive one being John Churchill, already one of the most influential officers in the army, and soon to be known as the Duke of Marlborough. Without the army James was helpless and his flight in December to France left William as the only possible remaining authority. A convention met in February and offered the throne jointly to William and Mary (daughter of James). The Convention declared itself a parliament and proceeded with a Bill of Rights and an Act of Settlement (limiting succession to Protestants) and laid down the conditions under which the monarchy was allowed to continue to exist. The King was no longer allowed to control the army or the judges and he was specifically forbidden to dispense with laws or suspend them. The control of finance passed over to the parliament and on these terms the Whigs again became loyal monarchists now that the monarchy depended on them for its existence. The *'Glorious Revolution'* brought in to power, along with William of Orange, the landed aristocracy who favoured promoting free trade in land, extending the domain of modern agriculture on the large farm system, and increasing the supply of farm labour to work it. Alongside the new landed aristocracy was their natural ally; the financiers, the banks, and the large manufacturers then dependent on protective duties. William was prepared to accept whatever conditions, provided he could secure the wealth and manpower he required for use against France with which Holland had entered a period of prolonged wars. But first he had to secure his hold, not only on England but upon Scotland and Ireland as well.

Talbot, Earl of Tyrconnell, it is considered, contributed to James's downfall by raising Irish Catholic regiments which were sent to England to support the Crown at the time of the crisis of the trial of the seven bishops. This attempt to introduce Irish Catholic regiments into England ensured what James had previously feared: the desertion of the English army. In addition, withdrawal of the Irish troops from Ireland gave the towns of Derry and Enniskillen the opportunity to close their gates and defend themselves against the troops of Talbot and James. James landed in Ireland in March 1689, on Talbot's invitation, from France with an army waiting and ready to hand. He was able easily to stir up a rising of the native and dispossessed Catholics against the Protestant *'garrison'* and ascendancy. In Scotland the new regime was accepted without much opposition, a rising in the Highlands fading after an initial success at Killiecrankie. The Covenanting lowlands were only too ready to welcome the expulsion of James the Catholic.[308]

William, James, and the First 'Patriot' Parliament – 1690/91

The accession of James II had been watched with great interest in Ireland because of its possible bearing on the Cromwellian Settlement. Charles II, his predecessor, had refused to upset or modify the Settlement arrangements for the dispossessed except to a negligible extent. Two-thirds of the good arable land was now in the possession of less than one-sixth of the population and this large owning minority were almost exclusively Protestant. In the provinces, the ratio Protestant to Catholic was 5:2 in Ulster, Leinster 2:13, Munster 2:20, and in Connaught 2:25. These ratios give some indication of the height of Catholic expectation and the depth of

[308] Ibid.

Protestant fears created by the accession of 1685. The appointment of Richard Talbot as Commander-in-Chief and later Lord Lieutenant added to the intensity of the situation.[309]

James landed at Kinsale on March 12th 1689 with a French fleet of over thirty warships, thirteen attendant vessels of 2,223 guns, 13,000 seamen, and provided with 500,000 crowns in money. He was met at Cork by his Viceroy Tyrconnell and they reached Dublin on March 24th. Tyrconnell had disbanded the Protestant militia and drove thousands of Protestant soldiers and officers out of the army, including Ormond's own regiment. They fled, many of them to Holland and some of course returned later with William of Orange. The Town corporations were also made predominantly Catholic and sheriffs, magistrates, and judges were appointed all over the country. The flight of the Protestant industrial classes had a devastating effect on the economy of the country and reduced rents and trade in turn. At the same time James had not come to Ireland for any particular Irish purpose other than solely to regain his English Crown. In the so-called *'Patriot'* Parliament in Dublin he was not of a mind to abrogate the laws against his co-religionists; *'lest it might alienate from him the hearts of his Protestant subjects in England'*.

The Act of Attainder against the Cromwellian Settlement was wrung from him against his will and it must also be borne in mind that he himself had benefited to the tune of 120,000 acres of the best land in the country from the Settlement. This new Act of Settlement swept away the 12,000,000 acres from the Protestant settlers and from those Catholics who had purchased land from them. It was accompanied by a general condemnation to death and confiscation of over 2,000 of the named landowners, albeit they were not all correctly identified. It was in effect a mirror image reversal of the Acts used to

---

[309] Jackson, T.A., Ireland Her Own.

dispossess the previous occupiers. Among the thirty-five Acts passed by the *'Patriot'* Parliament, were Acts recognising James as Sovereign, an Act for Liberty of Conscience, an Act repealing the Acts of Settlement and Explanation, an Act removing, *'all disabilities from the natives of this kingdom'*, an Act to regulate tithes and rent, and one to encourage industries.[310] It should also be said that the chief failure of the Irish *'Patriot'* Parliament was that it left the mass of the Irish people as it found them: landless. Neither was it the outcome James desired as the revocation of the Cromwellian Settlement alienated the Tory landowners in England upon whom he was counting for aid.

In any event both Ireland and England were pawns in a balance of power game fought out on the continent between Louis XIV and his allies on one side and a European Coalition which included Pope Innocent XI as temporal monarch as well as William of Orange on the other. Apart from the incidental question as to which of two rival kings would rule Ireland, the issue which the mass of the Irish fought to decide was in effect as to who they would be tenants of, an English Protestant landlord or an Irish Catholic one.

The Battle of the Boyne

The leaders of Europe had been overawed by the strength of France and so worried had they become that in 1686 the Emperor of Germany, the King of Spain, William of Orange, and Pope Innocent XI entered into the Treaty of Augsburg to protect themselves from French encroachment. Thus, the peculiar position arose that when William of Orange landed in England he was politically backed by the head of the Catholic Church and the Catholic kingdom of Spain in his efforts to overthrow the Catholic king of England. Whilst James

---

[310] Hull, E., A History.

had allied himself with Louis XIV of France with England as a semi-dependent state. William arrived in Ireland and at the Boyne River on June 30th and July 1st won a rather indecisive battle in the course of which James abandoned the field and three days later fled to France. The English Whigs did not wish to give William an army a long standing position of parliament for fear of absolutism, so his army, along with some English, Scotch, and Ulster regiments comprised of Dutch, Danes, Swedes, Prussians, and French Huguenots, his General Schomberg being one of the latter and a French exile. The one regiment on the Irish establishment which fought for William was Meath's, later the 18th Royal Irish. The most important part of his Irish contingent came from the irregular forces raised from the Protestants of Derry and Enniskillen and these 6,000 Protestants were put on the army's official establishment as nine regiments of foot and cavalry in January 1690.[311] William's army wore distinguishing green badges and the army of James wore the white cockade of the Bourbons and Stuarts. William's army was said to have numbered 36,000 and that of James 23,000 with far less equipment and artillery.

Patrick Sarsfield had advised James against accepting battle at the Boyne site, knowing the relative size of the armies, and advised a retreat behind the line of the Shannon, until the Irish troops had become better trained and equipped. James overruled Sarsfield's tactics and insisted upon a battle which he then proceeded to lose and abandon. The casualties on both sides were less than 2,000. When news of the victory for William reached Rome a *Te Deum* was sung in St. Peter's in celebration while similar celebrations were held at the great Catholic capitals of Madrid and Brussels and in the Catholic

---

[311] Denman, T., Hibernia Officina Militum, Irish Recruitment to the British Regular Army 1660-1815, The Irish Sword Vol XX, (Winter 1996).

cathedral of Vienna. The question as to whether religion played a major part in the conflict is moot. One Williamite commander quoted the Irish Jacobite leaders as saying they were not fighting for '*king or faith, but for our estates*'. William's regiment of Blue Guards who contributed largely to his success was made up chiefly of Dutch Catholic soldiers. When James asked them how they could serve on an expedition designed to defeat their own religion, it is said one replied '*his soul was God's, but his sword belonged to the Prince of Orange*'.[312]

Siege of Limerick – Aughrim

Tyrconnell decided after the Battle of the Boyne not to oppose William and shipped away his wife with all of his wealth to France. After the Boyne, with James gone, the Franco-Irish army fell back as Sarsfield had advised to the line of the Shannon. Tyrconnell and Lauzan, the French commander, along with the French forces, withdrew to Galway and Lauzans Deputy De Boissealeau was installed as Governor of the City of Limerick with overall charge of Sarsfield and the cavalry on the Shannon side of Clare. The first Siege of Limerick was commenced by William and his army and three epic stories emerge from this siege. The destruction of the Williamite siege train at Ballyneety, the role played by the women of Limerick in defence of the City, digging the earth, filling the gabions, piling the shot, and drawing up ammunition while around them showered bombs and grenades, and the rescue of wounded Williamite soldiers from a blazing hospital camp by Irish troops.

On the 27th August William gave orders for the assault on Limerick. The first assault and breach was led by a party of 500 Grenadiers who were followed closely on by between two and three thousand of the

---

[312] Ibid.

Williamite soldiers including the Brandenburg regiment. The news that they had penetrated into the town unleashed the citizens, women and men, the women like *'liberated furies'*, flinging stones, bricks, glass, and bottles with serious effect. The women, said George Story, the Williamite Chaplain, *'rushed boldly into the breach and stood nearer to our men than their own, hurling stones and broken bottles right into the faces of the attacking troops, regardless of death by sword and bullet, which many of them met'*. By seven o'clock in the evening the enemy had been driven out of the streets and back into the counterscarp where there escaped the last remnants of the Dutch battalions. A counter assault and breach by the Brandenburg regiment fell victim to heavily mined ground which exploded under their feet and resulted in severe casualties and fatalities. William, resolving to renew the assault the next day, could not persuade his men to advance though he offered to lead them in person. In rage it is said he left the camp and didn't stop till he came to Waterford, where he took ship for England, never to return. His army in the meantime retired by night from Limerick.[313]

The year closed with Sarsfield's successful defence of Limerick but this was somewhat offset by the Duke of Marlborough's capture of Cork and Kinsale from the sea. In 1691 the line of the Shannon was forced at Athlone by an Anglo-Dutch assault and the French General St. Ruth decided to risk a stand against the advice of Sarsfield, at Aughrim in Co. Galway. The Battle of the Boyne was not the decisive victory of the campaign for William, more so it was the Williamite victory at Aughrim on the 12th July 1691, when St. Ruth was killed and a pass for the English advance was provided by the English Jacobite cavalry commander Henry Luttrell, who it was later believed was in secret contact with the Williamites. St. Ruth's French guards withdrew from the field, followed by some of the Irish horse

---

[313] Sullivan, A.M., The Story of Ireland, Wentworth Press, (2019).

cavalry, and though the foot-soldiers still stubbornly held their ground they were unsupported and un-officered. Slowly, they were pushed back again up the hill toward their camp, dropping in numbers as they struggled upwards. The fall of night and a heavy rain alone put an end to their slaughter. Under a torrent of fire on the open hillside they gradually melted away. The battle of Aughrim was followed by the surrender of Galway and Sligo whose garrisons marched out with favourable terms to take part in the last scene of the great drama behind the walls of Limerick. After the first siege of Limerick, William had broken camp and ordered the men into winter quarters, and, with Prince George of Denmark and the Duke of Ormond, departed to England, hastened by reports of an intended landing by James on English shores but also to continue his conflict with Louis in Flanders. After Athlone and Aughrim, and the ending of the second siege of Limerick these events combined to mark the end of the war and this was followed by the signing of the Treaty of Limerick on October 3rd 1691.[314] During the siege of Limerick Colonel Luttrell, who had conspired with Williamite forces and received 2,000 crowns in return from the Prince of Orange, along with his elder brother's estate for his co-operation, was again at large and involved in treachery. He met his death in 1717, when he was assassinated by some unknown hand in the streets of Dublin. The imposing soldier Patrick Sarsfield went on to die in French service at the Battle of Landen in 1693.

The Treaty of Limerick

The Articles of Capitulation consisted of two parts: Military and Civil. The Military being signed first. On October 3rd 1691, after long

---

[314] Ellis, P.B., A History of the Irish Working Class.

discussion, the Military Articles, proposed by the Dutch Baron Ginkel, were signed by Sarsfield and others and by the Lord Justices who had replaced Tyrconnell on the Irish side and Ginkel on the other. The French Generals also signed. William wanted a speedy conclusion as his troops were needed in Flanders to check the rapid advance of the armies of Louis XIV and so a treaty was critical for him.[315] The Military Articles provided for the liberty of any officers and soldiers with their families to pass overseas to France or any other place they wished, and ships and money were provided for their embarkation. At the same time Ginkel made it clear that any who entered the service of the armies of France could never re-enter the country on pain of death. They left in their thousands and entered Irish history as the *Wild Geese*.

Social Change

A different view presented of the 'patriotic' efforts of the Catholic gentry is that what they were solely about was the return of their own rights to property as against the right of an English parliament to interfere with or regulate such rights. They wished to dispossess those who had dispossessed them, albeit they had previously taken their opportunity to dispossess the indigenous clans. In the same vein, the forces which battled beneath the walls of Derry or Limerick were not the forces of England or Ireland but were the forces of two English parties fighting for the possession of the powers of English government. Thus, the leaders of the *Wild Geese* on the battlefields of Europe were not shedding their blood because of their fidelity for Ireland but rather because they had been exiled as they had attached themselves to the defeated side in English politics. They had, for

---

[315] Hull, E., A History.

example, been offered the opportunity to transfer to the Williamite side and fight on accordingly as 'swordsmen' in his campaign.

Equally, William and his followers showed their actions were also animated by their considerations for land when they confiscated over one and a half million acres for distribution amongst themselves. The Dutch Lord Bentinck received 135,000 acres, Lord Albemarle 103,603, Lord Coningsby 59,667, Lord Galway 36,142, Lord Athlone 28,640, and Lord Mountjoy 12,000. These were some of the largest but amongst others. It also included the bestowing by William of 95,000 acres on his mistress Elizabeth Villiers, Countess of Orkney. The virtuous Irish parliament, however, intervened and took these back to distribute them amongst their Irish loyalist followers. [316]

After the reformation successive sovereigns and parliaments from Elizabeth I to the James's, both of the Charles's, and on up to George III, engaged in the passing of penal statutes to enforce conformity to Protestantism in England and Wales, Scotland and Ireland. These policies were pursued through fines and deprivations, death, and forfeiture of inheritance and property. This was their response to the threat of Catholicism and any attempted return to *'popery'* which was associated with invasion, reaction, and importantly attempts to return or restore property to the church and to the dispossessed Catholic landowners. The first Acts in the Elizabethan period were the Acts of Supremacy and Uniformity. Penalties of *Praemunire* included exclusion from the sovereign's protection and forfeiture of all land and goods. After Elizabeth's excommunication further penal legislation was passed and continued on up to 1585 when it was made high treason for any Jesuit or seminarian to be in England at all. Under this statute over 150 Catholics died on the scaffold between 1581 and 1603, exclusive of her other victims. Acts

---

[316] Connolly, J., Labour in Irish History.

on the oaths of supremacy and allegiance were also enforced which excluded Catholics from Parliament. The first Catholic Relief Act appeared in England in 1778. In Scotland the first Penal statutes were enacted by the Scottish parliament of 1560 and continued on and even after the Act of Union in 1707 when they were still in force and the first Act for the Relief of Scottish Catholics did not receive royal assent until May 1793.

In 1666 the Irish parliament stopped sitting and this may provide a possible explanation for the lull in the ongoing extension of Penal laws to Ireland during this period.[317] Ireland in effect became a colonial dependency of England until the Jacobite parliament resumed in 1688 and instituted a Catholic *revanche*.[318] The outcome of the Williamite wars meant that in 1692 the Protestant ascendancy, or *'new colonial interest'* parliament, was returned to its previous control with the Catholic interest excluded. In 1690 an Act in the English parliament declared all Irish Acts of the *'patriot'* or *'pretended'* parliament null and void and an Act passed in Westminster in 1691 prevented Roman Catholics from sitting in any future Irish parliament. The returned Irish *'Anglican'* parliament of 1692 refused to ratify the civil articles of the Treaty of Limerick which provided for religious toleration as set out similar to those available during the reign of Charles II. This provided that Jacobites taking an oath of allegiance could retain lands they held under Charles II and alongside this the right to bear arms were rights guaranteed to nobles and gentlemen. In other words, although lands acquired since 1685 would be lost the Catholic elite would be free from persecution even if they would not be full members of the political nation. The departure

---

[317] Barnard, T., The Kingdom of Ireland, 1641-1760, Palgrave Macmillan, (2004).

[318] Gillen U., Ascendancy Ireland, 1660-1800, The Princeton History of Modern Ireland, (2016).

from Ireland of the vast bulk of the Jacobite army meant in effect that there was no real chance of an effective Irish military force for decades to come or to ensure the enforcement of any of these agreed arrangements. Meanwhile, bands of dispossessed *tories* and *rapparees* wandered the countryside, gave challenge to the colonialist occupiers, and this attracted the extension and another raft of repressive legislation by the Ascendancy parliament and is represented by what became commonly known as the Penal Laws.

CHAPTER SEVENTEEN

THE PENAL LAWS – PROTESTANT ASCENDANCY – RISE OF A CATHOLIC MIDDLE CLASS

Although government was overseen by English appointees, the Irish Anglican elite had undisputed possession of the Irish parliament. The Irish parliament quickly turned to the Catholic question and over the next 35 years it passed a series of measures collectively known to their enactors as the penal or popery laws. Many of the parliamentary elite believed that violent conflict with Catholics was inevitable unless they removed permanently their capacity to rebel. As previously noted a comprehensive penal code only failed to emerge as the Irish Parliament did not meet after 1666 when these laws had been enacted in England. Parliament's first action was to refuse to ratify the Articles of the Limerick Treaty and did not do so until 1697, and even then only after certain Articles had been removed, including the guarantee to Catholics of the same toleration as under Charles II. The Crown, driven by financial motives, accepted this breaking of its commitments. The first session of the Irish parliament after 1692 was in 1695 and the first penal laws were passed in this session, including the infamous law that banned Catholics from keeping weapons and owning horses worth more than £5[319] – that is horses considered of use for military purposes. Both aimed ostensibly at the prevention of the re-arming of 'rebels'. Other legislation aimed at restricting Catholic access to local education and banned access to foreign education considered contingent to political ideas. All of these Acts mirrored the penal legislation already enacted in England and Scotland. Local Catholic schools were also banned as being nurseries for the Catholic religion and Irish language. Further penal laws were enacted in 1704 and 1707, respectively banning Catholics from Parliament and the legal profession, and in 1709 the *Banishment of Bishops* and the re-enforcement of the prevention of land being held in trust on behalf of Catholic landowners. The most important of these Acts was possibly the 1704 Act to *Prevent the Further Growth of Popery*, slipped in by English councillors in 1703, the aim of which was to substantially weaken if not eradicate the Catholic landed elite. It banned inheritance by primogeniture with land having to be divided by gavelkind (previously removed in favour of primogeniture) that is equally among all the sons. This process sub-divided and weakened the overall holding levels. On conversion to the established church, the eldest son could become owner, and in this case the Catholic parent became the tenant for life. This happened in many instances. Catholics were also banned from holding a lease for longer than 31

---

[319] This Act was still in force in 1773 and gave rise to the famous lament and call for revenge the *Caoineadh* for Airt Ui'Laoighire. He was educated abroad and a son of one of the few surviving Catholic gentry who had land leased near Macroom, Co. Cork. He returned from the continent after a commission had been purchased and he had served as a Captain in the Hungarian Hussars. He brought his horse with him and refused to sell this horse for the required £5 to Abraham Morris, Sherriff of Cork, who had him outlawed, subsequently ambushed and murdered. The soldier responsible, Green, was later decorated for his gallantry. Green was later found guilty but at that point he had transferred to the East Indies operation. Airt was married to Eibhlin Dubh Ni Chonaill of Derrynane, Co. Kerry, who wrote the lament (she was an aunt of Daniel O'Connell).

years. English Tory politicians used the 1704 Act to extend the sacramental Test to Ireland and so removed Catholics and Dissenters (mostly Presbyterians) from local government and holding any public office, civil or military. An attempted Bill to castrate or brand on the cheek Catholic clergy failed in 1719. Catholics were finally stripped of the vote, their last political right, in 1728.

Society Post-Penal Legislation

The Penal Laws aimed to secure the unchallenged political, social, and economic supremacy of the Anglican Protestant Ascendancy. This can also explain why Dissenters, mostly Presbyterian in north-east Ulster, were targets of the penal legislation.[320]

How did the Penal Laws affect the Catholic population? The purpose of the Penal Laws was not just to destroy the Catholic Church, in that object it failed, as the Church emerged more aligned and in sympathy with the population. Research has indicated that although attempts to enforce the Banishment Act had some effect in the early years, the Catholic clergy were by the 1720s mostly allowed to operate with impunity apart from times of crisis such as possible international intervention or the threat of invasion. Foremost, it did complete the elaborate legal substructure on which the Ascendancy dominance was built. The Penal Laws did ensure that the established church dominated public displays of religion, as evidenced by the growth of Anglican architecture in the towns and countryside and the decline of other faith buildings. In the main the laws affected only a small proportion of the Catholic community; priests, lawyers, gentlemen, and would-be gentlemen. Where the Penal Laws were much more successful was in altering the behaviour of the Catholic

---

[320] Gillen, U., Ascendancy Ireland.

elite and to deny them political power and ownership of land. In broad terms these laws did not apply to the vast majority of the Catholic population, amongst whom they made little or no impression on their already existing poverty-stricken lives. However, the picture painted by some historians that all were effected in the same way and the elevation of the imagery of mass rocks, hedge-schools, look-outs, and unwelcome visits from redcoats had frequent re-telling and entered the narrative. That is not to detract from the fact that the courage displayed and the work undertaken by hunted priests and hedge school masters is beyond question and the consequences for those caught was fatal. However, the Catholic elite in some cases, with the help of a sympathetic Protestant elite, educated their children abroad, and it is evident that more than half of the land-owning families affected by the inheritance provisions of the 1704 Act experienced a conversion to the established church.

Although the amount of land owned by Catholics fell from 14% in 1704 to 5% by 1776, the story is more complicated than the figures suggest. A variety of legal strategies evolved to get around the laws, including nominal conversion and land held in trust or under leases. Between 1702 and 1773 the number of those who conformed was shown to be 4,055 persons.[321] When the land leased was taken into consideration there was more land in Catholic hands by 1800 than in 1700. Official enquiries in 1731 measured the Catholic's strength and the personnel of the Catholic churches easily outnumbered those of the Protestant churches.[322] Also, it does appear that the Catholic elite had abandoned Jacobitism before the 1750s as there was no Irish rising in 1715 or 1745 as in Scotland which ended with the Battle of

---

[321] Hull, E., A History.

[322] Barnard, T., The Kingdom of Ireland, 1641-1760, Palgrave Macmillan, (2004).

Culloden in 1746.[323] Instead, the Irish Catholic elite sought an accommodation with the state as the Catholic Committee from 1757 to 1791 demonstrates. The vast majority of the Irish were small-scale tillers of the soil and out of necessity were tied to scanty holdings and conditions of tenure with no better outcome than some level of wretchedness. These people were considered the lowest strata of the Irish, segregated by poverty by language, by creed, by law, and, in the words of one commentator, by the arrogance of the class that *'knelt to England on the necks of their countrymen'*.[324]

The Irish population was divided into the rich and poor with no intermediate class. The system divided the country into landlords, small farmers, and cottiers and there was no middle-class as such. In England the great body of yeoman farmers, as we have noted, constituted the backbone of society and were determinant on occasion of the politics of the nation. They were the grand nursery of the fleets and armies, navigation and commerce, and referred to more generally as the *'middling sort'*. The people who might have been the Catholic Irish yeomanry were dispossessed and dissipated overseas by way of various conflicts and penal legislation. As one commentator of the time remarked, *'in Ireland we see the two classes of men, a pampered gentry and a starving commonalty'*. This was put in more stark and less sympathetic terms in the *Tribune*, a periodical in Dublin, in 1720 which *'lamented'* that the people who should have been Ireland's yeomanry *'are a generation of half-starved, half-naked, half-dead animals, and*

---

[323] The Act of Union between England and Scotland was effected in 1707. In October 1703, when the negotiations for the union with Scotland were proceeding, the Irish Commons sent an address to the Queen petitioning for a legislative union. After the completion of the union with Scotland in 1707, the Irish Commons sought a more comprehensive union. At the time England had no wish for a union with Ireland; the demands of commercial monopoly reigned supreme, (*Murray, A, E, A History of the Commercial and Financial Relations*).
[324] Jackson, T, A, Ireland Her Own.

a nursery for nothing else, but the whipping post, the plantations and the gallows'.[325] On the other hand, and indefatigably what can also be observed, is the rise of a Catholic mercantile class in Ireland's urban centres[326] and the extent to which a Catholic strong farming class emerged over the course of the latter part of the eighteenth century. In other words, the notorious poverty of much of the peasantry cannot be ascribed alone to the Penal Laws but to other less mentioned social and economic factors as well.

One thing about the Penal Laws is indisputable; they aimed to secure the unchallenged political, social, and economic supremacy of the Irish-Anglican Ascendancy and this may also explain why the Dissenters were the targets of penal legislation. In political terms, the Laws succeeded mostly in their goal of reshaping society to the power and control requirements of that Ascendancy.[327]

The Rise of a Catholic Middle Class

When the acts passed during the reign of Charles prohibited the export of live cattle, many in Ireland turned to the provision trade instead. Cork became the great centre of this export industry and in the other towns where it flourished, it was chiefly carried on by Catholics. Further legislation passed in England after the Williamite wars in 1699 – the *Woollen Act*, which prohibited the export of woollen goods to England and abroad, do not appear to have pressed unduly on Catholics. The manufacture of fine woollens which had been carried on largely by the Ascendancy class was all but destroyed.

---

[325] O'Brien, G., The Economic History of Ireland in the Eighteenth Century, Maunsell & Co, Dublin and London, (1918).

[326] Wall, M., The Rise of a Catholic Middle Class in Eighteenth Century Ireland, Irish Historical Studies, Vol XI, No. 42, (September 1958).

[327] Gillen, U., Ascendancy Ireland.

The Catholics still retained the biggest share of the *'not for export'* coarse woollen trade which they had been side-lined into and this was an important commodity for clothing an extensive home market. From the beginning of the eighteenth century the laws which prevented Catholics from buying land or from taking long leases drove many more Catholics to seeking a living in trade. So much so that the Anglican Archbishop King, writing in 1718, states: *'that the Papists, being made incapable to purchase lands, have turned themselves to trade, and already engrossed almost all the trade of the kingdom'*. A further reason why Catholics had opportunities in this field was that trade was held in considerable contempt in Britain as in Ireland in the eighteenth century. Samuel Madden, one of the founders of the Dublin Society in 1731, spoke of other countries where merchandising was considered honourable, *'whereas those in Ireland who make some money buy lands and turn country gentlemen'*. Though there were many attempts by the *'Protestant interest'* to prohibit Papist involvement in trade, the Irish parliament was not prepared to risk a collapse of the revenue generated, and the Catholic merchants of Cork and elsewhere continued to apply themselves to trade. Albeit, they were required under the navigation laws to use British ships and ports. On occasion this requirement was circumvented by the use of French or other shipping. It was unthinkable at the time that new taxes would be imposed on land in a parliament controlled almost entirely by landed gentlemen who could invest their revenues in England and had no interest in Irish trade or manufacturing. In another account, written in 1724, it was claimed that more than half the trade of the country was carried on by Catholics and that they *'pay more custom and duty than all the Protestants in it'*. Ireland's chief export during the eighteenth century, apart from linen, was provisions and although Limerick, Waterford, Dublin, Belfast, and Derry participated in it, Cork was the chief centre of the trade. Cork had become the second city of the country.

From 1717 on the Catholic merchants of Cork were beginning to take the offensive and the city became the chief centre of Catholic resistance to the demands of the guilds for *quarterage,* a heavy levy on Catholics, to become a quarter-share brother in order to participate in trade. This agitation spread to other cities and towns as the century progressed. The richest merchants in Limerick were the *Roches* and the *Arthurs,* both Catholic families. The *Roches* built an enormous warehouse on the quays and owned ships mounted with guns which they employed in the West Indies trade. Patrick Arthur built *Arthur's Quay* and a line of streets branching out from it. However, in the early part of the century Catholics were excluded under the popery laws from the main urban centres, and in many cases lived on the outskirts or in unfashionable parts of the city, notably as in Limerick and Galway. Neither did they belong to the guilds or city jamborees as they were prohibited from boroughs and Parliament. They could not buy land, there was little outward display of wealth, so they accumulated their wealth unostentatiously. Their opportunity for lavish living and spending opportunity were circumscribed and with the penal requirement of £5 for horses no Catholic was foolhardy enough to invest in horses or horse-racing.

Amongst other enterprising Catholic families in trade were the *Blakes* of Galway. Many younger sons of the Catholic gentry emigrated to various continental countries and the West Indies to pursue a life in trade, and in turn establish links in return with the home country. Michael Bellew of Galway, a wealthy Catholic landowner and miller, had a brother Patrick who was also a partner in the firm of *Lynch & Bellew* in Cadiz which carried on an extensive trade with Ireland. From the other perceived end of the social scale

Edward Byrne and *John Keogh* rose through the ranks from apprenticeships to merchants. Byrne died worth £400,000 and Keogh was regarded as the richest merchant in Ireland paying £80,000 annually to the revenue as a merchant distiller and sugar-baker. He retired in 1787 and acquired extensive landed interests in Sligo, Leitrim, and Roscommon and claimed to have 2,000 tenants on his estates in 1792.

It is considered that Belfast benefited in its prosperity from the trade connections it enjoyed with America through the hosts of Ulster dissenters (Presbyterians) who were subjected to the disabilities of the Test Act and driven over there by persecution and prohibitive legislation. Equally, the flow of Catholics from Ireland to the continent of Europe, to the armies (*the Abbe McGeoghegan estimated that 450,000 Irishmen fell in the service of France overall*), church, and trade correspondingly so. All of the foregoing activities, including the international links, contributed to the gradual rise of a wealthy Catholic middle class in Ireland.[328] Another area of activity which arose from Catholic inability to purchase land or spend their wealth was the involvement of Catholics in financial affairs. So much so that in 1763 a Bill was published to enable Catholics to provide lending facilities to Protestants on foot of securities. The Bill was defeated amidst anti-Catholic acrimony in the Irish parliament. (See: *A brief examination of the question whether it is expedient either in a religious or a political view to pass an act to enable papists to take real securities for money which they may lend, Dublin 1764.*)[329]

---

[328] Wall, M., The Rise of a Catholic Middle Class.

[329] Ellis, P.B., A History.

Mercantilism, Emigration, Famine, Debt, and Pension

Lists in the 18th Century

It is considered that English legislative interference with the Irish economy and trade in 1699 and after injured the Protestant Ascendancy far more, ironically, than the Catholic elite who had a lesser involvement in trade and commerce around this time. The different trades were in the hands of Protestants as Catholics were forbidden to have more than two apprentices though the provision trade was carried on by and large by Catholics. Although they profited accordingly, profits in the main went back to the great landowners who were the main suppliers. Additionally, the Navigation laws checked the development of Irish shipping. In 1698 Dublin had one ship, Belfast and Cork a few small ships, and there was no large ships held at all. In 1720 King George I by a Declaratory Act (later considered as the model for the *American Colonies Act of 1766)* affirmed the right of the British parliament to legislate for Ireland and transferred to the English House of Lords the powers of the Supreme Court in Ireland in appellate law. By 1723 Great Britain possessed about two-thirds of the carrying trade while by 1772 she monopolised seven-eighths of it. Restraints were laid on every industry which might possibly compete with British industry and Irish raw materials were sourced exclusively to the benefit of England manufacturers by the prohibition of their export to anywhere else, other than with the single exception of linen manufacture.

The cotton industry was monopolised and centred in Manchester and Irish manufacturers were again prohibited either to start a foreign export trade in cotton, or develop a home manufacture. A more severe policy was pursued in relation to the glass industry. Several glass houses were set up by English colonists in Ireland but the sand necessary had to be imported from England. Irish glass manufacturers were undersold in their own markets by English traders while a prohibition was put on the export trade. Another target of British commerce was the brewing industry. The British exported large quantities of beer to Ireland on payment of the usual duty of 10 per cent, while they prevented the Irish from exporting their beer to Great Britain, by means of a duty equal to a prohibition. A British Act also prohibited the import of hops into Ireland except from Great Britain, and Irish merchants had to pay much more than had previously when they were able to import from other countries. For the benefit of the British sugar colonies, Ireland was forbidden to import sugar or molasses from the colonies of other powers, and two and a half per cent fee was charged by English agents on sugar sent from English plantations which had to be then unloaded and shipped from English ports. The importation of rock salt for preservation was restricted which was disadvantageous to the Irish fishing industry and a further Act was passed prohibiting the export of sail-cloth. Only one industry, other than linen, was encouraged in any way and that was certain processes in iron manufacture. This proved disastrous in other ways as it led to the wasteful consumption of timber for smelting purposes until such time as there was insufficient timber available for use. In an earlier period forests had been cleared for naval, building, and military reasons but the depletion for smelting, and the fact that Irish timber could be exported to Britain with scarcely any duty, completed the destruction of the forests of Ireland.

Overall, this commercial policy led to an ongoing diminution in revenue which largely came from customs and excise. Revenue fell from over £500,000 in 1700 to £342,222, five years later and by 1715 still only amounted to this sum. Not until 1725 did it reach a revenue over the 1700s figure. The restraints placed on trade and industry were one of the chief causes that led to the large emigration of Protestants (Presbyterians) from the north of Ireland to North America and the West Indies. Protestant artisans and merchants found their foreign trade either denied them altogether or rendered unprofitable by English legislation while the poverty of the country prevented the development of a market for home goods. Those that settled in North America, the majority of them Presbyterian, settled in Maryland, Virginia, and North Carolina. It is considered that the Presbyterians that settled in the New England states as well as in the southern colonies proved to be critical participants in the American struggle for independence. At the same time those that remained in Ireland played a major part in the later struggle with England for free trade, a free parliament, and the formation of and recruitment into the United Irishmen.

Social Change

The well-to-do Catholic traders formed a small portion overall of the total Catholic population; below them were a mass of Irish peasants stricken by poverty and reliant on the potato as the staple of their diet. English commercial policy did not injure directly the poorer classes to the same extent as they didn't have wealth, but by checking industrial development it injured them indirectly by compelling them to remain entirely on the land, resulting in more and more sub-division for subsistence while closing off any other means of access to work and income. Famines in 1729 and 1740, caused by weather conditions and the absence of granaries, in which over 400,000 of the population were believed to have died also forced many of the poor, both Protestant and Catholic, to emigrate. Protestants in the main to America and Catholics to France and Spain. A contemporary pamphlet published in 1741 asserted, '*the universal scarcity was followed by fluxed and malignant fevers, which swept off multitudes of all sorts, so that whole villages of all sorts were laid to waste*'.[330] There were food riots, many of them localised, which didn't last very long. The rioters broke into '*bakers and meal men's shops*' and stopped boats loaded with goods for export in Dublin. During 1740-1741 food riots ensued in Galway, Youghal, and Munster in general, including Limerick, Waterford, and Carrick-on-Suir. Tenants also moved away from growing oats and barley as cash crops and instead potato cultivation intensified as it was the staple food source. The rural poor relied more and more on this subsistence crop and supplemented their income by selling cow and pig products for cash.[331]

Economic depression arising from prohibitions in the wool and silk industries forced many skilled weavers and artisans to emigrate in search of work. It is estimated that in the first fifty years of the 18th century 200,000 immigrated to the British colonies alone.

The other class in Ireland who were comparatively prosperous were the great graziers. This wealth had arisen from the conversion of large tracts of pasture farms into grazing land while a small middle class in the towns engaged in trade.[332] Rents remitted to absentee landlords rose from £100,000, about one-quarter to a sixth of all rents in 1698 to in excess of £300,000 by the 1720s. It was feared that in the effort to pay absentee rents the whole money supply in the country would be exported.[333] It was the general view that rank political corruption ran through the whole system of government during the Walpole (1721-1742) period. The sale of places and

---

[330] Connolly, J., Labour in Irish History.

[331] McDermott, C.B., An Ghaoth a Chriofidh an Eorna, The Moral Economy of Ireland's Whiteboys, 1761-1787 Bard, (Spring 2017).

[332] Murray, A.E., A History.

[333] Cullen, L.M., An Economic History of Ireland.

commissions was a public scandal and Parliament was managed by borough mongers, some of whom commanded an immense number of votes. This corruption was also reflected in the Government of Ireland but more so because *'none but Englishmen sent over for the purpose'* were allowed to have any effective voice in government. During the rule of Primates Boulter and Stone from 1723-64 the English Ascendancy all told were established in offices, whether secular or religious, so much so that even the infamous* Viscount Castlereagh was considered disqualified as he was born in Ireland: however, Cornwallis contended that an exception might be made for him because he was *'so very unlike an Irishman'.*[334]

It is when the roles played by the Ascendancy, penal legislation, and English commercial and financial policy are combined that we get a clearer picture of the forces preventing the development of Irish society and the economy in the first three-quarters of the 18th century. The absence of industrial development, related alternative work opportunities, the consignment to sub-division, and subsistence farming of the great mass of the population and reliance on the potato, had the effect of a double economic penalty in both the internal and external economy and was the background for the remaining decades of the eighteenth century.

---

[334] Hull, E, A History.

*Castlereagh did become Acting Chief Secretary for Ireland and was considered largely responsible for suppressing the 1798 Rebellion and forcing through the Act of Union in 1801, when £1 million and a half in bribes and many other 'persuasions' were dispensed to ensure its passage. Later, as Foreign Secretary, he was centrally involved in the Treaty of Chaumont and the Congress of Vienna ending the Napoleonic wars. As Leader of the Tories in the House of Commons, he was considered one of those responsible, along with other members of Lord Liverpool's cabinet, *'the Seven bloodhounds'*, for the events leading to the *Peterloo Massacre* in 1819. In Shelley's poem, *The Masque of Anarchy*, his role inspired the lines; *'I met Murder on the way, He had a mask like Castlereagh.'* Also the immortal lines, *'Ye are many—they are few'*. Castlereagh took his own life in 1822.

CHAPTER EIGHTEEN

18TH CENTURY – DECADES OF CHANGE: IRELAND

There were additional burdens placed on the country with the cost of the local army, which kept in power and control and maintained security, for the ascendancy regime. Alongside this was prolonged involvement in the long series of English wars, including the Spanish Succession for which a large sum of money had to be borrowed. Another £50,000 was borrowed towards crushing the Jacobite rebellion in Scotland in 1715 and this went on increasing until by 1731 the overall debt stood at £330,000. After the Seven Years' War in 1763 the Irish debt amounted to £520,000, the largest ever contracted in the country. Despite the succeeding years of peace, by 1773 it had reached £1,757,000 including funded and annuity debt. The duplicitous claims by Britain that it alone maintained the Empire ignored the underlying cost for Ireland of maintaining a military establishment in constant readiness to help England in her wars. All this was apart from funding the enormous pensions list of the King's favourites, funding for which he was unable to get support in the English parliament. This was also at a time when practically all remunerative offices in the Irish Government, Church, and Army were kept in the hands of Englishmen who hardly ever set foot in the country. All these factors acted as a huge cost on the Irish exchequer. In 1759 during the struggle between England and France in North

America, Ireland raised six new regiments and a troop of horse and a specific note of credit of £150,000 was given by Parliament. A little later a second vote of £300,000 was given and the interest on Government stock was raised by 1%. In little more than a year there was paid out of the treasury for military purposes more than £703,957. As a result three large banks in the country stopped payment and the remaining three did practically no business, paper stopped circulating and no bank would discount even first-class bills.

In 1761, after the conflict with Spain, and for the next two years, Ireland kept in pay an army of 24,000 men, 8,000 of whom were sent to fight abroad and 16,000 remained at home for defence. Ireland sent 33,000 recruits to fill up gaps which had been made in British regiments while over £600,000 was spent in Germany for the support of the war. From 1725 to 1759 the pension list steadily increased. In 1751 the Countess of Yarmouth was given £4,000 on the Irish establishment which continued for twenty years. In the same year a pension of £5,000 for life was given to the Princess of Hesse. Many large pensions were given to the King's favourites of German origin; Ferdinand Duke of Brunswick was given one of £4,000, afterwards increased to £6,700. In 1774 Caroline Matilda, Queen of Denmark, received a yearly pension of £3,000 during the King's pleasure, that is before she was banished from England. Despite protests the pension list increased further and from 1759 to the Act of union it had reached almost £100,000 per annum. The pension list increased far more rapidly than it had in the preceding half-century. From 1757 to 1777 the civil list nearly doubled, the pension list nearly doubled and the national debt increased to over £1,000,000. While a tax was imposed on absentee landlords, many of the members in the House of Commons disliked the tax as they feared it would lead to a depreciation in land value, however those appeals did not succeed in all of the circumstances.

Ultimately, it was to became a situation where the Protestant gentry could not find profitable employments for themselves or their sons, the recurring civil lists, seeing their taxes being squandered on the King's favourites (many of whom they considered disreputable) on the pension list, the burden of the military, the restrictions on trade, the combined collection of grievances began to foster a new 'national' spirit. The Protestant gentry found themselves as alienated from England as their elite Catholic fellow-subjects. This dissent had been given expression originally by Molyneaux[335] and was taken up later by Swift in his *Drapier* letters on the Woods coin scandal and his Modest Proposals (1724-29). Swift also observed with foresight, *'the Catholics were always defenders of the monarchy, as constituted in these kingdoms, whereas our brethren the Dissenters were always Republican both in principle and practice'.*[336] The 'national' spirit was continued by Lucas in his *Citizens Journal* from 1741 and created a new spirit of patriotism while at the same time he was supportive of the ascendancy elite. The *Citizens Journal* played a major part in leading Catholic elite opinion as well as Protestant opinion. It also started to form a public opinion outside Parliament which eventually made itself felt as a force inside Parliament. In the last quarter of the eighteenth century, for the first time, there appeared a disinclination on the part of alienated Protestants to enforce the Penal Laws. There were also those in the Protestant community who believed the Penal Laws, by inadvertently supporting adherence to superstition and general ignorance, were actually hindering the work of the enlightenment. That said, the Penal Laws were increasingly difficult to justify as the decades wore on as

---

[335] William Molyneaux, *The Case of Ireland's Being Bound by Acts of Parliament in England stated*, 1698. (The English parliament decided that a copy should be burnt by the common hangman).

[336] Swift, J, *Reasons for Repealing the Sacramental Test*.

there had been no *'rebellion'* for a lengthy period and even the threat of rebellion had declined.[337] Slowly a *'patriotic'* parliament was growing and from 1775 Henry Grattan took the leadership of a bourgeoisie driven by a fight for free trade and a free parliament. In essence, a desire for the repeal of the commercial restrictions on free trade with foreign countries and the colonies. The Catholic elite threw in their lot and in 1779 England was confronted for the first time by this bourgeois unity of purpose. The American War of Independence had created in Irish minds the belief that the power of England could be successfully challenged as had been the case in that conflict.[338] Additionally; *'the progress of American doctrines'* excited popular discontent and the raising of the Volunteers enhanced popular hopes not only of redress of constitutional grievances and also the lowering of rents was a matter of interest to the broader mass of the population. The emergence of a Patriot party in the Irish parliament was later considered a fatal break in the ranks of the governing class and a significant political development.[339]

Peasant Rebellions

In 1761 plague in England and the continent destroyed great quantities of cattle and the Government, fearful that the ensuing increases in the price of meat would lead to a demand for higher wages on behalf of the working class, removed the embargo from Irish cattle, meat, butter, and cheese at English ports, partly establishing free trade in these items between the two countries. The

---

[337] Bartlett, T, The Catholic Question in the Eighteenth Century.

[338] Murray, A, E, History of Commercial Relations.

[339] Miller, D, W, Armagh Troubles, Irish Peasants, Violence and Political Unrest, 1780-1914, eds. Clarke &Donnelly, Manchester University Press, (1983).

immediate result was that all such provisions brought a high price in England and tillage farming in Ireland became unprofitable by comparison. As a result every effort was made to transform arable land into sheep-walks or grazing land. The landlord class commenced evicting their tenants; breaking up small farms and even seizing upon village common lands and pasture grounds all over the country with disastrous results for the labouring people and cottiers generally. In reaction and almost immediately, there sprung up secret societies into which the dispossessed piled and set about reacting to these dispossessions. They met in large bodies, generally at midnight, and proceeded to tear down enclosures; to hough cattle; to dig up and render useless the pasture lands; and to burn the houses of shepherds. In short, to terrorise the landlord owners responsible and cause them to abandon the policy of grazing in favour of tillage so as to restore employment to the labourers and provide more security to the cottiers. Later, grievances in relation to rent and tithes were added to the demands. These secret organisations assumed different names and frequently adopted different methods. They commenced in County Tipperary and were at first called *Levellers* as they levelled ditches erected by landlords around common lands. Later they were called *Whiteboys* from their practice of wearing white shirts over their clothes when on their night-time exploits and so as to recognise one another. Their proclamations were signed by an imaginary female *Sadbh Oultagh (ghostly)* and other times they were in the name of *Queen Sadbh*.

Government responded to the rebellion without mercy with hangings, shootings, and transportations, raiding villages at dead of night and dragging suspects before magistrates. The magistrates responded with the vindictiveness of their privileged position and sentenced those they considered outside the law with no regard to evidence or hearings, nor were they obliged to by the legislation enacted. In the year 1762 the Government offered the sum of £100 for the capture of the first five *Whiteboy* chiefs. The Protestant inhabitants of the City of Cork offered in addition the sum of £300 for the chief and £50 for each of the first five of his accomplices arrested. Immediately, the wealthy Catholics of the same city added to the above sums a promise of £200 for the chief and £40 for each of his first five subordinates. This at a time when a former Lord-Lieutenant, Lord Chesterfield (1745-1746), declared that if the military had killed half as many landlords as they did *Whiteboys* they would have contributed more effectively to restoring the peace. Harry Flood, later hailed as the great Protestant 'patriot' in the Irish House of Commons, fiercely denounced the Government in 1763 for not killing enough of the *Whiteboys,* he called it *'clemency'.*[340] From 1761 to 1778 the landlords and the authorities waged perpetual war against the *Whiteboys* and Acts such as the 1763 Riot Act (passed originally in 1715 by the British parliament) and the Proclamation in 1764 along with a *Whiteboy Act* were passed imposing penalties including transportation and death for taking or administering the *Whiteboy* oath. The *Oakboys* appeared in Monaghan in 1762 and spread from there into Tyrone, Fermanagh, and Armagh as a reaction against the exaction of forced labour for the repair and upkeep of roads. This was followed subsequently by protests against tithes and cess tax. Catholics, Presbyterian, and some Anglican-Protestants joined in this movement which was suppressed but only after a bloody battle with the military in Armagh in which they were defeated. However, they won their point, thereafter a money-rate was levied instead of forced labour.

The *Steelboys* were Protestants of Antrim and Down who put up a mass resistance in 1769 to fines for the renewal of tenancies, to rack-

---

[340] Connolly, J, Labour in Irish History.

rents, to tithes and attempts to introduce grass-farming. They were strong enough to march into Belfast, break open the gaol, and liberate some of their number who had been captured. Juries in Belfast failed to convict *Steelboys* and when the trial was shifted to Dublin juries there also refused to convict. In the end, however, the landlords were strong enough to force most of them to immigrate to America. Many of them turned up later as combatants in and supporters in the American War of Independence.[341]

Subsequently, the Catholic Defenders and United Irishmen built on the traditions of the agrarian popular protest movements like the *Whiteboys* and *Steelboys*.[342] These organisations gave added force to the opposition waged in Parliament against the landed oligarchy.

Combinations of Workers (Trade Unions)

England is often considered the birthplace of trade unionism, yet the records of the Irish parliament show there were combinations of workmen in early eighteenth century Dublin and the oldest existing trade union document is the 1788 minutes-book of the Belfast Cabinet-Makers Club. The first of Ireland's anti-combination laws was passed by the Irish parliament in 1729 but was largely ignored both by employers and workers. The former continued to pay wages as they wished and the latter continued to form combinations, raise funds for the benefit of their members, and control the intake of apprentices.

In 1743 a further Act was passed where assemblies of three or more for the purposes of making by-laws respecting journeymen or apprentices were prohibited. Also prohibited was the collecting of

---

324 ibid
[342] Gillen, U, Ascendancy Ireland.

money for the support of unemployed journeymen or for any other purpose. Owners of inns and taverns used for trade union meetings could be treated like *'those who kept common bawdy houses'* and fined £20 for each offence.

In 1749 several hundreds of journeymen broadweavers in Dublin petitioned Parliament, but to no effect that *'the want of settled prices for their labour was causing them great discouragement and distress'*. Despite the hostility of Parliament which consisted mainly of large landowners or their nominees, trade union activity was increasing, especially in the main cities like Dublin, Belfast, and Cork. In August 1752 three journeymen woolcombers were brought before the magistrates for *'riotously assembling with several others and unlawfully forcing away from their work such as would not come into their illegal combinations'*. The three journeymen were sent to Newgate prison in Dublin and kept there for nearly 12 months followed by fines and further imprisonment. In 1757 Parliament imposed further penalties on workmen who formed trade unions and laid down terms of imprisonment for attempted recruitment or wage-setting. In the early 1760s the first Irish trade union to be identified by name appears in the records, the Regular Carpenters of Dublin.

Further penalties were imposed in 1763, and provided that anyone *'attempting to fix the price of labour, either by calling a meeting, making rules, or preventing others from working, should, on conviction, be sent to prison for six months and thrice whipped'*. The act contained 97 clauses, notwithstanding not one offered any benefit to workmen.[343]

In January 1770 two weavers were found guilty of forming a trade union, and were whipped through the streets from Newgate Prison to College Green. The whipping was done by the public hangman,

---

[343] Boyd, A, The Rise of the Irish Trade Unions, 1729-1970, Anvil Books, Dublin, (1976).

while the High Sheriff of Dublin walked alongside to make sure the punishment was fully carried out. In Cork, after considering a petition from employers, Parliament declared that anyone in the City of Cork who was found guilty of being a member of an unlawful trade union should be *'imprisoned not above six months, whipped in public, and only released on giving recognisance of good behaviour for seven years'*. In 1769 the Lord Mayor of Dublin received what he considered an alarming memorandum from the City's Common Council largely influenced by the Guilds, stating, 'an *outrageous mob have of late entered into unlawful combinations, particularly the weavers, bakers, and coopers of this city; they have quit the work of their respective employers for the purpose of advancing their wages, and have committed many acts of violence.'* [344]

In 1774 about one-third of all weavers in the country were unemployed. 10,000 had immigrated to America and, by 1779, the Sheriffs of Dublin informed the Lord Lieutenant there were 19,000 weavers in starvation in the city.

As the industrial revolution proceeded and machinery increasingly replaced skilled labour, handloom weavers and other crafts were driven into poverty. The employer's response to resistance to the introduction of machinery was to seek the suppression of trade unions using the full rigours of the law. With the passing of the Free Trade legislation in 1779, employers argued that Ireland's industries could only enjoy full advantage on the basis that workmen were restrained in their demands for higher wages, compelled to accept the new means of production (already underway) and persuaded to adopt more conciliatory attitudes towards their employers.

In response, in June 1780, a Bill was passed by the *'Patriot'* parliament suppressing combinations/trade unions and for the encouragement of trade. It received Royal assent in August 1780. Just

---

[344] ibid

one favourable amendment towards the journeymen tabled by Hely Hutchinson was permitted.[345] This legislation more than contradicted those who argued that Parliament alone would provide for the interests of working people.

(The Irish legislation was twenty years ahead of the Combinations Act of 1799 in Great Britain passed during the French wars which outlawed combinations/trade unions and was tabled by William Wilberforce, the British Empire black slave emancipator, who ironically was virulently anti-trade union and called it the greatest disease in the land).

For the next twenty-five years[346] the magistrates in all parts of Britain and Ireland did their utmost with fines, floggings, and imprisonment to destroy the nascent trade unions.

In June 1780, when the debate on the *Act to Prevent Combinations and for the Further Encouragement of Trade* opened, 20,000 trade unionists with their families and supporters assembled in the Phoenix Park and marched through the city to hand in their protest petitions at College Green. Apart from Hely Hutchinson, the member for Trinity College, no one else from Parliament turned out to meet them. Instead, the Dublin Corps of Volunteers were turned out at the request of the magistrates to maintain law and order and during the year 1780 three corps of the Volunteers in Dublin passed resolutions condemning the combinations/unions.

The middle classes were hostile, the landlords antagonistic, and the newspapers printed long columns of anti-trade union comment. The church, never far behind in these debates, in the person of Robert

---

[345] O'Connell, M, R, Irish Politics and Social Conflict in the Age of the American Revolution, University of Pennsylvania Press, (1965).

[346] In 1803, heavier penalties for combination offences were introduced in Ireland than were imposed in England. These Acts were repealed in 1824, but further Conspiracy legislation was introduced in 1825 which had largely the same prohibitive effect. It was not until 1871 that unions received some legal recognition.

Law, Rector of St. Marys Church in Dublin, argued that nothing should impede the freedom of trade which the Irish parliament had won from England. He described *'combinations of journeymen and working mechanics'* as *'the greatest of all possible evils'* and their only purpose was *'to exact higher wages for labour-iniquitous extortions'*.

The views of the Catholic Archbishop of Dublin, Dr Troy, who vehemently opposed oaths and combinations, are well documented. He abhorred the republicanism of the American revolutionists and condemned them for their disloyalty while equally opposing the French Revolution for their radical views. Troy also condemned and refused the sacraments to Catholics who joined the Defenders. (He also condemned and opposed the 1798 Rebellion and went on to actively support the Act of Union).

The upper and middle classes concluded that the prevention of trade unionism was in the best interest of working people. For the evangelicals it was justified by their belief that it led to drunkenness and idleness, a belief often fuelled by the fact that members met in pubs, even though as combinations were illegal there was nothing unusual about pubs as a meeting place. For others it was a matter of supposed equity, equity meaning that the price for labour would be set *laissez faire* style by embracing the *invisible hand* of the market, and the entrepreneurial vison and individual self-interest promoted by Adam Smith.[347] This was of course to the detriment of the greater collective interest and bargaining possibilities.[348]

During the 1790s Belfast also went through a period when the trades were every bit as active. On numerous occasions during the decade the carpenters, shoemakers, bricklayers, coopers, linen-

---

[347] Smith, Adam, The Wealth of Nations, (1776).
[348] Boyd, A, The Rise of the Irish Trade Unions, 1729-1970, Anvil Books, Dublin, (1976).

weavers, cotton-weavers, as well as workers in other trades, issued demands for higher wages and suffered the full rigours of the repressive legislation in return.

By the mid-1790s labour struggles had become so widespread that Judge William Downes, addressing the Dublin Grand Jury in 1795, denounced trade unionism as follows:

'... *these combinations, notwithstanding the repeated efforts of Parliament to suppress them, have increased in the most alarming manner and, at this moment, some important branches of industry are almost destroyed by them'*.

Others observed that the decline of many Irish industries were not caused by combinations but rather caused by restrictions imposed after the Act of Union (1801) and that the increasingly defensive activities of Irish trade unions were most likely the result of, and not the cause of, any industrial decline.[349]

---

[349] ibid

CHAPTER NINETEEN

18TH CENTURY – DECADES OF CHANGE: INTERNATIONAL COLONIAL WARS OF EXPLOITATION AND EMPIRE

French and British possessions lay alongside each other in three main areas of European expansion outside of South America, which remained in Spanish control. These were India, North America, and the West Indies where isolated French possessions could be easily seized. The only Scottish attempt at colonisation ended in disaster in the late 1690s at Darien in Panama and this failure encouraged Scotland to unite with England through the 1707 Acts of Union which also stipulated that the Darien investors would be reimbursed. This union in turn opened up new commercial opportunities for the Scots and especially for the Glasgow investors.[350] The Scottish union was in contrast to the continuing colonial approach to Ireland with its restrictive and protectionist controls and, despite the best efforts of the Irish House of Commons of the time, for a more formal union. The Irish, although considered royal subjects, were treated differently to other subjects of the kingdom when it came to commercial, financial, and other matters.

The main seats of war were India and North America. The East India Company which had grown steadily had a capital of £3,000,000

---

[350] Barry, Melissa, University of Paris, History of the British Empire, (2017).

and paid a dividend of seven per cent to shareholders. This represented only a small part of the profits taken from India. It was the practice of the Company to pay its servants a nominal wage: their real wage and in the higher grades known as *'nabobs'* vast incomes were derived from bribes, extortion, and private trade. Even the Directors of the Company, who had set up the system, were forced to admit that the vast fortunes acquired in the inland trade had been obtained by a series of the most tyrannical and oppressive conduct that was ever known in any country. By the time the French arrived with their armed forces the English company had set up its own private army and war over the rich spoils became the order of the day. Since the French main depot Pondicherry was close to Madras and a second Chandernagore close to Calcutta, a clash was inevitable. At the same time the Mogul Empire was breaking up and its local officials were establishing themselves as independent rulers.

The superiority of the weapons possessed by the French and English made it possible for them to intervene in the local wars of native rulers and both began to play at king-making by setting up puppet princes whom they could control. The victory at the Plassey in 1757 marked the beginning of British Imperial power later known as the Raj, and was followed by the conquest of the rich province of Bengal. The French controlled Pondicherry was captured in 1760. Plassey was preceded by the incident that gave rise to the infamous tale of the *'Black Hole of Calcutta'*. The *'Black Hole'* was the ordinary prison of the East India Company and a number of English imprisoned there because of a dispute between the *Nawab* of Bengal and the Company died owing to the prison being overcrowded in the hot season.

Hostilities with the French ended in 1763 with the Treaty of Paris. From this time on there were no limits to the exploitation possible. From Bengal alone the Company extorted over £6 million in bribes between 1757 and 1766. In 1769-70 the English created a famine over wide areas by cornering rice production and refusing to sell it except at exorbitant prices. The vaunted Clive of India amassed a vast fortune by taking bribes and *'presents'* from native rulers. In 1767 the British Government insisted on taking a direct share of the plunder, and the Company was forced to pay £400,000 a year to the exchequer. The Regulation Act of 1773 took the further step of securing to the Government partial control over the administration of the conquered provinces. When the Treaty of Paris in 1763 ended the Seven Years' War following the defeat of the French, England kept her Indian conquests, Canada, Senegal, and some but not all of the West Indian islands. The British also acquired Florida from Spain in exchange for Havana and Manila. Havana was returned later after the American Revolution.

American Revolution

The Seven Years' War left England with a vast National Debt and a burden of heavy taxation. The bulk of new taxation was placed on articles of general consumption. The Government, on the pretext that the war had been fought for the benefit of the colonies, even though the colonists had paid significantly towards the costs, decided to impose taxes on the colonies to cover part of the cost of the Army and Navy still kept in America. Grenville's Stamp Act of 1765 evoked immediate protests and was repealed in the following year although the right of the English parliament to tax the colonies was insisted on. The colonists who had representative bodies of their own raised the slogan *'no taxation without representation'*. With the fall of Quebec and the French threat gone, the colonists resented paying for an army and navy, which was now being used to curtail their very lucrative smuggling trade being used to circumvent the trade prohibitions. It was the Stamp Act issue ostensibly which gave rise to the revolution. There were, however, other issues which went deeper and were embodied in the Navigation Acts.

The economic organisation of the empire in the eighteenth century and the mercantile theories on which it was based were contained in the Navigation Acts, which had as their object the utilisation of the trade and wealth of the colonies for the exclusive benefit of the English ruling class. England's legal, commercial, and financial policy towards the Irish economy is instructive in this regard as many of the prohibitive Acts used in America replicated English colonial policy towards Ireland. The most valuable products of the colonies, the tobacco of Virginia, the rice of the Carolinas, the tar and timber of New England (priceless materials for naval construction), and the sugar of the West Indies could only be exported to England or Scotland. Equally, the colonies were forbidden to import manufactured goods from any foreign country and the development of colonial industry was checked where it might endanger an established home industry. Additionally, in the case of New England the manufacture of iron and steel goods was prohibited and the raw iron had to be shipped across the Atlantic to England. From there the Americans had to re-import the manufactured iron goods for their own use.

Just as at a previous opportune time for the English bourgeoisie in their history, the American bourgeoisie now took to the stage. They also had their upper-class leadership and its lower-middle-class rank and file. The colonial war itself would be fought mainly by the small farmers, traders, and artisans but its benefits went to the merchants and planters of whom Washington[351] was a typical representative.[352] So as far as America itself was concerned the Stamp Act was the beginning of a ten year conflict which culminated in a ban on English goods in 1775, an attempt to secure their importation by force through the *'Boston Tea Party'* followed by the outbreak of the War. The eventual surrender of Cornwallis, British Commander at Yorktown in 1781, was followed by American independence in 1783. France, Spain, and later Holland having entered as protagonists into the war on the colonist's side.

The Native Americans were significant losers from the conflict brought about in the main by their support for the British during the war. At the Peace of Paris in April 1783 the Native Americans weren't mentioned. Britain recognised the independence of the United States and transferred its claim to all the territories between the Atlantic and the Mississippi, the Great Lakes, and Ontario.

Jefferson, in the aftermath of the war, placed the Native Americans on the wrong side of the struggle for liberty and hence the wrong side of history. For the Native Americans who fought on the British side, the American settlers posed a greater threat than did a faraway king. The American war of independence was ironically a war of independence for them also. Ultimately, their fate can be best described in the words attributed to Red Cloud, a Chief from the Oglala Lakota, in the following century, *'They made us many promises, more than I can remember, but they kept but one; they promised to take our land, and they took it'.*[353]

The victory of the American Revolution was a blow to the whole corrupt, borough-mongering, oligarchic system of eighteenth-century

---

[351] Described by Wolfe Tone *'as a high-flying aristocrat'*.
[352] Morton, A, L, A Peoples History.
[353] Brown, D, Bury My Heart at Wounded Knee, Open Road, New York, (2000).

Britain and was followed by an immediate reaction at home. Corruption, however, had become too powerful a vested interest for change to be possible. The existing balance of class forces was preserved and within a few years the outbreak of the French Revolution had transformed most of the critics into defenders of the British *'constitution'* as a God-given and perfect masterpiece.

West Indies

The continuous increase in colonial wealth and trade provided a constantly rising market for British goods for which the hand-made small scale of production was inadequate. The West Indies were the most profitable of British possessions. In 1790 it was calculated that £70 million was invested there as against £18 million in the Far East and their trade with England was almost double that of the East India Company. The wars of the age created the need for regular uniforms which required hundreds of yards of cloth, boots and buttons, muskets, bullets and bayonets all standardised. These armies needed not only to be clothed and armed but also just as importantly to be fed. This supply chain provided golden opportunities for all those who had the capital and credit to take up army contracts and the floating of loans and subsidies to allied powers were equally profitable. There was the resultant interdependence of the landed aristocracy, the bankers and merchants, and in every generation city magnates acquired titles and bought landed estates. In the process they became indistinguishable from the existing incumbents, descendants of the robber barons, or victors of the sixteenth and seventeenth centuries wars respectively. At the same time the landowners began to invest their profits in industry and commerce while the younger sons often went into trade. The *'class of yeoman'* were also to fall victim to the establishment of agriculture on a capitalist basis. The revolution in agriculture had three results. First, it increased the productivity of the land and so made possible the feeding of the great industrial populations of the new towns. Second, it created a reserve army of wage-earners, disconnected from the land without ties of place or property, so the coming together of labour and accumulated capital combined with the large-scale production now possible was the essential composition of agricultural capitalism. Thirdly, there was the creation of a vast internal market for manufactured goods. These were the general conditions which brought England to the Industrial Revolution. The central period of the Industrial Revolution – 1793-1815 – was occupied by European Wars on a scale never before known. Britain entered these wars as an agricultural country and emerged from them as an industrial one.

French Revolution

The series of events in France under different circumstances had quite different outcomes. The *'victory'* in America was at huge financial cost and no real financial benefit. Without the benefit of colonial wealth, she was stripped one by one of her colonies and the State became top-heavy and perpetually on the verge of bankruptcy. The French bourgeoisie benefited though not to the same extent as their English rivals following the opening of the world to European exploitation. The result in France was a rising and ambitious capitalist class face to face with a discredited and bankrupt autocracy. Below the French bourgeoisie were the overtaxed, exploited peasantry and artisans who saw as their main oppressors the aristocratic supporters of the monarchy. The same chain of events, although differing in incidents and operation, produced both the French Revolution and the Industrial Revolution in England and with them produced the modern world.[354] In the year following the ratification of the U.S. Constitution, the people of Paris in July 1789 stormed the Bastille, defeated a military coup, and unleashed the French Revolution.[355] The Women's March on Versailles in October of the same year is considered the defining moment of this phase of the Revolution. They besieged the Palace and forced King Louis XVI, his family, and most of the French Assembly who were ensconced there to return to Paris as virtual prisoners. In the process they changed the balance of power and ended the privilege and power of the *ancien regime*.

---

[354] Morton, A., L., A People's History.
[355] Faulkner, N., A Marxist History.

CHAPTER TWENTY

IRISH PARLIAMENTARY INDEPENDENCE

Parliament had become an essential institution and government had to learn how to manage it, that is ensure a majority on important questions, particularly the money bill. For much of the century the task was devoted to *'undertakers'*, powerful figures like Conolly, Clare, and Beresford who delivered large numbers of votes in the Irish Commons for a share of government patronage.[356] From 1769 the poverty of Ireland had been increasing, the revenue had been declining, and the country had been getting into even more debt. In 1770 there was so much commercial difficulty being experienced, due to an embargo issued by the English Privy Council on the export of provisions, that the Lord Lieutenant sought a 'certain' amount of relief for Irish trade to get over these difficulties.

The American non-importation agreement of 1775, followed by the war, closed the chief market for Irish linens. The embargoes laid by England on Irish ports led to a stoppage of the provision trade. The financial consequences of the commercial impositions were soon apparent insofar as, in 1778, the Irish Government was nearly bankrupt and new troops were required to be raised, which in some way had to be funded out of the Irish revenue. Eventually, in June the Bank of England agreed to an advance of 50,000 guineas for six months on the security of debentures for the Government loan in

---

[356] Gillen, U., Protestant Ascendancy.

Ireland. In February of 1778 Henry Grattan placed his first motion in the Irish House of Commons for an address to the King on the state of the nation. He stated at length the financial situation and as to how, during the past twenty years, the whole charge of the civil list and also the pension list had nearly doubled. He complained of the number of additional salaries in the nature of pensions annexed to lesser offices, mostly sinecures, and the growing practice of annexing large salaries to obsolete offices. This motion was lost in favour of Government by 143 to 66 votes.[357]

The matters concerned were also taken up in the British Parliament by the opposition and they agreed to go into Committee to examine matters further. A number of limited proposals for relief emerged but no sooner were these read in the British House than storms of indignation arose all over the country and petitions flowed in from all the large manufacturing towns in England and Scotland. The Merchant Adventurers of Bristol petitioned against all the resolutions without exception, as did the merchants of Glasgow. It was insisted over and over again if the proposed relief was given to Irish trade, English workmen would be thrown out of employment, and the capital of English manufacturers would be useless as Irish goods would be undersold everywhere due to the low cost of labour and living. The fears of the British manufacturing classes were too much for the British Parliament. This rejection created great resentment in Ireland and from this time on the agitation for free trade took on a more '*physical*' form.

The Irish Protestants now realised that the matter lay with them and decided to take advantage of Britain's difficulties and press energetically for relief at a time when it would be dangerous for England to refuse it. The distress was particularly acute in Dublin and

---

[357] Murray, A., E., A History.

they pointed to the unemployment of many thousands of artisans. They suggested that the people of Ireland should be encouraged to consume only their own manufactures and as the American war proceeded Ireland had been stripped of troops.

The Irish Volunteers

Early in 1779 volunteer corps began to be formed all over Ireland. In April 1778 a Bill was passed to establish an Irish militia[358] as the condition of the northern counties appeared dangerous to Government but want of funds prevented the Bill from being carried into effect. In May 1779 the numbers of volunteers were 8,000 but by the end of the year they numbered 40,000. They were all loyal to the Crown at this time and declared themselves prepared to share their last drop of blood in defence of their king and country. Though loyal, and having taken on the arms provided for the non-existent militia, they were determined to obtain free trade and these 40,000 were now a force to be reckoned with. Side by side with the formation of these volunteers, another kind of volunteer association had been establishing itself; these were the non-importation leagues.

Women in Dublin, mostly wives of merchants and manufacturers, were determined to support these leagues and twelve of them began a movement by forming an association for the encouragement of the manufacturers of Ireland. The association spread amongst similar

---

[358] Ireland rarely had a militia during the eighteenth century until 1793, and for a good deal of the reign of George II, England was at peace with the chief *'popish princes'* in France and Spain. A petition from the Roman Catholics of County Kerry wrote to Parliament on the 20th June 1710 complaining of the heavy taxes they were under from the *'frequent ravages and depredations of the privateers'*. This was received sympathetically and the Lord Lieutenant was requested to put a barracks in Valentia. Catholics at the time were required to reimburse the costs for any robberies by *'popish privateers'* and to fund the required militia accordingly. (Wall, M, The Rise of a Catholic Middle-Class).

women all over Ireland and was believed by contemporaries to be one of the most important reasons for the extraordinary success of the non-importation agreements. At first the English manufacturers tried to neutralise the effect of the leagues by attempting to flood the Irish market with woollen manufactures at cost price but soon gave up for lack of take up. The imports from England to Ireland, which generally amounted to £2.1 million annually, had declined over the course of a year to £595,000 and continued to fall. Revenue also fell and as a result England had to support Irish troops abroad while the Irish government was continuously applying for financial aid. From the beginning of 1778 until June 1779 England had remitted £485,000 to Ireland with the concurrent losses.

Events in Ireland soon forced the British Government to consider the necessity of conceding the demands. On November 4th, on the anniversary of King Williams's birthday and round his statue, the Dublin Volunteers, commanded by James Napper Tandy, hung labels on the necks of their cannon with the inscription '*Free trade or a speedy revolution*'. Two cannons with the inscription '*Free trade or This*' stood before the front of the statute. On November 24th in the Irish Commons Grattan moved that, '*at this time it would be inexpedient to grant new taxes*'. The resolution was carried against the Government by a majority of 123. One of the government supporters spoke of the necessity of preserving peace, to which Hussey Burgh eloquently replied, '*talk not to me of peace, Ireland is not in a state of peace; it is smothered war. England has sown her laws like dragon's teeth, and they have sprung up like armed men*'. Eventually, the English government gave way and in December 1779 and January 1780 Acts were put through the English parliament abolishing almost all restraints on Irish trade.[359]

By the middle of 1780 there were 80,000 volunteers under arms

---

[359] Murray, A., E., A History.

and volunteer meetings all over the country passed resolutions asserting the independence of the Irish parliament. An incident in Kerry in 1781 exemplified the changed environment when a vessel loaded with rum was seized by the customs officers, it still being illegal by virtue of a British Act, to import from the West Indies. This action failed to be prosecuted by a jury on the ground that there was no *'Irish Act prohibitive of the trade'*. The jury went on to find damages against the customs officers for illegal arrest. During 1781, discontent with the continuing legislative situation increased and in February 1782 Grattan moved his Declaration of Irish Rights only to be defeated for a second time. In February also, a Convention of 243 delegates from every Volunteer corps in Ulster met in Dungannon, County Tyrone, and carried a number of resolutions. Conventions also met in other provinces and carried similar resolutions. The resolutions declared that '*English legislative control over the Irish parliament was unconstitutional, illegal and a grievance, the powers exercised by the Privy Council … under the pretence of Poyning's Law were unconstitutional, and as Protestants welcomed the relaxation of the Penal Laws against their Roman Catholic fellow-subjects.*' It was January 1783 before the Bill was passed by the British parliament renouncing explicitly all legislative and judicial supremacy over Ireland.[360]

Catholic Relief and the Penal Laws

Throughout the 1770s, as the war in America progressed, Catholics were taken into the British Army in increasing numbers. In 1770 Chancellor Townshend's wish for the recruiting of Catholics was dealt with in the context '*that now the necessity of recruiting to the army is so pressing*', he was to '*authorise the recruiting parties of the marching regiments on*

---

[360] Ibid.

the British establishment to beat up in the three provinces of Leinster, Munster, and Connaught', and Townshend noted in *'which all the lower class of people are Roman Catholics'*. Catholic recruitment got a boost at the end of 1775, when important Catholics petitioned the Irish government offering to encourage enlistment and individual Catholics gave bounties in support of recruiting. Lord Kenmare, the wealthiest Catholic landlord, asked Major Boyle Roche (later an Irish MP) to raise a regiment from his retainers and gave a bounty for each recruit. Furthermore, at the end of 1775 the King approved plans to recruit 2,000 Irish for North America mainly from the West of Ireland. By 1776, 16 of the 44 battalions on American service had originated in the Irish establishment and were full of Irish Catholics and Protestants.[361]

Irish Protestants openly protested against this development for fear of their own security and condemned the use of Catholic recruits to put down fellow Protestants in America, albeit it was acceptable for Irish, German, or English Protestants to do so. Their anger was directed at Catholic recruitment into the East India Company as well and what was believed to be George III's support for the recruitment of Catholics, including recruitment in the defence of Ireland. They also began to suspect that the British Government was offering Catholic relief in return for Catholic recruits to the army. There was in fact a British plan to offer concessions to the Catholics of England, Scotland, and Ireland and it was this scheme which formed the background to the Catholic Relief Act of 1778, the first major breach in the Penal Code.

This Act repealed some of the Penal Laws concerning land ownership by Catholics but its main aim was to encourage the

---

[361] Denman, T., *Hibernia officina militum,* Irish Recruitment to the Regular British Army, 1660-1815.

Catholic gentry to beat the recruiting drum for enlistment into the British Army and for their onward transfer to war in the American Colonies. Luke Gardiner (Mountjoy, later killed at the Battle of New Ross in 1798), long on record as a supporter of Catholic recruitment. introduced the Relief Bill in the Irish Parliament in 1778. This Bill firmly established the principle of Catholic relief as a key element of war-time strategy.[362] The attempt to gain passage for a Bill entitling Catholics to rights of mortgage and lease-holding had been attempted previously in 1774, but had many opponents amongst Protestant churchmen and merchants. The case against was made by George Ogle, member for Co. Wexford, who said that Catholics had previously only received toleration, this Bill would mean that popery *would be established by law*. The Catholic Committee, founded in 1757 to repeal the Penal laws, but strictly supportive of King and Government, in a letter to the Chief Secretary, tendered their duty, zeal, and affection to the King and declared their abhorrence of the *unnatural rebellion* among his American subjects. Ogle surfaced again with an amendment to the Relief Bill, which was carried, where the right to purchase and outright ownership by Catholics was prohibited and which left the lease period at 999 years.[363]

Social Change

In any event, the great mass of Catholics received no benefit from the Act other than the opportunity to put their lives on the line fighting for king and Empire, that is other than for the occasional recruit who liked to hear *'cannon-balls a roaring'*. In some Protestant

---

[362] Bartlett, T., The Catholic Question in the Eighteenth Century, History Ireland, Issue 1, (Spring 1993), Volume 1.
[363] Hull, E, A History.

quarters it was argued that it was preferable to send papists to be killed instead of Protestants who were in short supply. The forces of economic change, the steam engine, mass industrial production, and commercial farming pushed large numbers of artisans, trades, weavers, and farm labourers into unemployment and penury and these became a welcome target for the recruiting sergeants. A steady stream of recruits were also made available through press gangs and for others it was offered as an alternative to prison.

Towards the end of the American war another Catholic Relief Act was passed and this, the 1782 Act, repealed those Penal Laws directed specifically at the practice of the Catholic religion. On this occasion the concession was granted with an intention of keeping Irish Catholics detached from the Volunteers. If this was the plan, it failed when the Volunteers Convention in Dungannon took up the Catholic cause and declared their support for the removal of restrictions on their fellow-subjects. The Catholics, having been supported by the Volunteers, however, were soon abandoned by them as the Volunteer plan for parliamentary reform made no attempt to include Catholic franchise or representation. The Volunteer campaign soon ran out of steam, having failed to enlist the support of the mass population of Catholics, but from the failure of that campaign certain lessons were learned by the more committed reformers.

In this resolution lay the seeds of the future Society of the United Irishmen. In the words of Wolfe Tone, *'the Revolution of 1782 was a Revolution which enabled Irishmen to sell at a much higher price their honour, their integrity, and the interest of their country ... it left three-fourths of our countrymen slaves as it found them ... formerly we had our distress, our injuries, and our insults gratis at the hands of England, but now we pay very dearly to receive the same with aggravation, through the hands of Irishmen'.*[364] In another

---

[364] Tone, T.W., *An Argument on Behalf of the Catholics of Ireland.*

pamphlet Tone had written that '*the influence of England was the radical vice of our government,*' comments on which Sir Henry Cavendish remarked that '*if the author of the work was serious he ought to be hanged.*'

The radical volunteers of Dublin, led by James Napper Tandy, tried to organise a reform convention made up of delegates elected by the people in October 1784 but the leadership of Henry Flood and Lord Charlemont (Commander-in-Chief of the Volunteers) who had extensive property interests in Armagh, completely deserted the radicals. This elite leadership had obtained what they had sought a fairly independent Ireland, still ruled by the aristocracy and a capitalist class now free from the English commercial restrictions which had interfered with their development. In short, Henry Flood believed in a Protestant democracy and opposed religious freedom and Henry Grattan believed in religious freedom but opposed democracy in so far as he advocated landowners only having the franchise.

The policies pursued by Grattan's Parliament in the last two decades of century were nothing new and their influence on the overall economy has also been questioned. Once again the benefit to the great mass of the population, cottiers, labourers, and artisans was of little consequence.

There is also an argument that the industrial development of the period owed little to legislative measures or to the financial assistance of the legislature. The emergence of bigger firms with their consequent economies of scale was a factor in the growth of glass, milling, and brewing in this period. The stimulus to expansion in the cotton industry was similar to the technological developments that had taken place in the industry in Britain. This was already underway before 1782 and cotton locations were being established rapidly in many locations in the Eastern half of Ireland. Agricultural prices were rising sharply relative to industrial prices. In industry itself the technological features of the industrial revolution were being adopted rapidly in the 1770s and 1780s. An inflow of British capital and skilled labour were also contributing factors. Developments in agricultural productivity contributed to the population sharply increasing in the last decades of the century and this continued into the first decades of the following century. This was reflected in a disproportionate increase in the number of cottiers and labourers and in a sharp contrast between social classes. Unemployment was rife in the Dublin Liberties in the 1790s.[365] In three streets of the parish of St. Catherines, *'no less than 2,000 souls had been found in a starving condition'*. At a very numerous and peaceable meeting of the Munster peasantry, held in July 1786, a resolution was passed to *'oppose the oppressors .... and raise her angry voice in the councils of the nation to protect the toiling peasant and lighten his burden'*.[366]

The great mass of the Irish peasantry lived in a state of desperate poverty and were driven beyond endurance, first by the enclosures which robbed them of common land, and afterwards by the rapid rise in rents that followed the Corn Laws (1784). England had progressed from being a corn-exporting country to becoming an importing one to feed the growing numbers of industrial workers. In Munster the rent of an acre of potato ground was £6 and the tenant had to work his rent out in labour for the landlord at the rate of 6d per day. It required therefore 240 days' work to pay a year's rent, so that the peasant had to spend two-thirds of their labour power for the landlord. Even the remaining third was not their own. Direct taxation in the form of hearth tax was levied on 400,000 out of 475,000 houses in Ireland and indirect taxation was required to support the military. There was also the most hated burden of all the payment of

---

[365] Cullen, L.M., An Economic History
[366] Connolly, J., Labour in Irish History.

tithes for the Protestant clergy. Out of a population of five million by the end of the century, three and a half million were Catholics, one million were dissenters – mainly Presbyterian and other faiths – and half a million were Protestant Anglican. This church had to be supported as well as by those of their own faith, by the remaining non-Anglican ninety per cent of the population.[367]

The future of the domestic textile industries, vital as a source of employment for the population, not sharing in the country's agricultural prosperity by landlords and graziers, was not reassuring. Rising imports of woollens severely affected the weaving branches in the 1780s and 1790s. The textile industries were especially important for rural welfare as they were labour-intensive and the preparatory work was critical in supplementing agricultural earnings. In England in 1785 the steam engine was first used to drive spinning machinery and the discovery of large coal deposits rapidly drove water power out of favour. Soon steam began to be the main motive power for all industries where power was needed. The main source of recruitment for these industries was child labour, the labour of craftsmen who were losing their occupations, the emigrant Irish reduced to starvation level by English colonial policy, and above all the rural proletariat fleeing from the vast distressed area that enclosures had created.[368]

A critical point for Ireland was as to how a country that showed fair if uneven development potential in the later part of the eighteenth century could not participate in the type of nineteenth-century industrialisation that would sustain such a population growth. By 1780 the potato was the year-long staple diet of the cottier class as it was also a good crop for reclaiming marginal land and one acre

[367] Burns, E, British Imperialism in Ireland, Cork Workers Club, (1976).
[368] Morton, A.L., A Peoples History.

could support a family of six. They were consumed at a rate of ten pounds per person per day and often supplemented with milk or buttermilk when available.[369] The boom of the war years from 1793 to 1815 was in the future, so to understand the emerging character of pre-famine Ireland what needs to be noted is both the growth in population and dependence on subsistence farming and the crisis which by 1815 was already affecting domestic industries.

[369] Foster, R.F., Modern Ireland, 1600-1972, Allen Lane, London, (1988).

CHAPTER TWENTY-ONE

THE FOUNDATIONS OF UNIONISM AND REPUBLICANISM

The Orange Society arose out of the earlier societies known as *'Protestant Boys'*, *'Peep-o-Day Boys'* and *'Wreckers'* whose activities since 1784 had created havoc for Catholic communities in Armagh, Tyrone, and Down in particular. It was evident by 1780 that numerous members of the Protestant gentry had ceased to consider Catholics a grave menace to the security of the established political and religious order. They no longer considered it necessary to choose tenants on religious grounds but rather their ability to pay rent, to restrict Catholics to the less lucrative branches of the linen industry or even to keep inviolate the Protestant's right alone to bear arms. This was heresy to the Protestant working classes whose privileges depended on Protestant hegemony. They considered the landed elite had abandoned Protestant ascendancy as they had been led to understand it. Their objective under a banner of opposition to rent increases and weaver unemployment was mostly sectarian and was one of ejecting the Catholic peasantry from their lands and homes, visiting them at night, breaking up their furniture, looms where present, ostensibly seeking arms which were banned under the Penal Laws, and forcing evictions. Some Protestant landlords had provided looms for work and arms for defence to Catholic tenants whereas the *'Protestant Boys'* proposed to plant colonies of Protestants on the farms of ejected Catholics.

This in turn gave rise to the growth of a Catholic *'Defenders'* organisation and the two organisations regularly came into conflict. In addition, under the impact of the French Revolution, the political, economic, and religious tensions of the previous fifty years came to a head. Members of the chiefly Presbyterian textile and mercantile elite, joined by professionals, sought to break the political power of the Anglican aristocracy and gentry. Alternatively, the middle-class Presbyterian radicals appealed for support to the Protestant *'lower orders'*, mainly by exploiting the traditional agrarian grievances of rents, tithes, and taxation. To the Catholics they appealed partly on the same grounds but mostly by embracing the cause of full civic and political equality for those of that faith. Later, as long as the United Irishmen demanded only reform as they did until 1795, they could rely on the backing of most middle-class Presbyterians or the growing capitalist class but once the commitment to revolution was made much of this support fell away. This drift took its toll later in the struggle as many middle-class had been appointed Colonels and Majors and their departure left the ordinary recruits without officers or leaders. The encouraged fear and hatred of Catholics and hegemony amongst the Protestant *'lower orders'* prevailed over agrarian grievances. When the Protestant gentry, mobilised in the yeomanry and took control they led the ordinary Protestants into the Orange Order. The landlords also placed themselves at the forefront of this movement and took control of disaffected Protestants using the resources of the Orange Order.[370]

Lord Gosford, who was Governor of Armagh in 1795 at the time of the *'Disturbances'*, denounced the Protestant extremists: *'It is no secret that a persecution is now raging ... the only crime is profession of the Roman*

---

[370] Miller, D.W., The Armagh Troubles.

Catholic faith. Lawless banditti have constituted themselves judges … and the sentence they have denounced … is nothing less than a confiscation of all property … and immediate banishment'.[371] On the other hand, for the ordinary classes, Jemmy Hope, a Downpatrick weaver, observed economic conditions were *'the real basis of the persecution in the County Armagh, religious profession being only a pretext to banish a Roman Catholic from his snug little cottage, or spot of land and get possessed of it'*.

The Battle of the Diamond (September 1795), the loyalist celebrated conflict between the opposing sides, had little it appears to do with politics. It was a local attempt on the part of Catholics to hold a semi-secret assembly which was sniped at by Protestant sharpshooters which brought on desultory fighting which lasted for a numbers of days. After a peace had been negotiated a further body of Catholics, misunderstanding the situation, intervened which prolonged the dispute. It then escalated when a party of Defenders arrived and a good number were killed by the Protestants who were better armed. It was subsequent to this the first Orange Lodge was formed at Loughall, in Co Armagh.[372] These events came later to symbolise the distinction between loyalty to the Crown and disaffection. The Orange Society had been formed to support the Protestant Ascendancy. Their oath of allegiance made as a condition the defence of the king and his heirs as long as they supported their cause, despite the fact that the Catholics in general and the Catholic elite were, at that time, no less loyal to the Crown. It is, however, well established that the Orange Society was encouraged by Castlereagh and the Clare-Beresford *junto*[373] in Dublin Castle who provided them with considerable sums of money to spread their organisation. They

---

[371] Hull, E., A History.

[372] Jackson, T.A., Ireland Her Own.

[373] As described by Edmund Burke.

sought in this sectarian way to separate ordinary Protestants from the growing movement of United Irishmen. The effect of their treatment of the peasantry and the cover provided for their acts by local magistrates, and supported by Dublin castle, stimulated the opposing societies into greater activity. Where an Orange lodge sprang up, branches of the United Irishmen would follow. Lord Castlereagh, during the examination of Arthur O'Connor (1798), denied that they had anything to do with the Orange Society or with the *'oath of extermination'* (of Catholics) but did not deny its existence.[374] The Orange Order was the means by which the Protestant *'lower orders'* were used to break up the solidarity engendered by the United Irishmen. In turn it was used to halt the struggle for democratic advance, to support the interests of the controlling Ascendancy and restrict the influence and growth of the developing capitalist class. This class were represented in particular by the Presbyterian manufacturers, merchants, and traders, the class of republicans earlier identified by *Swift*.

United Irishmen and Catholic Defenders

The organisations the Order had been founded to disrupt and destroy were the United Irishmen and the Defenders who had now joined forces with them; the former a revolutionary body on the American and French model and the latter a tenant's defensive and representative organisation. Together these radicals were working to end the control of the landed aristocracy and their supporters in the British Government. Their aims were to replace them with a democratic government under universal (male) suffrage and ultimately *'break the connection with England'*. Tone put it as follows: *'If*

---

[374] Hull, E., A History.

the men of property will not support us, they must fall: we can support ourselves by the aid of that numerous and respectable class of the community – the men of no property'.[375] On the other side Fitzgibbon (*Clare*) put the Ascendancy position starkly in 1789 during the Regency (temporary insanity) crisis, when he reminded the *'gentlemen of Ireland, that the only security by which they held their property, the only security they have for the present Constitution in Church and State, is the connection for the Irish Crown, with and its dependence upon, the Crown of England. The Act by which most of us hold our estates was an Act of violence … the Act of Settlement … every acre of land which pays quitrent to the Crown is derived by title acquired under the Act of Settlement … how far it may be prudent to pursue successive claims of … independence for Ireland. We are committing ourselves against the law and against the Constitution, and in such a contest Ireland must fall'.*[376]

The stage was now set for what was in essence a class war between opposing interests. In Ireland the Anglo-Irish elite needed a highly restrictive political and legal system in order to secure their Ascendancy. This inhibited the development of capitalist social relations and acted as an obstacle to the development of a more modern form of bourgeois government with popular support. However, in any conflict the Dublin-based elite could not rely on a secure base of popular consent in their relations with London or indeed any meaningful support from the majority of the Irish population.

The Influence of the French Revolution

In 1794, during the French wars, Pitt had suspended Habeas Corpus and this lasted for eight years. The Rights of Man (Paine) was

---

[375] Jackson, T.A., Ireland Her Own.
[376] Foster, R.F., Modern Ireland.

banned, the Corresponding Society and other radical organisations were declared illegal. Troops were frequently used to suppress disorder but were often found to be unreliable because of their sympathy with the crowds they were ordered to attack. They were now housed in barracks away from the community whereas previously they were quartered in homes and in Inns. For this reason a new body, the yeomanry, a mounted force drawn from the upper and middle classes, was created at the beginning of the French Wars. It was intended as a class body with the suppression of *Jacobinism* as its main object. This object was pursued with an enthusiasm and an unfailing brutality, which earned them common hatred. The anti-Jacobin fury of the Government and ruling class was all the keener because of the continued success of the French armies.

As the revolution in France became increasingly violent and popular, the dominant sections of the bourgeoisie in Britain and Ireland became increasingly agitated. '*Jacobinism*' meant an attack on privileges and in these countries privilege was not only aristocratic but bourgeoisie as well and more so in the former after the *'Glorious Revolution'*. Britain was one of the last countries to become involved in the counter-revolutionary war but, once involved, was the most determined in carrying it through. The willingness of European sovereigns to intervene grew with the spread of revolutionary ideas among their own subjects and the threat to absolutism or continuing feudal reign. It was the conquest of Belgium and the denouncing of commercial treaties that brought revolutionary France into direct conflict with British commercial and financial interests. The main source of Britain's strength was the modern and capitalist economic organisation which enabled trade and industry to increase even under war conditions and vast sums of money to be raised without bankruptcy. Pitt's war finance was an extension of that practice throughout the eighteenth century: heavy and increasing taxation on the necessities of life, a huge national debt and subsidies totalling £50 million to other European powers who were prepared to raise supportive armies.[377]

Early in 1793 Britain entered the war joining with Austria, Prussia, Spain, and Piedmont to form the first coalition. Before the war began the radical and republican agitation which arose in Britain as a reflection of the revolution in France had been met with a pogrom and severe legal repression by Pitt. After the overthrow in France of the *Jacobins,* on the 9th *Thermidor,* power was assumed by the Directory, representing the most disreputable sections of the bourgeoisie, namely the land speculators, currency crooks, and fraudulent army contractors. Later, risings over 1794 and 1795 by the *'sans culottes'* [378] – the original backbone of the revolution – were also put down. The new bourgeoisie regime could rely on the support of the peasantry as the revolution left many permanent gains above all the division of the great feudal estates from which they benefited, and for the merchants and traders when restraints were ended, on the development of trade and industry. The way lay open for the creation of the *Code Napoleon,* the legal framework for bourgeoisie development. The settlement of the agrarian question had given a firm basis for any government that was opposed to the return of the Bourbons and the nobility.[379]

---

[377] Morton, A.L., A People's History.

[378] 'Sans culottes' was a name given to those people 'without' culottes, a form of clothing worn by the wealthier members of French society. The 'sans culottes' as a class were a critical element in the French revolution.

[379] Ibid.

The Society of United Irishmen

The Society of United Irishmen was set up in Belfast in October 1791 and aimed to curb the influence of England in the government of Ireland through a thoroughgoing parliamentary reform. The Belfast reformers had already hailed the French Revolution and in July 1791 had celebrated the Fall of the Bastille with special ceremonies involving the Volunteers.[380] Central to its formation was, as Tone observed, that *'no reform is practicable that does not include the Catholics'.* It pre-dated by a year the formation of its nearest English counterpart, the London Corresponding Society, the starting point of all organised working-class radical-democratic and revolutionary political struggle in England.[381] Within a month Tone, Russell, and Napper Tandy were assisting other notables to found a Dublin Society. Between them they began to spread a network of affiliated individuals and local societies throughout the country. The Society stood broadly on the principles of Paine's *The Rights of Man* and through their paper *The Northern Star* (founded by Samuel Neilson in Belfast in 1792). They gave a welcome on their first appearance to Mary Wollstonecraft's *Vindication of the Rights of Woman* and to Paine's *Age of Reason.* They corresponded with the Jacobin Society in Paris and reported its proceedings regularly in their Journal.

By late 1791 members of the professional and mercantile bourgeoisie had seized control of the Catholic Committee from the clerical-aristocratic leadership and began campaigning more aggressively for political rights. While its immediate aim was parliamentary reform, Tone's desire was *'to break the connection with England, the never failing source of all our political evils ... and to substitute the*

---

[380] Cronin, S., The Revolutionaries, Republican Publications, Gardiner Pl, Dublin 1.
[381] Jackson, T.A., Ireland Her Own.

common name of Irishman in place of the denomination of Protestant, Catholic, and Dissenter – these were my means'. The political elite had already considered and rejected the idea of change after the 1782 *'reliefs'* and persisted with the consolidation of Protestant Ascendancy for the following decade. In response the Catholic Committee organised elections on the basis of one man one vote, known as the Catholic Convention or the Back Street Parliament. When it met in December 1792 in Tailor's Hall in Dublin, Wolfe Tone, as Secretary of the Committee, was one of the main organisers. A delegation crossed to London to petition King George III and Tone was also among them.

Catholic Relief Act 1793

The British Government was sufficiently alarmed at the possibility of an alliance between the Northern Dissenters, Irish Catholics, and Dublin radicals that it urged that major concessions be made to the Catholics in order to head off this development. The Castle resisted this argument and the concessions offered in 1792 fell far short of those which the Catholic Committee – now much more assertive than before – demanded and indeed were far less than the British government considered necessary. The decision to petition the sovereign over the heads of the administration shocked Chief Secretary Hobart in Dublin Castle. Later the Viceroy said the King wished Parliament to consider the grievances of his Catholic subjects. Then, on Administration insistence, the Catholic Relief Bill of 1793 was carried by a two-thirds majority. Catholics were given the right to bear arms, to vote if they held a freehold the valuation of which was 40 shillings, which enfranchised 200,000, to act as grand jurors, to take degrees at Trinity College, to join the Outer Bar and to get army commissions. They still could not enter Parliament or hold state office. Tone was dissatisfied with the terms but he was in a minority. The Castle played on the fears of the wealthy Catholic traders for the most part, however, Grattan was annoyed that the measures barred the upper-class Catholic elite from Parliament.

Iron Hand in a Velvet Glove – Suppression

The price paid for the Catholic Relief Act was a measure banning future delegate assemblies. A series of coercion bills including a Militia Act were also passed to deal with what Castlereagh called *'the insurrectionary spirit in the North'*. This Militia was largely composed of Catholics while officered by Protestants, whereas the yeomanry was set up as an armed force of loyal Protestants to which Orangemen were encouraged to join. The Relief Act itself ended Tone's usefulness to the Catholic Committee which voted him £1,500 and a gold medal. A critical factor in these concessions was the reality that France and England had gone to war in 1793. This was also the reason why the Volunteers were suppressed and disarmed as their potential loyalty was questioned. Meanwhile, the Dublin Parliament supported Britain's position and the Opposition declared its loyalty.

The Dublin Society of United Irishmen declared that the object of the war was *'to produce a counter-revolution in France'* and stifle liberty in Europe. The Belfast United Irishmen repeated that *'radical reform in the representation of the people has long been, and still is, the great object of all our wishes and endeavours ... all Irishmen of every description shall be equally and fairly represented'*.[382] An angry Grattan claimed that arming *'the poverty of the kingdom'* besmirched the original Volunteers *'the armed property of the nation'*. The radicals, however, proved incapable of forcing change from the native parliamentary elite who were supported by the

---

[382] Cronin, S., The Revolutionaries.

resources of the state and an influential segment of public opinion.[383]

In this new scenario, the radicals, through a raft of repressive legislation, were to be removed, and an Arms and Gunpowder Bill was also passed, requiring the Volunteers to give up their arms.[384] In Dublin there were three divisions of Volunteers corresponding to the three popular divisions of the 'patriotic' forces. There was the Liberty Corps recruited exclusively from the working class, the Merchants Corps composed of the capitalist class, and the Lawyers Corps comprised of members of the legal fraternity. The Government seized the artillery of the Liberty Corps, made a private arrangement with the Merchants Corps, by which it got possession and induced the Lawyers to give up theirs. But first the Lawyers made a public procession through the streets with their arms to the public cheers of the credulous Dublin workers before they were privately handed over. As Connolly observed: *'In Dublin working men fought, the capitalists sold out, and the lawyers bluffed'.*[385]

After successfully passing the Convention, Militia, and Arms Acts, by the beginning of 1794 the authorities were ready to suppress the United Irishmen by force. On May 4th 1794 a party of soldiers, headed by one of Dublin's military magistrates, forced their way into Tailor's Hall in Back Lane, the regular meeting place of the United Irishmen, and ordered the meeting then proceeding to disperse. A proclamation was issued for the Dublin Society and the Attorney General announced in Parliament any similar association in Ireland would be dealt with in the same way. He charged the United Irishmen categorically *'with treasonable association with the King's enemies'.* The evidence was based on charges which had been secured earlier by the

---

[383] Gillen, U., The Protestant Ascendancy.

[384] Ellis, P.B., A History of the Irish Working Class.

[385] Connolly, J., Labour in Irish History.

arrest of Rev. William Jackson, an emissary from France. Pitt's secret service had planted a spy named Cockayne as Jackson's secretary and a copy of a memorial on the state of the country drafted by Tone was intercepted by Cockayne (he was later to die of poison in the dock) and forwarded to Pitt. This laid the basis for the charges.

A week after the raid on the Dublin United Irishmen, the English Government swooped down on Thomas Hardy, Horne Tooke, and the other leaders of the English *Jacobin'* societies.

Tone's secretaryship of the Catholic Committee and the support of the influential John Keogh, despite Grattan's pleadings to sever the relationship, provided him with some cover as the Government wished to placate this Committee. Tone ended up voluntarily going into exile with his family to the United States. At this time, Pitt, faced with the continuing success of the French abroad and growing opposition at home, decided to broaden the base of his support by making an alliance with the moderate Whigs. They demanded in return for their support the direction of Irish affairs.[386] Towards the end of 1794 Westmoreland was recalled and Fitzwilliam, who had previously inherited large estates in Ireland, came as Lord Lieutenant in January 1795 with a policy which he did not conceal, to emancipate Catholics.

He removed Cooke and Beresford and others of the Castle *junto'* as well as the most bigoted of the Protestant Ascendancy who were identified as obstacles to progress. In response to these developments, Parliament voted a large sum of money for the expenses of the navy in the war with France and 20,000 men for the army. A Bill was also brought in by Grattan in February for the admission of Catholics to Parliament. However, a Bill in order to become law required the agreement of the three branches – the King,

---

[386] Jackson, T.A., Ireland Her Own.

the lords, and the commons. Beresford, it was said, managed to convince the King that this was in contravention of his constitutional position and his royal veto was exercised against accordingly.

When Fitzwilliam was recalled and Beresford was restored, the Ascendancy received another lease of life and the policy of coercion was resumed. Camden, who replaced Fitzwilliam, returned to the policy of suppression and fomenting sectarian division. (Camden is also remembered for laying the foundation stone of Maynooth College in 1796, this favour being returned by Troy and the Irish Bishops in general who repaid with their loyalty both in 1798 and their support for the Act of Union.) In some quarters it was considered that the whole Fitzwilliam scheme was part of a plan by Pitt in order to obtain large supplies from the Irish parliament, particularly for the army for the French wars.[387] It was considered that Pitt had begun formulating his policy for an Act of Union after the rejection of Catholic emancipation by the Castle *junto*. This reflected his desire to end the Protestant Ascendancy opposition and their control of the Irish Parliament which he considered unreliable.

The Society of United Irishmen itself was beset with paid informers and much of what was taking place was known to the authorities although not the critical decisions. This infiltration was supported by Pitt's secret service and spies in France. Many, even prominent members of the Committee, were in receipt of regular sums of money for giving information to Government. Thomas Reynolds, a silk manufacturer in Dublin, on whose information several of the Leinster leaders were taken in March 1798, and who subsequently gave evidence against them, was one of their most trusted leaders. On his information, the members of the Provincial Committee meeting at Oliver Bond's house of whom he was one

---

[387] Joyce, P.W., A Concise History of Ireland, (1910).

were arrested. Soon afterwards, Thomas Addis Emmet, Dr W. J. McNevin, and later Lord Edward Fitzgerald were arrested; Lord Edward suffered wounds during his resistance and arrest which later proved fatal. Even some of those who were employed as professional advocates at their trials were at the same time taking money from the Government for the betrayal of their secrets. Councillor McNally, at whose house the meetings were held, and the Northern lawyer James McGucken were among those paid and pensioned for their services.

The magistrates in the north also procured witnesses against United Irishmen, Neilson, Russell, and McCracken who were especially detested by the Ascendancy party in Belfast. Bribes were offered to give evidence that would lead to their capital conviction and it was later revealed that this money was paid by Lord Hillsborough. An informer by the name of Bird, alias Smith, was persuaded to come forward against Neilson (editor of the Northern Star) and was placed under the tutelage of the Crown solicitor. Fortunately, for the accused they also had their own spies who provided information and they were able to rebut testimony. Bird was also to give evidence against two others in State custody – Charles Kennedy and Daniel Shanahan, however Bird, alias Smith, did not appear on the day he was to give evidence in Court. It was said he had returned to England, his native country, and as he was only a bird of passage and not of prey, his flight was deemed by no means extraordinary. Bird subsequently engaged in extensive correspondence exposing the plot and the reasons for his non-appearance and unwillingness to testify. He was eventually captured and despatched in chains to an English dungeon.[388] The accused prisoners, after eighteen months in custody, were released. Despite

---

[388] Madden R.R., The United Irishmen, Their Lives and Times, Madden & Company, (1843).

the threats and the bribes, informants generally delivered no solid evidence of United Irishmen strategy to Dublin Castle, and this was the position right up to hours before the time of the rebellion.

Before leaving Ireland for Philadelphia via Belfast, Tone had met his friends in Belfast at Mac Art's Fort. Most of the inner circle of the United Irishmen were present, including Russell (later immortalised in the poem *The Man from God Knows Where*), Neilson, Henry Joy McCracken, Robert and William Simms. They urged him to go to France for aid as soon as possible. After some months in America, Tone made the onward journey to France.

CHAPTER TWENTY-TWO

THE RISE AND FALL OF REPUBLICANISM – 1798

The French outfitted three expeditions for Ireland largely based on the powers of persuasion of Wolfe Tone who had struck up a friendship with Lazar Hoche, the French General. All three expeditions failed. The first reached Bantry Bay in December 1796 and was scattered by storms. The land forces were commanded by Hoche, considered at the time the greatest general of the Revolutionary wars next to Bonaparte. This was the expedition considered to have had the most chance of success as the regular troops in Ireland were considered second-rate due to general redeployment for the French wars and the colonies. The militia were considered unreliable and the yeomanry also of doubtful quality. The spring of 1797 passed without any move by the French to prepare a second expedition, even though the seas were open, and the British navy were paralysed by mutinies at Spithead and the Nore. The Crown garrison in Ireland was demoralised, discontent was high, and the United Irishmen were well-organised along military lines in Ulster. In the summer of 1797 a new expedition was fitted out in Holland of 26 ships and 15,000 men and Tone joined it in July. Bad weather, delayed departure, supplies ran low, and the British, now over their various mutinies, were able to rally offshore. By September Tone had gone on a mission to Hoche who was now dying.

When news of the Rising of May 1798 reached France, Tone urged that an expedition be sent immediately but none was forthcoming. Humbert did sail, against orders, eventually with a small force but not until August and landed at Killala in Co. Mayo with his 1,000 men. After an initial victory at Castlebar, the French and the Gaelic-Irish, who had now rallied to his side, were defeated at Ballinamuck by a much superior force. The French received terms while all the Irish involved were massacred, including Wolfe Tone;s brother Mathew who was hanged along with Bartholomew Teeling, the son of Luke Teeling, a linen merchant from Lisburn. Mathew Tone was buried, it is believed, along with many other casualties at the Croppies Acre near Arran Quay in Dublin.

On September 20th 1798 Tone himself sailed with a 3,000-man expeditionary force from Brest. They sought to avoid the much superior British fleet by making a great sweep to the northwest arriving at Lough Swilly, County Donegal, on October 10th. The British navy was waiting and after a six-hour battle Tone's ship was seized. He was recognised, put in irons, and on November 10th 1798 he was tried by the courts martial and sentenced to be hanged two days later. In the early hours of November 12th he was found with a deep knife wound in his neck. He remained alive for a further seven days and died on November 19th. The circumstances of his death remain a mystery. His son wrote later, *'in consequence of the attempts to withdraw him from the jurisdiction of the military tribunals, my father's end may have been precipitated by the hands of his jailers ... no one was allowed to approach after his wound, no medical attendant to come near him other than the prison surgeon ... no coroner's inquest was held on his body ... what passed in that Provost's prison must remain for ever amongst the guilty and bloody mysteries of that pandemonium'.* [389]

---

[389] Cronin, Sean, The Revolutionaries.

The Dragooning of Ulster and the Defenders

In response to the arrival of the French Fleet at Bantry Bay, County Cork, and in a session which lasted from January to April 1797, the Irish parliament occupied itself with two Acts, providing an Act Of Indemnity for *'all such persons as had, in the previous half-year, exceeded their legal powers in the preservation of the public peace'* and with it an Insurrection Act, *'one of the most severe and comprehensive in Irish history'*. The first Act provided legal indemnity for Orange magistrates where they had exceeded their powers and had refused to convict the Orange military who had embarked on a campaign of terror through Armagh and then extended through adjoining counties into Connaught. The magistrates refused to convict for these acts, even when there was plain evidence of murder, and, at the same time, awarded sentences of transportation for life to Catholics who had procured arms to defend themselves.

The second, the *Insurrection Act*, was designed to complete this work and to cope with the consequences of the terror which had driven the Defenders organisation over to the United Irishmen as a body and which was now fast becoming an oath bound society. The *Insurrection Act* also gave the Government powers to suspend *Habeas Corpus* and impose martial law on any area proclaimed as *'disturbed'*. It imposed death as the penalty for administering any *'seditious oath'* and transportation as the penalty for taking one. It ordered the registration of all arms which magistrates could confiscate at will, it imposed transportation or imprisonment for possession or concealment of arms, *'tumultuous assembly'* or for possessing, distributing, or selling seditious papers. Magistrates were given large powers of arrest on suspicion.

The Administration (Dublin Castle) appointed General Lake, Military Commander for Ulster, and he issued a proclamation imposing martial law on the greater part of the province, with sign-up and compliance to terms required by June. The Crown establishment used sectarianism as a divisive instrument to prevent the involvement of Protestants in the United Irishmen. This was officially encouraged and General Knox, writing to General Lake, stated, *'I have arranged ... to increase the animosity between the Orangemen and the United Irishmen, or liberty men as they call themselves. Upon that animosity depends the safety of the centre counties of the North'.*[390] The Castle had also given permission to the country magistrates and gentry to form corps of *'Yeomanry'* on the English model. In practice these corps were little more than Orange Lodges and Peep-O-Day Boys put into uniforms and given an official licence to work their will on the countryside in the name of law and order. To secure a parallel end, Orange Lodges were established in each Militia battalion, and a systematic purge was instituted, beginning with the officers to weed out those considered the unwilling or disloyal.

Yeomanry and militia regiments were also brought over from Britain, amongst them the Ancient Britons, who were considered little other than *'Church-and-King'* mobs supplied with weapons, pay, and rations. When the date of the proclamation expired and on General Lake's orders, all of these forces were let loose in the proclaimed area to search for arms and for tactical and efficiency reasons were concentrated on the towns. They soon moved from simple assault, where they removed any green clothing from women, and robbery to arson, rape, and murder. To exhort confessions, they resorted to floggings, picketing – a variety of crucifixion and pitch-capping. When the terrified victims fled or slept-out in the fields at night, they resorted to burning down their houses. Adding to this and

---

[390] Lecky, W.E., A History of England in the Eighteenth Century, Volume VII, Appleton and Co, New York, (1890).

included were the magistrates arrests on suspicion. When the jails could hold no more, they were cleared-out on a simple magistrate's order by the expedient of *'impressing'* all the prisoners for service in the fleet. Many of these *'impressed'* men were later labelled *'Jacobins'* and blamed by Pitt, along with the London Corresponding Society, for being the instigators of the mutinies at Spithead and the Nore.[391]

Estimates of Irish in the British navy vary from under 16,000[392] to 24,000. A fifth of those concerned were believed to be Irish but the vast bulk of those involved in the mutinies were English sailors. In the regular army, disaffection was mostly linked to the prospect of being sent to the West Indies, which was perceived as a veritable death sentence. Some 80,000 troops were said to have perished there.[393]

The dragooning of Ulster had unintended consequences. People gathered in *'great masses'* to stack the hay, cut the corn, and lift the potatoes of men detained in jail. If the military dispersed these *'seditious assemblies'* by day, they came back and did the work by moonlight and these *meitheals*[394] soon turned into secret drillings. The wish that *'the French would come'* was openly expressed, and one Honourable member told the House that there existed *'a generally-expressed determination to abolish all taxes, and all tithes, and reduce rents to a standard of 10s an acre for the best land, and so downwards in proportion'*. Another honourable member added, *'they were facing a war of the poor against the rich'*. The legislation created the basis for the final suppression of the Northern Star paper and the wrecking of its machinery by the Monaghan Militia. It also had the effect of scaring

---

[391] Jackson, T.A., Ireland Her Own.

[392] Thompson, E.P., The Making of the English Working Class, Vintage Books, New York, (1966).

[393] Cannon, D., Irish Catholic Service and Identity in the British Armed Forces 1793-1815, Thesis M.Litt., NUI, Maynooth, (2014).

[394] *Meitheal*, an Irish word for a mustered body of workers.

out of the *United* ranks, a number of the better-off supporters who in some cases turned informers. However, many of the deserter's places were taken by more resolute recruits roused to indignation by the dragooning.

The panic spread by the atrocities and official terror drove many of the peasantry in the other provinces in to taking measures for self-defence. The partial disarming of Ulster was set off by a secret re-arming of the rest of Ireland, even into some of the remotest points.[395] The spread of Defenderism was helped and infused with revenge by the Armagh outrages of 1795-96, in which several thousand Catholics from Armagh, Tyrone, Down, and Fermanagh were driven from their homes by the recently formed Orange order. These migrated to Connaught and other districts and brought tales of the experiences suffered and stories of the atrocities with them. It was in the cauldron of these expulsions that the alliance between the Defenders and the United Irishmen was forged sometime in early 1796.

The Politicising of the Defenders

The importance of the Defender movement in the history of Irish rural protests is beyond dispute. It is the link between the *'conservative'* protest movements of the period 1760-1790 and the revolutionary or so-called subversive movements of the nineteenth century. On the one hand, the Defenders drew on the traditional grievances of the small farmers, cottiers, and labourers and, like the Whiteboys and Rightboys, they sought to regulate tithes and refused to deal with tithe proctors or tithe farmers. They fought bitterly the price of conacre land and the level of labourer's wages. They criticised the high level of priest's fees, which probably contributed to their

---

[395] Ibid.

excommunication by the pro-state Catholic Church. In August 1795 Archbishop John Troy of Dublin issued an address to be read in all Catholic chapels, condemning all Catholic members of any combination of *Whiteboys*, *Rightboys*, Defenders, or any others '*as scandalous and rotten members of our communion*'.[396] There were a few notable clerical exceptions who also suffered the effects of the terror and were excommunicated.

Social Change

The Defenders challenged graziers and often houghed their cattle. Their anti-state ethos marked the Defenders off from previous agrarian protest organisations and were a response to the sectarian nature of the repressive apparatus employed by a panic-stricken gentry and a fearful Dublin Castle. As Defenderism emerged from its origins in sectarian conflict and began to expand in north Leinster, it became an increasingly self-conscious revolutionary movement, inspired by the radical ideas circulating during the early 1790s. In Dublin, Defenderism appealed strongly to a significant body of radical artisans and petty shopkeepers. Thus the movement began to shed some of its exclusively rural associations and merged with the strain of plebeian radicalism developing simultaneously in Dublin, London, and Paris. In the early 1790s political associations of mechanics, artisans, and petty shopkeepers were proliferating in Dublin. Newspapers were readily available to artisans and labourers, who interested themselves in the revolution in France, the reform movement in Dublin and Paine was widely read. Republicanism was

---

[396] Curtin, N.J., Transformation of the United Irishmen into a Mass-based Revolutionary Organisation, 1794-96, Irish Historical Studies, Vol. 24, No. 96, Nov. (1985).

taking root among Dublin's working classes long before the United Irishmen raised the standard.[397] There is evidence that as early as 1792 the Defenders were in touch with the French authorities with a view to obtaining military aid from that quarter. There is also evidence to support the view the Defenders would have welcomed an opportunity to *'plant the tree of liberty in the Irish lands'* and *'French Defenders will uphold the cause and Irish Defenders will pull down the British laws'*. The Defenders, importantly, drew on popular Gaelic Irish culture as well. In the Defender oaths and catechisms the theme of deliverance, the central feature of Gaelic literature for over two hundred years, was fused with the very real prospect of French help to form a revolutionary dynamic. It was this fusion in the final analysis that made Defenderism an altogether new force in Ireland.[398]

It was not that long, however, before the internal contradictions in the United Irishmen emerged between those who sought Government to be rationalised to suit their entrepreneurial needs and political aspirations and the more working-class radicals seeking a levelling of wealth and property. Crucial desertions took place among the middle-class who dominated the upper ranks of the movement. As early as March 1796 northern magistrates began to observe daily defections among gentlemen, prosperous farmers, and substantial tradesmen along with increasing moderation of their political views as the movement spread among the lower ranks. Within two years the United Irishmen became a secret revolutionary organisation which struck terror into the hearts of the Irish administration. Over the next two years, however, the movement collapsed under the strains of

---

[397] Ibid.

[398] Bartlett, T., Select Documents XXXVIII: Defenders and Defenderism in 1795, Irish Historical Studies, Vol. 24, No. 95, (May 1985).

severe government repression, repeated disappointment of hopes of French assistance, and the murder, arrest, or defection of its ablest leaders.[399] It is also considered that its failure to organise in the west and south of the country was beset by a combination of literacy issues and its failure to translate into Gaelic its policies to a largely Gaelic-speaking community. This was notwithstanding the absence of a Gaelic version of Paine's *Rights of Man* which was also sorely missed. Overall, these issues had the effect of not enabling or mobilising potentially more support in these areas. Laterally, the local support for Humbert in the west was pointed to as evidence of the potential support which could have been rallied.

Jemmy Hope wrote, '*the appearance of a French fleet in Bantry Bay brought the rich farmers and shop keepers into the societies and, with them, all the corruption essential to the objects of the British Ministry ... they alleged as their reason for their reserve, that they thought the societies only a combination of the poor to get the property of the rich*'. He continued, '*it was my settled opinion that the condition of the labouring class was the fundamental question at issue between the rulers and the people, and there could be no solid foundation for liberty, till measures were adopted that went to the root of the evil, and were especially directed by the restoration of the natural right of the people, the right of deriving a subsistence from the soil on which their labour was expended.*'[400] It was another hundred years and not until after the mass campaign of the Land League that the foundation for these rights were laid.

---

[399] Curtin, N.J., The Transformation of the Society of United Irishmen.

[400] The memoirs of Jemmy Hope; An Autobiography of a Working-Class United Irishman, B.I.C.O., (1972).

CHAPTER TWENTY-THREE

TONE'S REPUBLIC TO CASTLEREAGH'S UNION

Under the leadership of Wolfe Tone, the United Irishmen, now strengthened with Defenderism, combined the demand for Irish independence with radical republicanism. Tone had an understanding of the relation of class to the national struggle and was rightfully distrustful of the aristocracy and middle-class after the betrayal of the Volunteers. He made his appeal to *'that large and respectable class of the community – the men of no property'*. The United Irishmen took the lead for the whole national movement and for a time succeeded in breaking down the hostility between Catholics and Protestants and combining both against the British Government and the Ascendancy *'junto'* in Dublin Castle. Tone's journey to France in 1796 was to persuade the Directory to send an expedition to Ireland and to co-operate with the rebels there. However, he had to contend with the empire building preoccupation already stirring in Napoleon's mind with his designs on Egypt and India. In Tone's words, he *'was trying to reach London by way of Calcutta starting from Egypt'*. Napoleon's support for Ireland was not whole-hearted, a fact he had plenty of time with regret to muse on later in his exile on St. Helena. Having said that, he did provide a force of 15,000, with arms for another 20,000, and these departed Brest for the Munster coast in December 1796. Bad weather and poor seamanship prevented the landing at Bantry Bay and the fleet returned to France. It was within striking distance of shore with only a few hundred Galway Militia there to resist them. After the failed landing the year 1797 advanced with increasing tensions within the United Irishmen, between those who wanted to strike the rebellion and those who wanted to wait for French support. For those who wanted to wait, information was circulated that a force was being prepared and would be despatched to Ireland no later than May of 1798. It would consist of 10,000 men and there would be arms for many more.

The sudden death at the end of 1797 of Lazar Hoche cleared the way for Bonaparte and his Imperial schemes. As the rebellion in Ireland was ongoing Napoleon sailed for Egypt and the destruction of his fleet at the Battle of the Nile in August 1798 cut his troops off from home and into a position from which they could not be extricated. The *'army for England',* which had been assembled in the North of France, to which Tone was attached since the end of 1797, was broken up and marched elsewhere. When this news reached Dublin a special meeting of the Leinster Directory was called for March 12th 1798 to devise means of coping with the crisis. The entire Directory – with the exceptions of Arthur O'Connor who was in prison in England, Thomas Russell, who was also in prison, and Lord Edward Fitzgerald, who was on his way – were betrayed by Thomas Reynolds, who was in attendance, in a surprise raid by a military magistrate supported by a strong force. From this moment onward it can be said that the rebellion in effect had begun.

Putting Down the Rebellion

The Government announced to an appropriately horrified House of

Commons that a diabolical conspiracy to *'bring in the French'* and *'plunge the country into the horrors of civil war'* had been discovered. They sent to England for more troops and extended the *Insurrection Act* to the whole of Ireland.

Pending the arrival of the troops (which, when they arrived, included as well as Dragoons and infantrymen, a number of conscript-serfs of the Grand Duke of Hesse and Brunswick, hired to the English government at so-much-per-head), the troops in Ireland were ordered *'to repress disturbances'* especially in Kilkenny, Tipperary, Limerick, Cork, Kilkenny, King's County, and Queen's County. In Dingle, County Kerry, a company of South Mayo Militia was pitched to ward off the *'catching contagion'*. In Kerry overall it was reported that the county which had been quiet was now disposed to rebellion and in Limerick two regiments which served on the continent were sent against the insurgents. The government-directed troops were ordered to crush rebellion in every shape and form and forcibly to disarm all rebels. Officers were ordered to *'quarter'* their troops without payment on anybody they thought fit; to requisition horses, carriages, and carts; to demand forage and provisions; to hold courts martial; and to issue proclamations. All that had previously happened in Ulster was now repeated in the Midlands and South but on a more wholesale scale and with even greater ferocity. Homes were burned, stores of provisions were looted, hundreds were murdered, and thousands were arrested and subjected to *'half-hangings'* carried out by the notorious *'Walking Gallows'*, Lieutenant Hempenstall of the Wicklow Militia. These were added to the pitch-cap introduced by the North Cork Militia, floggings, and other depraved acts of torture.

One magistrate was said to have scoured the countryside, at the head of a party of Yeoman cavalry, accompanied by a regular executioner on the back of a cart with a hanging rope and a cat-o-nine-tails, flogging and half-hanging suspects till confessions were elicited and arms surrendered.[401] The imposition of *free quartering'* was of itself sufficient to ensure ruin and starvation to any region in which it was imposed. The victims were warned that the troops would remain not only until all arms were surrendered, and showing the underlying class basis of the policy, '*all rents, taxes, and tithes had been completely paid up'.* All of this state-sponsored, counter-revolutionary terror was imposed much of it even before the rebellion of May 23rd 1798 had begun.[402]

Lord Edward Fitzgerald, who preferred to be known as Citizen Fitzgerald (he had repudiated his courtesy title) held a commanding position in Irish minds, as the younger brother of the Duke of Leinster and one of the senior line of the Geraldine family. His political sympathy with France went beyond that of his cousin Charles James Fox. The mothers of Fox and Fitzgerald were sisters and grand-children of Charles II. On the eve of the swoop of March 12th it is interesting to note the Directory contained the three main strands of Irish history; the old Gaelic Irish, the Norman-Irish or *old English,* and the planted *new English-Irish.* The arrests of March 12th left the Directory in the hands of Fitzgerald who had avoided capture. He set to work, considering no further delay was possible and proceeded to arrange the rising. He gathered a new Directory, including the Sheares, brothers from Cork, and William Lawless amongst others, and fixed upon the night of 22nd-23rd May for the rebellion. Fitzgerald and the others, along with Samuel Neilson, spread the word as best they could. On May 19th Fitzgerald was followed and arrested in a house in Thomas Street, Dublin. In the course of the arrest he was wounded

---

[401] Lecky, W, A History of England in the Eighteenth Century, Chap. XXIX, vol. VIII, Longman Green & Co, London, (1890).

[402] Jackson, T.A., Ireland Her Own.

while resisting arrest and was carried in a dying condition to jail. The Sheares brothers were arrested on May 22ⁿᵈ on the information of their so-called friend Captain Armstrong (King's Co Militia) who had infiltrated their company and were later hanged. Lawless, escaped, and boarded, a ship bound for America. Neilson was captured while rounding up a party to free the captives in Newgate prison in Dublin. In effect, the whole central Directory of the rising had now been captured or were dispersed. There were concerns in the Castle as to the reliability of the Irish militia which was largely Catholic, however, it had been reinforced in 1797 by staunch Scottish and English fencible regiments.

Jemmy Hope – Organising Workers

Earlier, in 1796, Neilson had sent Jemmy Hope to Dublin to help organise the workers in the capital with a letter of introduction to Oliver Bond, a wealthy Dublin Presbyterian, who was recruiting workers into their revolutionary committee based at Pill Lane (now Chancery Street). In sending Hope to Dublin, Neilson believed he was sending his best man to organise the working class. Hope stayed for a time in Balbriggan and then moved into the City centre where he helped develop a large working-class membership for the United Irishmen under the direction of the Pill Lane group. He particularly targeted the *'illegal'* workers combinations and this accounted for the spread of the organisation south of the river into the Liberties and also for its significant Protestant artisan membership. Many of them were weavers and Hope's fellow Presbyterians.[403]

---

[403] Whelan, F., Jemmy Hope – The Most Radical United Irishman, *lookleft*, (24 September, 2011).

The 1798 Rebellion

Central to the overall plan for the Rebellion was for those in the city to seize the capital on the night of the 23rd May. They would be aided by reinforcements from the adjoining counties where diversionary tactics would take place. An outer ring of Leinster counties would then rise to hamper, or prevent, the movement of military reinforcements from the provinces to the city. There were also to be risings in Ulster two days earlier to draw away troops from Dublin as they had partially recovered from the dragooning of 1797. Cork was perceived as another strongpoint in Munster, albeit it was the location of a large number of Crown army concentrations. For those outside Dublin, the non-arrival of the regular mail-coaches from the capital would be the signal to confirm the rising. Upon this signal all else was contingent and confirmed that the capital had acted as planned. Neilson, before he was captured, had given the orders to the city and county Colonels at a meeting in Church Lane. The Dubliners gathered their forces and moved towards prearranged mobilisation points from where they intended to mount a wave of attacks at 10 p.m., but this was hastily cancelled when it was discovered that the yeomanry, following information, had occupied the predesignated rallying sites of Smithfield, Newmarket, and a number of other locations. Unable to mass in forces sufficient to overcome an alerted garrison, thousands of city rebels melted away into the lanes of the south city, abandoning their weapons on the way.

An estimated 10,000 weapons were recovered at first light on May 24th and 500 pikes were found in Bridgefoot Street, Dublin, alone. The plan for Dublin was upended but in the absence of viable communications the Rebellion had begun. Street fighting, ambushes, and skirmishes killed hundreds that night in Naas, Prosperous, Ballymore Eustace, Fox-and-Geese, Rathfarnham, Tallaght, Kilcullen, and Fingal. Scores of other risings materialised across Leinster. By dawn tens of thousands of United Irishmen commandeered all the major approaches to the capital and initiated a fresh wave of assaults in Wicklow, Carlow, and Meath. The rising spread quickly to the north-west and south, but the failure to halt all the interprovincial mail coaches and other communication difficulties ensured that the first news the vast majority of United Irishmen received was of the collapse of the rising in Dublin. Within 24 hours of the start of the Rebellion it was clear to the military that the campaign was dispersed and uncoordinated.[404]

The Wicklow contingent had risen on the night of May 22nd but as they approached Dublin they realised something had gone wrong with the plans. They signalled the surrounding counties by lighting fires, indicating that they were holding out. At Boolavogue, infuriated by the militia persecution, the rebels waited as a body on their local parish priest, Fr Murphy, and called upon him to lead them. It was at his command the fire was lit at Boolavogue. The following morning they successfully ambushed a party of Yeomanry and then moved to capture the seat of Lord Mount Norris at Camolin Park. Here they found the greatest prize of all, the weaponry surrendered since March 17th and other weaponry intended for the use of the Camolin Yeomanry. The news of this success was widely circulated and brought further recruits. The North Cork Militia, who were posted to the area and who despised the ill-armed peasantry, pursued some outlying parties and were engaged at the Battle of Oulart Hill. Of the total militia force only a small number it was reported escaped alive, including Colonel Foote, their commanding officer. After this success the rising became practically universal throughout Wexford and parties

---

[404] O'Donnell, Ruan, *Day in May that saw the disastrous beginning of Irish rebellion in which 30,000 were to die*, Irish Times, (May 23rd 1998).

from nearby counties made their way to join in the fight. Their handicap was lack of firearms and cannon and even lack of gunpowder for the firearms they had. That the supporters of the Ascendancy faction should represent the Wexford rising to all and sundry as a Catholic war against Protestants plainly followed their pursuit of their sectarian agenda. The Wexford peasantry, prior to the rebellion, had been faced with a continuous war from the Yeomanry and Militia so it was as much a rising in self-defence. The peasantry, in retaliation for the burning of thatched cottages, inevitably occupied by Catholics who made up 90 per cent of the population, and burnings which had been organised by the local gentry magistrates and other supporters of the Castle, responded by burning all the slated houses on the corresponding theory that the occupants were either 'Orangemen' or gentry sympathisers. It was in this way more class related than religion related, the owners against the dispossessed.

At the same time the peasantry sought out Protestant leaders who had played a role in the United Irishmen, some willing and others not so, as in the case of Sir Edward Crosbie in Carlow who was hanged without trail in a case of mistaken identity. Bagenal Harvey, who had figured with distinction in the Dublin Society of United Irishmen, was morally forced to take the leadership of the rebel army. His plans for the taking of New Ross were well-designed but he was outmanoeuvred when confronted by a disciplined opposition force. It was considered many women participated in the rebellion as combatants and in other roles. One of the notable combatants was Moll Doyle, who it was said replaced her feeble father. According to Cloney, who referred to her as an Amazon, '*if only every tenth man we had that day leaving Corbet Hill had the courage of the gallant Miss Doyle, the battle would have ended in a speedy victory to us'.*[405] Even though there were feats of reckless bravery by the peasant army, not unlike the clans of old running cattle and reliant on a strategy of hurling itself upon the enemy *en masse,* coupled with lack of supplies of arms and ammunition, the rebels were compelled to retreat but not until the battle had raged for ten hours. For some these losses were the turning point of the battle and not Vinegar Hill. They won at least at least half a dozen successes against Yeomanry, Militia, and Regular army forces, but were overpowered in the end by the combined operation of much superior forces, cannon, and twelve war-experienced English generals, amongst them Moore, Lake, Loftus, Eustace, Wilford, Needham, Trench, Johnstone, Fawcett, and Dundas. The rebellion ended in effect when the rebel headquarters of the men and women at Vinegar Hill near Enniscorthy was stormed by Lake's forces on 21st June, pikes being no match for grape shot and fused shrapnel shells from cannon, fired relentlessly into their midst, and the combined assault of serried rows of troops. Although, some did escape through what became known as Needham's Gap, to continue the struggle in nearby counties.[406]

While the Wexford rising was in progress, a rising broke out in Antrim and Down on June 7th, more than a fortnight after the date set by Fitzgerald. The Antrim Republicans took to the field under the leadership of Henry Joy McCracken. The Defenders in Antrim turned out in force and in general ordinary people responded to the call, while the well-to-do who should have occupied the posts of Colonels and Generals, were nearly all missing or had defected earlier. In Ballymena, Kells, and other places the rebels took the

---

[405] Cloney, Thomas, A Personal Narrative of Those Transactions in the County Wexford, Dublin, (1832).
[406] Jackson, T.A., Ireland Her Own.

towns but as no one came to lead them they dispersed to their homes. McCracken and Hope led forces gallantly and captured Antrim town but a false alarm caused the rebels to retreat. The government forces rallied and were reinforced. At the second attempt the rebels were beaten off. Although McCracken initially escaped along with Jemmy Hope and was hidden by his sister Mary (a notable person in her own right who accompanied him to the scaffold), MacCracken was betrayed, arrested, court-martialled, and hanged on the 17th July. In Down, 7,000 had assembled ably led by a Lisburn linen-draper Henry Munro. The rebels scored two inconclusive successes in two hard-fought engagements but were defeated and scattered on June 14th at Ballynahinch. This signalled the end of the rebellion in Ulster. Amongst those killed in the battle was the later lamented Betsy Gray, another notable combatant. All the leaders were hanged; Munro at his own shop door.

The Castle organised forces of yeomanry and militia pursued the *'rebels'* relentlessly throughout the country for months and in some cases years afterwards. In Kerry the captured rebels were hanged, decapitated, and their heads impaled on the big iron gates of the Old Market House in Castleisland. Similar incidents of hangings, decapitations, and impaling were reported from other towns around the country. Hundreds of United Irishmen were transported, many to Botany Bay in Australia, to serve out their sentences. In some cases they rose to leadership in foreign Governments and society, or as in the case of Philip Cunningham from Moyvane in County Kerry who was to lead the first rebellion in Australia in 1804 at the aptly name *Vinegar Hill* (Castle Hill in New South Wales) with the republican battle-cry, *Death or Liberty*.

CHAPTER TWENTY-THREE

The Tone Expedition – France

Three weeks after Humbert's defeat at Ballinamuck, a larger French force making its way for Lough Swilly was intercepted near Tory Island by a greatly superior English navy force. After four hours fighting, the French flagship was reduced to a wreck and forced to surrender in a sinking condition. Among the prisoners taken was Theobald Wolfe Tone. He was sent first to Derry and then onward, chained, to Dublin, tried by court-martial, and sentenced to be hanged. He died in questionable circumstances on November 19th 1798, and was buried by his father in the local Bodenstown churchyard in County Kildare.

Tone had written with foresight, '*When the people come forward, the aristocracy, fearful of being left behind, insinuate themselves into our ranks and rise into timid leaders or treacherous auxiliaries*'.

As in other parts of Ireland, the peasants rose in force, but the Irish '*sans culottes*' were left leaderless mostly through a combination of torture, murder, imprisonment, exile, and defection. In the end they were defeated by an Ascendancy counter-revolution organised and directed by the '*junto*' in Dublin Castle, ably supported by the Government in London. The Irish Parliament in their triumph, knowingly or unknowingly, wrote their own epitaph as these events were followed shortly afterwards by the Act of Union of 1801.

Social Change

During the rebellion of 1798 the Catholic Hierarchy led the way in expressing its '*detestation*' of the rebellion and proclaimed its '*unswerving loyalty*' to the Crown. It ordered its parish priests to check the spread of the rebellion and to secure the surrender of arms.[407] There were many instances where rebels were refused the sacraments until they had proved their *'repentance'* and they were encouraged to inform on their compatriots. In the case of Archbishop Troy, he did not consider the confession to the priest alone as sufficient atonement and *'that either the priest ought to insist on such confession to the State or police being made, or to enjoin the making of such disclosure subsequent to absolution in like manner as penance is enjoined under similar circumstances'.*[408]

Later, W. P. Ryan wrote, *'the most brilliant thing ever done by Irish Catholic priests was the invention of the legend that they had always been on the side of the people.'*

The democratic revolutionary challenge to the aristocracy in the latter part of the eighteenth century came from the *'middle'* and *'lower orders'*. It was a class war on an international scale and 1798 can be said to be the culmination of that struggle in Ireland. However, unlike America, France, England itself, or the Dutch Revolts beforehand where bourgeoisie revolutions had succeeded in displacing or replacing the *ancien regimes* of monarchy, aristocracy, and church, the separation of Ireland from Great Britain did not succeed against the wel-ensconced Protestant Ascendancy supported by the counter revolutionary Government in Britain. Neither did the battle to establish a democratic secular republic under French protection succeed.

In other words, a political and social revolution, placing revolutionary bourgeoisie democrats in power with the support of the so-called *'lower orders'*, was not achieved as in some other countries. Instead the union between Great Britain and Ireland,

---

[407] Jackson, T.A., Ireland Her Own.

[408] Ellis, Beresford, Ed. James Connolly Selected Writings, Pelican Books, (1973), P.63.

opposed by some sections of the Orange Order, for insular reasons, was taken forward by Cornwallis and Castlereagh. They were supported by the Catholic elite and clergy who were promised Catholic emancipation in return. The Protestants, to gain their support, were told Catholics would now be a minority in the new union. In any event, both of these elites were fearful of the drive for a French-supported democratic secular republic. To gain the Union with Britain and in the words of Edward Cooke, under-secretary for Ireland, it would have to be *'written up, spoken up, intrigued up, drunk up, sung up, and bribed up'.*[409] Castlereagh had one and a half million pounds or more at his disposal for these purposes apart from titles, sinecures, pensions, and other *'persuasions'*. Despite some stumbling blocks during 1799-1800, at the end of January 1801, instead of Tone's Republic, Ireland got Castlereagh's Union.

An insight on this epoch goes to Jemmy Hope, the Downpatrick working-class radical, he observed: *'You may live to see Ireland what she ought to be, but, whether or not, let us die in this faith'.*[410] It was also Hope's narrative that, *'the fire of 1798 was not quite extinguished – it smouldered and was ready to break out anew'.*

Emmet Rebellion

In the summer of 1803 the remnants of the United Irishmen, still at large, made a last attempt to establish an Irish Republic under the leadership of Robert Emmet, Jemmy Hope, and Thomas Russell.[411] This rebellion, often derided as a revolt of a *'Dublin mob'* was how the Ascendancy described it, was in fact much more proletarian than

---

[409] Gillen, U., Ascendancy Ireland.
[410] Madden, R.R., The United Irishmen.
[411] Cronin, Sean, The Revolutionaries.

that. Connolly described it as follows: '*Emmet believed the national will was superior to property rights, and could abolish them at will; and also … he realised that the producing classes could not be expected to rally to the revolution unless given to understand that it meant their freedom from social as well as political bondage.*'[412]

After Emmet's failed rebellion it was the Catholic Nationalism of O'Connell,[413] Archbishop Troy, and his successor Archbishop Murray, and their efforts through the Catholic Association in combination with the Ascendancy and Crown-established and - promoted Orange Order, who took centre stage and left the struggle for an Irish Republic in their wake. The suppression of the 1798 and 1803 rebellions, and the Act of Union, set the future course for political events in Ireland. The Protestant and Catholic working classes were separated '*divide et impera*' style by sectarianism. The former by an engendered sectarianism based on a perceived privilege, loyalty to Church and Crown and to a lesser extent to the Ascendancy (who had supported the Act of Union). In the latter case it was led by O'Connell and the newly discovered nationalism of the Catholic Church. The Catholic Church hierarchy had also supported the Act of Union and the putting down of the 1798 and 1803 Rebellions. O'Connell used the church gates very effectively for the collection of his popular '*penny a month*' subscription to the Catholic Association. This was a collection which reached £50,000 per annum at one point and in the process reinvigorated a moribund church organisation.[414] What both of the elites, Protestant and Catholic, had

---

[412] Connolly, James, Labour in Irish History, New Books, Dublin, (1973). P.66.

[413] Daniel O'Connell had been a member of the lawyers Yeomanry Corp and was turned out on duty on the night of Emmet's failed rebellion in 1803. (ibid, P.63).

[414] McNally, Vincent J., Who is Leading? Archbishop John Thomas Troy and the Priests and People in the Archdiocese of Dublin 1787-1823, CCHA, *Historical Studies*, 61 (1995), 153-170.

in common was their abhorrence for democratic republicanism and in particular that of the French revolutionary variety.

The formative beginnings of the key constituencies in Irish politics; unionism and loyalism, republicanism, democratic and physical force, and Catholic nationalism, can all be said to have had their origins in the latter half of the eighteenth and early nineteenth centuries. The events that unfolded during this epoch shaped then, and continue to shape now, the course of Irish society – socially, economically and politically.

BIBLIOGRAPHY

Anderson, Perry, (1974), Lineages of the Absolutist State, NLB, London

Anderson, Perry, (1974), Passages from Antiquity to Feudalism, NLB, London

Barnard, T., (1974), The Kingdom of Ireland, 1641-1760, Palgrave Macmillan

Barnett, C., (1974), Britain and Her Army, 1509-1970, Penguin

Barry, Melissa, (2017), University of Paris, History of the British Empire

Bartlett, T., Select Documents XXXVIII: Defenders and Defenderism in 1795, Irish Historical Studies, Vol 24, No 95, May 1985

Bartlett, T., The Catholic Question in the Eighteenth Century, History Ireland, Issue 3, (Spring 1993), Vol. 1

Bede, Ecclesiastical History of the English People, Oxford University Press, 2008

BICO, The Memoirs of Jemmy Hope: An Autobiography of a Working-class United Irishman, Dublin, 1972

Bonwick, J., Irish Druids and Old Irish Religions, Library of Alexandria, USA, 1894

Bourke, C., CORPOREAL RELICS, TENTS AND SHRINES IN EARLY MEDIEVAL IRELAND, Ulster Journal of Archaeology, Vol 74, 2017-2018

Bradshaw, B., Nationalism and Historical Scholarship in Modern Ireland, *Irish Historical Studies*, Vol 26 No (104), Nov 1989

Boyd, A., (1976), The Rise of the Irish Trade Unions, 1729-1970,

Anvil Books, Dublin

Brown, D., (2000), Bury My Heart at Wounded Knee, Open Road, New York

Burns, E., (1976), British Imperialism in Ireland, Cork Workers Club

Campbell, B., Benchmarking Medieval Economic Development, QUB, 2006

Cannon, D., Irish Catholic Service and Identity in the British armed forces 1793-1815, Thesis M. Litt. NUI, Maynooth, 2014

Charles-Edwards, T, M, (2000), Early Christian Ireland, Cambridge

Churchyard, T., *A General Rehearsal of Warres,* (1579), Edward White, London

Cloney, T., A Personal Narrative of Those Transactions in the County Wexford, Dublin. 1832

Coakley, M., (2012), Ireland in the World Order, Pluto Press, London

Connolly, J., (1973), Labour in Irish History, New Books, Dublin

Cox, N., Vikings, Undergraduate Reward Library, NUI, Maynooth, 2012

Cronin, S., (1971), The Revolutionaries, Republican Publications, Gardiner Pl, Dublin

Cullen, L.M., (1972), An Economic History of Ireland since 1660, Barton Manor, Bristol

Curtin, N.J., Transformation of the United Irishmen into a Mass-based Revolutionary Organisation, 1794-96, Irish Historical Studies, Vol. 24, No.96, Nov. 1985

Curtis, E., Richard Duke of York, As Viceroy of Ireland, 1447-1460, Government War and Society, P. Crooks, (ed.), Four Courts Press, 2008

Denman, T., Hibernia Officina Militum, Irish Recruitment to the British Regular Army 1660-1815, The Irish Sword, Vol.XX, Winter 1996

DePaor, L. and M., (1964), Early Christian Ireland, Thames and Hudson, London

DeRe, E., The Roman Contribution to the Common Law, Fordham Law Review, Vol.29, Issue 3, 1961

Doherty, C., The Problem of Patrick: History Ireland, Issue 1, Spring, 1995

Dorney, J., The Munster Plantation and the MacCarthys, 1583-1597, The Irish Story

Downham, C., (2018), Medieval Ireland, Cambridge University Press

Dunlop, R., The Plantation of Leix and Offaly, The English Historical Review, Vol. VI, Issue XXI, January, 1891

Edwards, D., (2010), *Age of Atrocity: Violence and Political Conflict in Early Modern Ireland,* Four Courts Press, Dublin

Ellis, P.B. (1985), A History of the Irish Working Class, Pluto Press

Ellis, P.B. (Ed.), James Connolly Selected Writings, Pelican Books, 1973

Ellis, S.G., Economic Problems of the Church: Why the Reformation Failed in Ireland, Journal of Ecclesiastical History, Vol. 41, No. 2, April, 1990

Ellis, S.G., Thomas Cromwell and Ireland 1532-40, Historical Journal, 23, pp 497-519, NUI, Galway

Engels, F., A History of Ireland, Preparatory Work Varia on the History of the Irish Confiscations, Progress Publishers, Moscow, 1974

Falls, C., (1996), Elizabeth's Irish Wars, Constable, London

Faulkner, N., (2013) A Marxist History of the World, Pluto Press, London

Foster, R.F., (1988), Modern Ireland 1600-1972, Allen Lane, Penguin Press, London

Fox, R., Marx, Engels, and Lenin on the Irish Revolution, Cork

Workers Club, Modern Books, London, 1932

Frame, R., (2012), Colonial Ireland, 1169-1369, Four Courts Press, Dublin

Gillen, U., (2016), Ascendancy Ireland, 1660-1800, The Princeton History of Modern Ireland

Greaves, Desmond, C, (1971), Liam Mellows and the Irish Revolution, Lawrence and Wishart, London

Grunke, K.R., The Effect of Christianity on the British Celts, UW-L Journal of Undergraduate Research XI, 2008

Healy, J., INSULA SANCTORUM ET DOCTORUM, Sealy Bryers and Walker, Dublin 1912

Holm, P., The Slave Trade of Dublin, Ninth to Twelfth Centuries, Peritia, January 1986, Dublin

Hughes, K., (1966), The Church in Early Irish Society, ACLS, Cornell

Hull, E., A History of Ireland and Her People, 1931, A Project Gutenberg Australia eBook 0800111.h.html, Feb 2008

Jackson, T.A., (1976), Ireland Her Own, Lawrence and Wishart, London

Johnston, E., Ireland in Late Antiquity: A Forgotten Frontier, Studies in Late Antiquity, Summer, 2017

Joyce, P., A Concise History of Ireland, 1910

Kearney, H., (2012), The British Isles, Canto Classics

Kerr, T.R., McCormick, F, O'Sullivan, A, The Economy of Early Medieval Ireland, EMAP Report, 7.1, 2013, Research Repository, UCD, Dublin

Kostick, Conor, (2009), Revolution in Ireland, Cork University Press

Law and Marxism: 800 years since the Magna Carta, www.marxist.com

Lecky, W.E., A History of England in the Eighteenth Century, Volume VII, Appleton and Co. New York, 1890

Leland, T., A History of Ireland Vol. III, London, 1773

Lynch, B., A Monastic Landscape: The Cistercians in Medieval Leinster, Thesis, NUI Maynooth, December, 2008

Lydon, J., (2008), Ireland and the English Crown, 1171-1541, Government, War and Medieval Society, Crooks, P, ed. Four Courts Press, Dublin

Lydon, J., (1973), Ireland in the Later Middle Ages, Gill and Macmillan, Dublin

Marx, K., (1990), Capital Volume 1, Penguin Classics

Marx, K., and Engels, F., (1971), *Ireland and the Irish Question, R. Dixon (ed.), Progress Publishers, Moscow*

Mathur, C., and Dix, D., (2009), *The Irish Question in Karl Marx's and Friedrich Engel's Writings on Capitalism and Empire*, in: Social Thought on Ireland in the Nineteenth Century, University College Press, Dublin.

MacCaffrey, J., History of the Catholic Church: From the Renaissance to the French Revolution, Library of Alexandria, USA, 1912

MacCurtin, M., The Fall of the House Of Desmond, Journal of the Kerry Archaeological and History Society, No. 8, 1975

McDermott, C.B., An Ghaoth a Chriofidh an Eorna, The Moral Economy of Ireland's Whiteboys, 1761-1787, Bard, Spring, 2017

McNally, V., Who is Leading? Archbishop John Thomas Troy and the Priests and People in the Archdiocese of Dublin 1787-1823, CCHA, *Historical Studies,* 61, (1995)

Miller, D.W., (1983), Armagh Troubles, Irish Peasants, Violence and Political Unrest, 1780-1914, eds. Clarke & Donnelly, Manchester University Press

Moorhouse, G., (2002),The Pilgrimage of Grace, Weidenfeld

Morrisey, J., Contours of Colonialism: Gaelic Ireland and the Early

Colonial Subject, Irish Geography, Vol. (37) (1), 2004

Morton, A., L., (1989), A Peoples' History of England, Lawrence and Wishart, London

Muirchu, *Vita S Patrici*, ed. and tr. L Bieler, *The Patrician Texts in the Book of Armagh, MS 52,* Trinity College Library, Dublin

Murray, E., A., History of the Commercial and Financial Relations between England and Ireland from the period of the Restoration, P S King & Co., Westminster, 1903

Mytum, H., (1992), The Origins of Early Christian Ireland, Routledge

Oakley, M., (2012), Ireland in the World Order, Pluto Press

O'Connell, M., R., (1965), Irish Politics and Social Conflict in the Age of the American Revolution, University of Pennsylvania Press

O'Corrain, D., (1972), Ireland before the Normans, Gill and Macmillan, Dublin

O'Corrain, D., (2013), Island of Saints and Scholars, Myth or Reality? ed. Rafferty O., P., Irish Catholic Identities, Manchester University Press

O'Corrain, D., Orosius, Ireland and Christianity, Perita 28, 2017

O'Corrain, D., (2017), The Irish Church, Its Reform and the English Invasion, Four Courts Press

O'Croinin, D., (1995), Early Medieval Ireland, Longman

O'Hannrachan, T., War of Religion or Ethnic Wars? Religious Conflicts in Ireland 1500-1650, Historical Review 2009/1, No. 649

O'Rahilly, T.F., (1981), The Two Patricks, DIAS, Dublin 4

O'Ruairc Og, P., "The Pope is the Enemy of Irish Republicanism And Irish Independence" Should We Commemorate the Catholic Church's Role in the War of Independence? The Irish Story, 11 February, 2019

Peden, J.R., Property Rights in Celtic Irish Law, Journal of Libertarian Studies, Vol. 1, No. 2, Pergamon Press, 1977

Petty, W., The Political Anatomy of Ireland, Irish University Press, Shannon, 1970

Pierse, J. H., The Pierse Family, Eltham, London, ed. Richard G Pierse, 2006

Poirteir, C., (1995), (ed.), The Great Irish Famine, p10, RTE/Mercier Press, Cork

Remonstrance of the Irish Chiefs to Pope John XXII, CELT, UCC, Cork

Ruthven-Otway, A. J., (1968), A History of Medieval Ireland, Ernest Benn, London

Smyth, W. J., Atlas of Family Names in Ireland, UCC, Cork

Sullivan, A.M., (2019), The Story of Ireland, Wentworth Press

Tacitus, Agricola, Harvard University Press, 1989

Tacitus, Germania, Penguin Books, 2010

Tirechan, Collectanea ed. and tr. L Bieler, *The Patrician Texts in the Book of Armagh,* MS 52, Trinity College, Dublin

Tone, T.W., An Argument on Behalf of the Catholics of Ireland, *The Society of United Irishmen of,* Belfast, 1791

Swift, C., Ogam Stones and the Earliest Irish Christians, Maynooth Monographs, Series Two, 1997

Vinogradoff, P., ed G, Pacillo, Roman Law in Medieval Europe, Ampere Publishing, 2015 (1909)

Wall, M., The Rise of a Catholic Middle Class in Eighteenth-Century Ireland, Irish Historical Studies, Vol. XI, No. 42, September, 1958.

ABOUT THE AUTHOR

Jerry Shanahan spent the past seven years as a Worker Member of the Irish Labour Court which resolves industrial relations disputes and adjudicates on employment law. Prior to that he was National Officer with the trade union Unite, on the Executive Committee of the Irish Congress of Trade Unions, and a former President of the Dublin Council of Trade Unions. He has had a lifetime interest in politics including the Connolly Youth Movement, Irish Communist Party, the Irish Labour Party, and was Chair of Labour Party trade unions. He also served on the Board of the National Economic and Social Council and the European Foundation on Living and Working Conditions. He holds a professional diploma in employment law from UCD and an MA from Keele University.

Printed in Great Britain
by Amazon

36634590R00188